CASSELL'S PINK DIRECTORY

LESBIAN AND GAY ORGANIZATIONS, BUSINESSES AND SERVICES IN THE UK AND EIRE

CASSELL

Cassell
Villiers House
41-47 Strand
London WC2E 5JE

387 Park Avenue South
New York NY 10016-8810

First published 1994

British Library Cataloging-in-Publication Data
A catalogue record for this book is available from the British Library

ISBN: 0-304-33085-X

Typeset by Liz Gibbs and Tim Purcell
Printed and bound in Great Britain by Hartnoll's Ltd, Bodmin, Cornwall

Contents

Acknowledgements

Without the support, help and advice of the following individuals and organisations, *The Pink Directory* would never have been completed. Thank you to all of the following: Will Anderson, Steve Cook at Cassell, Jeff Evans, Julian V Hows, Chris Markham at Rubberstuffers, Robert Pennock and Lisa Power, London Lesbian and Gay Switchboard, London Lesbian Line, National AIDS Manual, Aberdeen Lesbian and Gay Switchboard, Brighton Lesbian Line, Cardiff Friend, Edinburgh Lesbian and Gay Switchboard, Gwynedd Lesbian and Gayline, Leeds Lesbian and Gay Switchboard, Leicester Lesbian and Gay Community Centre, Manchester Lesbian and Gay Centre, Manchester Lesbian and Gay Switchboard, Manchester Lesbian Link, MESMAC Newcastle, Milton Keynes Lesbian and Gay Switchboard, NGLF Dublin, Nottingham GAI Project, Strathclyde Lesbian and Gay Switchboard, UMIST and West Midlands Lesbian and Gay Switchboard.

Notes on Contributors

Liz Gibbs is a list consultant and publicist for Cassell's Sexual Politics and Lesbian and Gay Studies Lists. She edited a collection of essays on contemporary lesbian culture, *Daring to Dissent* (Cassell, 1994). She also works for Scarlet Press, London.

Tim Purcell recently escaped a finance career. He has presented features for BBC Radio 1FM and worked on *The Big Breakfast*. He aims to pursue a broadcasting and writing career.

Foreword

Information is the lifeblood of the lesbian, gay and bisexual communities. Setting up a helpline and publishing a magazine are two of the things that any emergent community tackles. Whenever more than two or three of us are gathered together, a new social group springs up and we get going on how best to pass the word round about it - whether it be in Bulgaria or Birmingham (Alabama *or* West Midlands).

Gay guides of a sort have long existed and early listings can be found in 'gentlemen's' magazines and in *Arena Three* for lesbians (which even managed to discreetly advertise in *The Times*). But our information systems really came into their own in the UK after the birth in 1970 of the Gay Liberation Front which, whatever its shortcomings, was loud and proud and would have nothing to do with hiding ourselves away. I remember in my early days as a lesbian being told not to leave out leaflets about a social event where heterosexuals or naffs ('not a fairy') might see them, in case they came along and were disruptive. GLF would have no truck with such a ghetto mentality; so what if straights found out about our events ? They were welcome to come and learn about liberation and, if they were lucky, they might even end up coming out themselves.

So from the Gay Liberation Front came forth *Gay News*, the first and still the best of our community newspapers over the years. It became a fat fortnightly treat whose central section was a massive 'Gay Guide' to the whole of the UK, updated with meticulous regularity by a genteel lady called Jo Hodgkinson. There must be half a dozen PhD theses lurking in the analysis of the changing gay scene that this guide charted for more than a decade as the movement grew from a back page of alternative student groups and wholefood bookshops into helplines and discos in every town.

Gay helplines also began to emerge in the early seventies, often simply because of the pressure of calls to any phone number that dared to publicise itself as gay. Other kinds of phonelines were a central part of the counter culture; BIT could tell you about alternative living; Release helped you if you got busted for a drugs offence; Rape Crisis began for women who had been sexually assaulted. It was only to be expected that gay people (as we all were then) would expect a similar self-help service.

The first gay helpline in the UK was Oxford Switchboard which was set up in 1972 by students and gay liberationists. The idea spread rapidly. The GLF central office had a phone, answered, more often than not, by anyone who happened to be passing. But it was run ever more chaotically as the central apparatus fell apart and *Gay News* found itself swamped by callers who needed a helpline, not a subscription department. So they appealed in the paper for people to come and found a separate line. On 4 March 1974 London Gay Switchboard (now London Lesbian and Gay Switchboard) went on line with a shoebox full of file cards, operating what was from the start a national service which rapidly expanded to offer 24-hour service under pressure of callers. From 1974 to 1993 it remained in the same building where it was founded out of the ashes of the GLF Office Collective and it still retains the GLF structure of Working Groups and a Co-ordinating Committee.

It is from the knowledge of these Switchboards and other helplines, such as Lesbian Lines and Friend networks around the country, that the information in *The Pink Directory* is drawn. Using the basic framework of the London Switchboard files, now a computerised database, entries have been cross-checked and added from many local helplines, some only open a few hours each week - but which have unrivalled up-to-date knowledge of their own local area. Nothing changes so fast as what's in and what's out in the lesbian and gay scenes in the larger cities; and while rural pubs may be a little more stable in their attractions, they can disappear or become unwelcoming overnight with the transfer of a tenant manager or the death of an owner. The collaboration between helplines and Cassell will help all parties to remain as up-to-date as is humanly and electronically possible.

My own early experience on a helpline was founding Lancaster Switchboard in 1976. Up until then, we had used two local phone numbers (one for women, one for men) printed on little stickers surreptitiously stuck in the local public toilets. We were subject to strange calls at all hours - especially the lesbian one, which seemed to fascinate a number of middle-aged men and led to the phone owner feeling threatened and unsupported. We bound the relevant pages of *Gay News* (then at its fullest and most informative), found a free phone in the local wholefood and right-on bookshop that we could use one evening a week, drew up a rota and sent a press release to the local paper.

How could we fail ? But homophobia can be quite inventive. The paper printed our press release - but some wag had substituted our phone number for that of Harry Ball, Leather Merchant of Lancaster. Mr Ball was as unimpressed as we were and refused to let us borrow his phone for even that first evening. So it was back to the little stickers but at least we had a more regulated and supportive service. We were also soon listed in *Gay News* with the other helplines and Friend groups around the country.

Arriving in London in the late 70s, I eventually fetched up at London Switchboard and got quite a shock. For a start, they had a rigorous selection procedure, though I discovered afterwards that they were so anxious to recruit an obvious feminist, they forgot to ask if I was a lesbian. For another, lesbians were going through that rigorous separatist stage in which independent Lesbian Lines emerged, often via women who had left the previously mixed helplines. I turned out to be one of only two lesbians at Switchboard. The gay men ranged from married ones in suits to dopehead hippies and Marxists and the emerging 80s breed of new men, who believed everything lesbians said as gospel and had a nervous breakdown if we disagreed with each other. Personally, I took to the dopehead hippies.

Diverse as we were as information gatherers and providers, we were also remarkably puritanical in ways that changed over the decade. We became increasingly intolerant, on an organisational level, of drag and camp (I remember censuring a man who has since become Vice-Chair for backcombing his beehive hairdo while I was trying to chair a meeting) and sometimes censoriously concerned about the rise of disco culture (many of us certain that young people coming out needed a good political discussion rather than a pub). The married men disappeared from our ranks and bisexuality became taboo.

Now, as we head towards the millennium, helplines seem mostly to be becoming more genuinely open and flexible. Most make a conscious effort to recruit a range of people whose races, ages and sexualities reflect the callers. Most accept that there are many ways to be gay or lesbian. Most have taken on board the heavy load of HIV/AIDS information and counselling that inevitably fell on us in the absence of any early government response and as a result of continuing homophobia in much health provision. An increasing number are lesbian, gay and bisexual realising that sexuality is not the monochrome, polarised simplification that we sought to impose in the 80s.

Guides, too, have become more sophisticated but not at the same rate. Most have been woefully low on lesbian content. Those specifically for women have often been more right-on feminist than comprehensively lesbian. Many have dealt with either services or entertainments but few have been comprehensive. This one seeks to deal with those shortcomings and to finally strike up a relationship between the written and the spoken word and to support London Lesbian and Gay Switchboard with a percentage donation from sales and an improved database.

We will continue to need our helplines and our guides because knowledge is power. The more we know, the better we can control our lives in what is sometimes still a hostile environment and the better we can learn from one another. The information here is not just an introduction to a gay ghetto; it is the source of our strength, our sustenance in going out into the world and living on equal terms with others, proud of ourselves and what we can achieve. Use it to find a lover, a lawyer, a language teacher or just a good night out in a strange town. Or, if you are lucky, all the above in one!

Lisa Power
Volunteer, Lancaster Gay Switchboard 1976
Volunteer, London Lesbian and Gay Switchboard 1979 - 1994.
November 1994.

Introduction

How many times have you heard the words 'lesbian and gay community'? What *is* the 'lesbian and gay community'? Where does it meet ? What does it do when it meets ? Who sells to it, represents it in the courts, gives it medical care, teaches it, speaks up for it, counsels it, advises it, informs it, entertains it, gives it financial advice and accommodates it ? How big is it ? Some of the answers to these questions are scattered in the pages of the lesbian and gay media. Further answers lie in the records of numerous organisations and businesses up and down the country. This book is, as far as we are aware, the first attempt to collate this information and publish it in a single format. It is the result of the (rather frenzied) efforts of two people to compile and process it all with the generous assistance of hundreds of individuals, businesses and organisations up and down the country. As such, it is not infallible, particularly as it is the first edition of what we hope will become an annual directory.

Information

The information listed comprises both exclusively lesbian and gay ventures as well as those which are lesbian and gay friendly. Hence, *The Pink Directory* includes everything from the Joy Club in Edinburgh and guest houses in Mull, to lesbian and gay friendly lawyers in Leicester and AIDS projects on the Isle of Wight.

We have excluded services such as telephone sex lines and businesses which supply sexual services on the grounds that this information is readily available elsewhere. Additionally, we have excluded counselling services where we were unable to verify the professional qualifications in relation to the services offered. London Lesbian and Gay Switchboard has this information should you want it.

The original information was drawn from the database of London Lesbian and Gay Switchboard who are receiving a proportion of royalties from sales. All information was then verified by follow-up questionnaire. We received a huge response. We have only included information in *The Pink Directory* from sources which have been researched and checked in this way. London Lesbian Line, numerous regional Switchboards, Lesbian Lines and Friend organisations throughout the country were then contacted and asked for their assistance. The level of co-operation was overwhelming. This information was further checked and verified to ensure the highest level of accuracy as possible. Finally, both OutRage! London and National AIDS Manual gave us generous unlimited access to their extensive records.

Region and Information Span

Our aim was to achieve as wide a regional spread of information as possible. We were struck by the existence of 'hotbeds' of lesbian and gay activity in parts of the country where you might not expect it (see the Medway towns and Barnstaple). We are both Northerners and we are conscious of the little prominence and attention that is paid to the huge number and diversity of lesbian and gay activities north of Watford ! This is why *The Pink Directory* begins with Scotland and proceeds southwards throughout the rest of the UK.

How to use *The Pink Directory*

The information is split into ten broad geographical regions which are defined as follows :

* Scotland
* North-West England
* North-East England
* Wales
* Midlands
* East England
* South-West England
* South-East England
* London
* Ireland

In the listings for Edinburgh, Glasgow, Manchester, Leeds, Birmingham, London and Dublin, the following sub-divisions occur:

* Hotels, guest houses, bed and breakfast accommodation
* Bars, clubs, pubs, cafes, restaurants
* Businesses
* Organisations

Elsewhere, the information is listed by town name in alphabetical order with the name of each entry in alphabetical order. To make *The Pink Directory* easier to use, there is an index of towns and cities.

We have not used codes and symbols as this can become confusing. Each entry gives a brief outline of the services provided. Where we refer to switchboard in the text, we refer to the local switchboard (unless otherwise stated). You will usually locate this in the listings under 'L' for Lesbian and Gay Switchboard or Helpline and occasionally under 'G' for Gay Switchboard or Helpline.

Where possible, we have indicated which group of people each business or service primarily serves, this may include lesbians, gay men, bisexuals, straight (heterosexual) people or a combination of these groups. We have also made reference to transsexual or transvestite people where this information was specifically given by services and businesses. We recommend, particularly for bars and clubs, that this information is checked with a quick telephone call if you are unfamiliar with the venue.

We must point out that *The Pink Directory* is merely a listing of businesses and services which fulfil our criteria for inclusion. *The Pink Directory* does not recommend any of the services listed.

Finally, we should be extremely grateful for your comments and any other information which may be relevant to a new edition. The more information you can help us find, the better !

Liz Gibbs and Tim Purcell
Cassell
November 1994

SCOTLAND

Sexual Politics

ORDER FORM

To order titles direct from Cassell see the form at the back of the directory : here we list some 30 innovative and acclaimed new books in our Lesbian and Gay Studies, Women on Women and AIDS Awareness series.

PUB QUIZ

Throughout 1995 Cassell and *The Pink Paper* shall be running a nationwide tournament of pub quizzes. If you run a pub and would be interested in taking part, contact Cassell's Sexual Politics Quiz, Villiers House, 41/47 Strand, London WC2N 5JE.

MAKE CASH! HOLD A BOOK PARTY!

If you are interested in hosting a book party for you and your friends contact Cassell's Sexual Politics Book Party, Villiers House, 41/47 Strand, London WC2N 5JE.

MAILING LIST

For regular information about our forthcoming titles, catalogues and news of special offers and book events in your area, fill in the form below and return to Cassell's Sexual Politics Mailing List, Villiers House, 41/47 Strand, London WC2N 5JE. No charge and no obligation.

Please include my details on the Sexual Politics Mailing List for receipt of details of forthcoming titles, news of special offers and of Cassell book events:

Name ....

Address ....

....

....

....

Send to Cassell Sexual Politics Mailing List, Villiers House, 41/47 Strand, London WC2N 5JE.

Edinburgh

Hotels, Guest Houses and B&Bs

13 Howe Street

13 Howe Street. T:0131-556-0930. Guest House. Lesbian, gay, straight. Open all year. No car park. No credit cards.

Amaryllis Guest House

5 Upper Gilmore Place. T:0131-229-4669. Lesbian, gay, straight. Open all year. No car park. No credit cards. Disabled access.

Amardillo Guest House

12 Gilmore Place. T:0131-229-6457. Lesbian, gay, straight. Open all year. No car park. Accepts Visa, Access.

Henderson Terrace

Henderson Terrace Dalry. T: 0131-556-7980. Lesbian bed and breakfast.

Linden Hotel

9/13 Nelson Street. T:0131-557-4344. Lesbian and gay. Open all year. No car park. Accepts Visa, Access, AMEX, Diners. Disabled access.

Mansfield House

57 Dublin Street. T:0131-556-7980. Lesbian and gay guest house. Open all year.

Pollock Halls

Reservations Office Pollock Halls of Residence 18 Holyrood Park Road. T:0131-667-1971. Hall of residence accommodation open during Edinburgh Festival. Lesbian, gay, straight. Write for details.

Bars, Clubs, Pubs, Cafes, Restaurants

Blooms

23 Greenside Place. T: 0131-556-9331. Lesbian and gay bar. Mon - Sat noon - 2am. Sun 12.30pm - 2am.

Blue Moon Cafe

36 Broughton Street. T:0131-556-2788 and new cafe at 1 Barony Street. Lesbian, gay, straight cafe. Mon - Sat 11am - 11pm. Sun noon - 10pm. Thurs 7.30pm - 11pm women only.

Chapps Club Bar

22 Greenside Place. T:0131-558-1270. Mon to Sat 9pm - 4am. Sun 9pm - 2am. Gay bar.

Covenanter

158-160 High Street. T:0131-225-1782. Mon-Thur 11am - midnight. Fri - Sat 11am - 1am. Sun 2pm - 11pm. Thurs women only 8pm - midnight. Lesbian and gay bar with club on Sat only.

French Connexion

87-89 Rose Street Lane North. T:0131-225-7651. Mon - Sat midday - 1am. Sun 1pm - 1am. Gay bar.

Insinvendoes

QT's 2 Picardy Place. T:0131-556-0499. Mon, Thurs - Sat 9pm - 2am. Gay cabaret club.

Joy Nightclub

Calton Studios Calton Road. T:0131-556-2788. Sat 10pm - late. Lesbian and gay club.

Laughing Duck

24 Howe Street. T:0131-225-6711. Mon - Wed midday - 1am. Thurs - Sat noon - 1.30am. Sun 6pm - 1am. Gay cafe, bar,

club (Fri & Sat only).

Lord Nelson

Linden Hotel 9 - 13 Nelson Street. T:0131-557-4334. Mon - Sat midday - 2pm, 4pm - 11pm. Sun midday - 11pm. Women only Mon. Lesbian and gay bar.

Network Disco

Calton Studios Calton Road. T:0131-556-2788. First Fri of each month 10pm - late. Lesbian club.

Newtown Bar

26a Dublin Street. T: 0131-538-7775. Daily midday - 12.30pm. Gay bar.

QT's

2 Picardy Place. T:0131-556-0499. Daily midday - 2pm. Gay bar.

Star Tavern

1 Northumberland Place. T:0131-539-8070. Mon - Sat midday - 12.30pm. Sun 12.30pm - 12.30am. Lesbian and gay bar.

Sunday Club

The Red Hot Pepper Club 3 Semple Street. T:0131-229-7733. Sun 11.30pm - 4am. Gay club.

Women Only Disco

Wee Red Bar, College of Art Lauriston Place. Contact Lesbian Line for information.

Businesses

Bobbies' Bookshop

220 Morrison Street. T:0131-229-1442. Mon - Sat 10am - 1pm, 2pm - 5.30pm. Sells lesbian and gay magazines.

Drondale Ltd.

60 Broughton Street. T:0131-556-1471. Mon - Sat 11am - 8pm. Sells leather clothing.

Edge

60 Broughton Street. T:0131-556-0852. Daily midday - midnight. Lesbian, gay, straight cafe.

McCourts Solicitors

53 George IV Bridge. T: 0131-225-6555 daytime, 0131-334-7774 or 0131-334-2431 (emergency). F:0131-225-5054. Solicitors for criminal law, accepts legal aid work. Contact Alistair Duff or Alex Prentice. Mon - Thurs 8.30am - 5pm, Fri 8.30am - 4.30pm otherwise contact emergency numbers.

Massow Ivan Associates

45 Moray Place EH3 6BQ. T:0131-226-2001. Gay financial consultant.

West and Wilde Bookshop

25a Dundas Street. T: 0131-556-0079. Mon - Fri 10am - 7pm Sat 9am - 7pm. Sun noon - 6pm. Lesbian and gay bookshop which also sells magazines. Mail order service.

Organisations

ACT UP ! (AIDS Coalition to Unleash Power)

P O Box 135 Edinburgh EH8 9XJ. Political direct action group to effect change to end the AIDS crisis.

A D Group

P O Box 301 Edinburgh EH9 1ND. Meets first Sat of each month 2pm - 6pm. Social group for older lesbians and supportive younger lesbians.

Bifrost

Bisexual Resource Centre 58a Broughton

Street. T:0131-557-3620. Tues - Thurs noon - 5pm. Lesbian, gay, bisexual. Bisexual information organisation. Produces a bisexual magazine and has a library which holds a collection of worldwide bisexual publications.

Body Positive

Contact via Switchboard. Lesbian, gay, straight. Self-help group for those affected by HIV.

Business Group

Holds lesbian and gay social events. Contact via Edinburgh Switchboard.

Bisexual Group

Meets Thurs at the Lesbian and Gay Centre 7.30pm - 9.30pm. T:0131-557-3620 (Helpline Thurs only).

Cause (The)

Meets Fri at the Lesbian and Gay Centre 8.30pm - 9.30pm. Lesbian social group.

Contact Point Gay Mens' Group

Contact via Switchboard. Social group for unemployed and low paid gay men.

GALAS (Gay and Lesbian Action Scotland)

Meets at The Edge 60 Broughton Street 7pm first and third Monday of each month. Support and campaigning group.

Gay Men's Running Club

Contact via Switchboard. Meets Sun for a 3 or 4 mile run.

Gay Outdoor Club

T:0131-556-8705 (Grant). Local branch of the Gay Outdoor Club.Social group which organises outdoor sporting and associated events.

Icebreakers

Meets at Blue Moon Cafe 36 Broughton Street second and fourth Wed of the month 7pm - 8pm. Lesbian and gay social group which enables people to meet without the pressures of the commercial scene. Also for those who have recently come out.

Indykement

Meets at the Women's Centre 61a Broughton Street. Lesbian discussion group. Meets second Sun of the month at 7.30pm.

Lantern Group

Meets at the Lesbian and Gay Centre. Mon 7.30pm - 9pm. Gay political group. Meetings include slides shows and speakers.

Lesbian and Gay Centre

58a Broughton Street Edinburgh EH1 1AA. T:031-557-3620. Centre for local lesbian, gay and bisexual social and political groups, events and information.

Lesbian and Gay Switchboard (Edinburgh)

T:0131-556-4049. Daily 7.30pm - 10pm. Telephone service offering advice, information and counselling.

Lesbian Line (Edinburgh)

T:0131-557-0751. Mon, Thurs 7.30pm - 10pm. Telephone service offering advice, information and counselling to lesbians.

Lillidots

Contact via Switchboard. Women's hill walking group.

LLGYM

Lothian Lesbian and Gay Youth Movement. Contact via Switchboard. Social group. Target age group 20-26. Meets 2pm Sat Blue Moon Cafe.

MSC Scotland

P O Box 28 Edinburgh EH1 1AA. Gay men's leather social group.

Names Project

86 Constitution Street EH6 6RP. T:0131-555-3446. Aims to illustrate the impact of AIDS pandemic, provide a positive and creative means of expression for those affected by HIV/AIDS and to raise funds for people living with HIV/AIDS.

National HIV and AIDS Information Centre

2 - 4 Abbeymount EH8 8EJ. Mon, Tues, Thurs, Fri 11am-4pm, Weds 5pm -8pm. T:0131-659-5116. F:0131-652-1780. Information and resource centre operating as a drop-in and by telephone. Aims to provide accurate, relevant information concerning HIV/AIDS to all who need it. Offers enquiry service, referral service, information surgery, reference library, monthly newsletter, current awareness bulletin and press cutting service.

Outright Scotland

58a Broughton Street Edinburgh EH1 3SA. Lesbian and gay rights campaigning group.

SAM (Scottish AIDS Monitor)

26 Anderson Place EH6 5NP. T:0131-555-4850. F:0131-555-4850. Voluntary HIV/AIDS organisation. Services include buddying, welfare rights advice and legal referral, hardship fund for anyone with HIV/AIDS, health education and training, speakers, conferences and consultancy, production of safer sex leaflets, safer sex roadshow, newsletter (*SAM*), outreach and action research in the gay community throughout Scotland.

Solas

2 - 4 Abbeymount EH8 8EJ. T:0131-661-0982. F:0131-652-1782. Mon, Tues, Thurs and Fri 10am-4pm, Weds 5pm - 9pm. A centre offering support services, information and informal meeting place for people living with HIV/AIDS. Support services include cafe, information centre, counselling service, complementary therapy, emotional support, child care, arts programme and training events.

TV/TS Group

Contact via Switchboard. TV/TS social and support group. Meets last Sat of each month 1pm - 5pm.

Women's Aid

12 Torpichen Street EH3 8JQ. T:0131-221-0401. F:0131-221-0402. Mon - Fri 10am - 1pm (office open until 4pm). Information support and refuge for abused women and their children (regardless of sexuality).

Women's Centre

61a Broughton Street. Centre for lesbian and

straight women's social, support and information groups.

Glasgow

Hotels, Guest Houses and B&Bs

B&B / Studio Flat

32 Riddrie Knowes. T:0141-770-5213 (Alan / Hugh). Lesbian and gay bed and breakfast. Open all year.

Bars, Clubs, Pubs, Cafes, Restaurants

Austins

183a Hope Street. T:0141-332-2707. Mon - Sat 11am - midnight. Sun 7.30pm - midnight. Lesbian and gay bar.

Bennetts

80 Glassford Street. Tues - Thurs 11pm - 3am, Fri - Sat 11pm - 3.30am. Lesbian, gay straight club.

Club X-Change

25 Royal Exchange Square. T:0141-204-4599. Mon - Sat 11pm - 3am, Sun 11pm - 3am. Lesbian, gay, straight club.

Court Bar

69 Hutchinson Street. T:0141-552-2463. Mon - Sat 11am - midnight, Sun 12am - 2.30pm 7pm - 11.45pm. Lesbian and gay bar.

Delmonica's

68 Virginia Lane. T:0141-552-4803. Daily 11am - midnight. Lesbian and gay bar.

Squires

106 West Campbell Street. Mon - Fri midday - midnight, Sat midday - 2.30pm 7pm - 11.45pm, Sun 8pm - 11pm. Lesbian and gay bar.

Tunnel

84 Mitchell Street. Mon 11.30pm - 3am. Gay club.

Waterloo Bar

306 Argyle Road. T:0141-221-7395. Mon - Wed & Sat 11am - midnight. Thurs Fri 11am - 2am, Sun 12.30pm - 2.30pm 7pm - 11pm. Gay bar.

Businesses

John Smith

57 St. Vincent Street G2 5TB (T:0141-221-7472) and 252 Byres Road G12 (T:0141-334-2769). Bookshop that stocks lesbian and gay literature and magazines.

Organisations

ACET (AIDS Care Education and Training)

PO Box 725 G20 9PX. T:0141-945-5286. F:0141-945-4358. Branch of Christian AIDS charity which provides practical home based help to people affected by HIV/ AIDS.

Alternative Wrestlers

P O Box 437 Glasgow G42 8HU or contact via Switchboard. Gay social group.

Befrienders

c/o SLGYG P O Box 69 Glasgow G4 0TY. Young (under 28) befriending group for lesbians and gay men.

Body Positive

P O Box 190 Glasgow G4 9QR or via Switchboard. Self-help group for those affected by HIV/ AIDS.

Bisexual Group

Contact via Switchboard. Meets first and

third Mon of the month.

City Liaison Group

53 Cochrane Street. T:0141-553-2010. Aims to help and advise on lesbian and gay unemployment, education, homelessness, social and legal problems. Disabled access.

FROGALS (Friends of Gay and Lesbian Switchboard)

c/o SGLS P O Box 38 Glasgow G2 2QF. Funding raising and social group for Switchboard.

GALLUS (Gay and Lesbian Liberation and Unity)

P O Box 38 Glasgow G2 2QF. Campaigning group for lesbians and gay men.

Gay and Lesbian Project

GLC Project P O Box 463 Glasgow 12. Group which meets on the first Sat of each month at 2pm.

Gay Caledonia Association

Details from Switchboard. Meets at Squires Bar 106 West Campbell Street on the first and third Wed of each month. Gay social group for kilt fans.

Gay Football Supporters Network

GFSN c/o Gay Times 116 Bayham Street London NW1 0BA. Glasgow branch meets monthly at Squires Bar 106 West Campbell Street.

Gay Outdoor Club

T:0141-848-6643 (Douglas). Glasgow branch of the Gay Outdoor Club. Social group which organises outdoor, sporting and associated events.

Gay Wrestling Group

T:0141-423-3532 (Ian). Meets Tues 7pm - 9.30pm. Gay men's wrestling group.

HIV Carers Support Group

Church House 340 Cathedral Street. T:0141-353-2979. Lesbian, gay, straight. Support group for carers of people who have HIV/AIDS.

Icebreakers

Contact via Switchboard. Meets at Austins Bar monthly. Lesbian and gay social group which enables people to meet without the pressures of the commercial scene.

Lesbian Cycling Group

Contact via Switchboard. Social group for lesbians who enjoy cycling.

Lesbian and Gay Christian Movement (Glasgow)

T:0141-649-6616. Support and social group for lesbian and gay Christians.

Lesbian and Gay Switchboard (Strathclyde)

P O Box 38 Glasgow G2 2QF. T:0141-221-8372. F:0141-204-4423. Daily 7pm - 10pm. Telephone service offering advice, information and counselling to lesbians and gay men.

Lesbian Line

P O Box 686 Glasgow G3 7TL. T: 0141-552-3355. Wed 7pm - 10pm. Telephone service offering advice, information and counselling to lesbians.

Lesbian Mothers Group

Contact via Lesbian Line. Meets alternative Mondays at 7pm. Creche facilities available.

Lesbian Networking Meeting

Contact via Lesbian Line. Social group for lesbians.

Lesbian Sports Group

Contact via Lesbian Line. Weekly squash,badminton and tennis for lesbians.

Lesbian Youth Action

Contact via Lesbian Line. Young campaigning group for lesbians.

Long Yang Club

Contact via Switchboard. Social group for gay orientals and their western friends.

Outright

c/o SLGYN P O Box 69 G4 0TY or via Switchboard. Lesbian, gay, bisexual campaigning group for equal rights.

Older Women Group

Contact via Lesbian Line. Social group for older women.

SAM (Scottish AIDS Monitor)

22 Woodside Terrace G3 7XH. T:0141-353-3133. F:0141-353-1699. Provides buddying service and individual counselling, welfare rights advice, legal advice, prison work, hardship fund, gay outreach action research, conference speakers, training, education roadshow, safer sex leaflets.

Scottish Gay and Lesbian Sports Association

c/o Alternative Sports PO Box 437 G42 8HU. Lesbian and gay sports association which has regular events and newsletter.

SLGY (Strathclyde Lesbian and Gay Youth)

Contact via Strathclyde Switchboard. Tues 7pm. Social group for young lesbains and gay men up to the age of 26.

Steve Retson Project

Glasgow Royal Infirmary Department of GU Medicine 16 Alexandra Parade G31 2ER. T:0141-304-4754. F:0141-304-4978. Mon - Fri 5.30pm - 8pm. Project which provides GUM clinic service for gay men.

Women's Softball Group

Contact via Switchboard. Meets Sun 2pm - 4.30pm. Lesbian group which meets to play softball.

Aberdeen

Body Positive Grampian

PO Box 83 AB9 8DD. T:01224-404408. 24-hour helpline. Self-help support group for people affected by HIV/AIDS.

Club Caberfeidh

Hadden Street. T: 01224 - 212181. Lesbian and gay club. Sat & Sun 10pm - 2am.

Cross Dress Group

Contact Switchboard for details. TV social group.

Exchange

Guild/Chapel Street.

T:01224-213009. Mon - Sat 11am - 3am. Lesbian and gay club.

Flannies Lounge

Stirling Street. T:01224-571266. Open Mon - Sat 11am - midnight, Sun 11am - 11pm. Lesbian and gay bar.

Gay Group

Contact Switchboard for details. Meets first and third Sun of the month. Gay social group.

Grampian AIDS Line

P O Box 250 Aberdeen. T: 01224 - 574000. Tues & Fri 7pm - 9pm. AIDS/ HIV support and advice line.

Grampian Buddy Group

PO Box 353 AB9 3DD. T:01224-404407. 24-hour support and counselling to anyone with HIV/AIDS and their partners, families, friends.

Grant and Co

1 Albert Street. T: 01224 - 645066 (day) 01224 - 740281 (emergency) F: 01224 - 642525. Solicitor practice covering all aspects of law, particularly estate agency, commercial business, private client succession. Speaks French and Portuguese. Does not accept legal aid work. Disabled access.

Lesbian Gay and Bisexual Switchboard

P O Box 174 Crown Street Aberdeen AB9 8UZ. T:01224 - 586869 F: 01224 - 212333 (minicom). Wed & Fri 7pm - 10pm. Telephone service offering advice, support and counselling.

Lesbian Group

Contact Women's Centre for details. Meets second and fourth Wed of the month 8pm - 10pm at the Women's Centre.

Young Lesbian Group

Contact Women's Centre for details. Meets Wed at the Women's Centre. Social and support group for young lesbians.

Women's Centre

Shoe Lane Aberdeen AB1 1AG. T:01224 - 625010. Lesbians and straight women. Operates a drop in 9.30am - 2.30pm and various groups meet at other times. Supports women's groups and womens's initiatives.

Ayr

Roseland Guest House

15 Charlotte Street Ayr. T: 01292 - 283435 (Ron). Lesbian, gay, straight guest house.

Buckie

Glenelg Guest House

26 Richmond Terrace Portgordon. T:01542-33221. Lesbian, gay, straight guest house. Pets welcome.

Dundee

Club Cruise

Douglas Street Dundee. Sat 11pm - 3am. Gay club.

Edge

85 Commercial Street Dundee. Fri 10.30pm - 2.30am. Gay club.

Gaugor

75 Seagate Dundee. Mon - Wed 11am - 11pm. Thurs - Sun 11am - 2.30am. Gay

bar. (Pronounced *Gay - Jor*!)

Lesbian, Gay and Bisexual Network

Contact via Switchboard. Social group that meets regularly at Dundee College of Further Education.

Lesbian and Gay Switchboard

P O Box 53 Dundee DD1 3HG. T: 01382 - 202620. Mon 7pm - 10pm. Telephone service offering advice, support and counselling.

SAM (Scottish AIDS Monitor)

c/o Social Work Department Northern College Gardyne Road Broughty Ferry DD5 1NY. T:01382-461167. F:01382-454839. Mon - Fri 9am - 12.30pm. Offers buddying, support and advice/ information on HIV/ AIDS and related issues.

Tay Friend

P O Box 182 Dundee DD1 9UP. Lesbian and gay. Friendship, social and support group.

Women's Disco

Contact Switchboard for details. Lesbian and straight women's disco held monthly at West Port Bar.

Elgin

Easterton Farm House

Thomhill IV30 3SP. T:01343-86294. Lesbian and gay bed and breakfast.

Glenrothes

Social Work Department

Glenrothes House North Street KY7 5PB. T:01592-630639. Mon - Fri 9am - 4.45pm. Offers information about services available for people affected by HIV/AIDS.

Inverness

Gay Outdoor Club

T:01463-230651(Michael). Local branch of Gay Outdoor Club. Social group which organises outdoor sporting and associated events.

Out and About

P O Box 91 Inverness IV1 2GJ. Lesbian and gay social group which organises socials and trips.

SAM (Scottish AIDS Monitor)

28 Huntly Street IV3 5PR. T:01463-241000. F:01463-711793. Mon and Fri 7pm - 9.30pm. Offers information on HIV/ AIDS, telephone helpline, face-to-face emotional and practical support, support work for parents, hardship fund for people living with HIV/AIDS, free condoms and lubricants, monthly support groups for gay men and for women.

Isle of Skye

B&B

Tigh na Coille Dunan Skye. T: 01471 - 822547 (Ian). Lesbian, gay, straight bed and breakfast.

Kirkcaldy

Fife Friend

P O Box 19 Kirkaldy KY1 3JF. T:01592 - 266688. Fri 7.30pm - 10.30pm. Support and social group which organises local events.

Glenrothes and Levenmouth Support Group for Mental Health, Addictions and

HIV/AIDS

Viewforth Centre Viewforth Street KY1 3DH. T:01592-266688. Fri 7.30pm - 10.30pm. Telephone service offering advice support and information for people affected by HIV/AIDS.

Young Gay Christian Group

Contact via Fife Friend. Gay Christian social group.

Mull

Ardeck House

Dervaig Isle of Mull. T: 01068 - 84254 (Neil). Guest House. Lesbian, gay, straight.

Perth

Friend

P O Box 46 Perth PH1 2YH. T:01738 - 828840 (lesbian) 01738 - 23917 (gay). Lesbian and gay social group which operates a phoneline on Mondays 7pm - 10pm.

Rosebank Guest House

53 Dunkeld Road Perth. T:01738 - 621737. Lesbian, gay, straight guest house.

Stirling

Forth Friend

P O Box 28 Stirling FK9 5YW. T: 01786 471285. Mon 7.30pm - 9.30pm. Telephone service offering counselling and information. Organises social events and befriending for lesbians gay men and bisexuals.

Gay Outdoor Club

T: 01786 - 823021 (Bill). Local branch of Gay Outdoor Club, the gay social group which organises outdoor sporting and associated events.

Stornoway

Lifestyle Centre

Town Hall Point Street PA87 2BE. T:01851-701010. F:01851-704209. Offers confidential HIV/AIDS counselling and HIV/AIDS awareness campaigns.

NORTH-WEST ENGLAND

Sexual Politics

ORDER FORM

To order titles direct from Cassell see the form at the back of the directory : here we list some 30 innovative and acclaimed new books in our Lesbian and Gay Studies, Women on Women and AIDS Awareness series.

PUB QUIZ

Throughout 1995 Cassell and *The Pink Paper* shall be running a nationwide tournament of pub quizzes. If you run a pub and would be interested in taking part, contact Cassell's Sexual Politics Quiz, Villiers House, 41/47 Strand, London WC2N 5JE.

MAKE CASH! HOLD A BOOK PARTY!

If you are interested in hosting a book party for you and your friends contact Cassell's Sexual Politics Book Party, Villiers House, 41/47 Strand, London WC2N 5JE.

MAILING LIST

For regular information about our forthcoming titles, catalogues and news of special offers and book events in your area, fill in the form below and return to Cassell's Sexual Politics Mailing List, Villiers House, 41/47 Strand, London WC2N 5JE. No charge and no obligation.

Please include my details on the Sexual Politics Mailing List for receipt of details of forthcoming titles, news of special offers and of Cassell book events:

Name ....
Address ....
....
....
....

Send to Cassell Sexual Politics Mailing List, Villiers House, 41/47 Strand, London WC2N 5JE.

MANCHESTER

Hotels, Guest Houses and B&Bs

Carlton House Hotel

153 Upper Chorlton Road Whalley Range M16 7SH. T:0161-881-4635. Lesbian and gay hotel.

Merchants Hotel

Back Piccadilly M1 1HP. T:0161-236-2939. Lesbian and gay hotel.

Monroes/The International

38 London Road. T:0161-236-0564. Lesbian, gay, straight hotel.

Rembrandt Hotel

Canal Street Manchester. Lesbian and gay hotel.

Bars, Clubs, Pubs, Cafes, Restaurants

Austins

Richmond Street. T:0161-236-1547. Mon - Sat 10pm - 2am. Gay membership club with dance floor.

Bloom Street Cafe

39 Bloom Street. T:0161-236-3433. Lesbian and gay cafe.

Boodles

Canal Street. T:0161-237-9117. Lesbian and gay restaurant.

Cellar Bar

Bloom Street (under Napoleons). Gay bar. MSC leather, denim, rubber dress code.

Central Park

Sackville Street. T:0161-236-5196. Lesbian and gay club.

Churchills

37 Charlton Street. T:0161-236-5529. Lesbian and gay pub

Clarence Hotel

St Michael's Square Ashton-under-Lyne. T: 0161-339-559. Lesbian gay straight pub.

Club La La @ The Venue

17 Wentworth Street West. Fri until 8am. Lesbian and gay club.

Cruz 101

101 Princess Street. T:0161-237-1554. Gay members-only club open until 2am Mon - Sat.

Dammes

North-West England Deaf Centre Crawford House Precinct Centre. Details from Lesbian Link. Bi-monthly lesbian disco.

Dickens

74a Oldham Street. T:0161-236-5196. Club for lesbians, gays, TVs TSs. Mon - Sat 10am - 2pm.

Ethos @ The State

6 Whitworth Street . T:0161-236-7418. Fri 11.30pm - 6am. Lesbian, gay, straight club.

Euro Cafe

Whitworth Street. Mon - Sat midday - 10pm, also Thurs - Sat midnight - 6am. Lesbian and gay cafe.

Equinox

Bloom Street. T:0161-236-4445. Tues - Sat 10pm - 2am. Gay club.

Flesh @ The Hacienda

11-13 Whitworth Street West. T:0161-236-5051. Lesbian and gay club (run by A Bit Ginger). Last Wed of the month, 10pm - 4am.

Follies

Whitworth Street. T:0161-236-8149. Bar

and disco. Mon - Sat 9pm - 2am. Lesbian and gay (mainly women). Women only Sat.

Grand Central

80 Oxford Street. T:0161-236-2592. Open usual pub hours. Lesbian, gay, straight pub.

Green Room

54/56 Whitworth Street West. T:0161-236-1676. Arts centre with theatre, bar and cafe. Disabled access.

La Cage

Bloom Street. T:0161-236-4445. Mon - Sat midday - 11pm, Sun midday - 3pm, 7pm - 10.30pm. Gay wine bar. Wed - Sat opens after the clubs close as a cafe serving drinks.

Libido @ No. 1

Central Street. T:0161-834-6187. Lesbian club every second Thurs 10pm - 2am.

Manto

46 Canal Street. T:0161-236-2667. Lesbian and gay cafe and bar. Open all day.

Napoleons

Bloom Street. T:0161-236-8800. Mon - Sat 10pm - 2am. Gay and TV/TS club.

New Union

Princess Street. T:0161-228-1492. Mon - Sat midday - 11pm, Sun midday - 3pm, 7pm - 10.30pm. Gay pub (hosted by Joyce of the Immaculate Hairdo).

New York New York

98 Bloom Street. T:0161-236-6556. Mon - Sat midday - 11pm. Sun midday - 11pm (food in the afternoon). Gay pub.

No. 1

Central Street. T:0161-834-6187. Lesbian, gay, straight club.

Oscars

5 Cooper Street. T:0161-236-6007. Daily 6pm - 2am. Gay bar, club, restaurant.

Paddy's Goose

Bloom Street. T:0161-236-9709. Open usual pub hours. Lesbian, gay, straight pub.

Paradise Factory

112 Paradise Street. T:0161-273-5422. Thurs - Sat 10pm - 2am. Lesbian, gay, straight club with women only space on Fri.

Q Bar

28 Richmond Street. T:0161-237-9329. Gay bar. Open until 1am.

Rembrandt

33 Sackville Street. T:0161-236-2435 / 1311. Mon - Sat midday - 11pm, Sun midday - 3pm, 7pm - 10.30pm. Lesbian and gay bar. Women only space Fri (Sapphos), TV / TS space Wed (Concorde), deaf lesbian and gay space fortnightly Sat.

Rockies

4-6 Whitworth Street. Mon - Fri 10pm - 2am (except Tuesday). Sat 10am - 3am. Sunday 1pm - 4pm. Women only space on Saturday. Lesbian and gay club.

Subway

Oxford Road (below Grand Central pub).Mon-Sat 6pm-11pm. Lesbian, gay, straight bar.

That Cafe

1013 Stockport Road.T:0161-432-4672. Tues-Sat 7.30pm-late. Sunday midday-2.30pm. Gay run cafe.

Businesses

A Bit Ginger

Studio 115 Ducie House M1 2JW. T:0161-237-9460. Lesbian and gay nightclub promoters (Flesh etc).

Bookloft

160a Wellington Road Withington M20. T:0161-445-2772. Stocks lesbian and gay books.

Churchill's

425 Bury New Road Prestwich M25 1AH. T:0161-773-3173. Individual tailoring for TV/TS.

Clone Zone

38 Bloom Street. T:0161-236-1398. Gay shop which sells fashion, cards, leathers and magazines. Mon - Sat 11am - 6pm (Thurs until 9pm). Also Fri and Sat evening 9pm - 11pm. Sun 2pm - 6pm.

Collyhurst Law Centre

Community Centre Paget Street. T:0161-205-5040. General law centre. Legal aid available.

Corner House

70 Oxford Street. T:0161-228-2463. Open 11am - 11pm daily. Arts centre with gallery, cafe, bar and cinema.

Debbie the Decorator

T:0161-476-2906. Woman painter and decorator.

Elles Belles

T:0161-226-8888. All women 24-hour taxi firm.

Ethos

427 Bury New Road Higher Broughton. T:0161-792-9494. TV /TS service offering various facilities.

Euro Sauna

202 Hill Lane off Victoria Avenue Blackley. T:0161-740-5152. Gay sauna.

Frontline Books

1 Newton Street M1 1HW. T:0161-236-1101. Fax:0161-236-1103. Mon - Sat 10am - 6pm. Lesbian, gay, straight bookshop which also sells magazines, cards, t-shirts etc. Regular readings.

Funky Crops

Bloom Street. T:0161-237-1032. Lesbian and gay friendly hairdressers.

Glaisyers and Glickman

6th Floor Arkwright House Parsonage Gardens M3 2LE. T:0161-832-7046. Contact Anthony Sacks. Solicitor practice specialising in conveyancing, life policies, living together agreements, family law, custody, employment and crime. Accepts legal aid work.

Ingham and Co

37 Bloom Street. T:0161-237-3594. General solicitor practice.

Keynes (Dr G)

217 Hulme Walk. T:0161-227-9785. Medical practice.

Ladycars

T:0161-442-1442. Women's taxi service.

L' Homme Escort Agency

T:0161-736-1546 office hours. After hours 01378-144171. Male escort, kissograms, male strippers, party design and catering services. 24-hour service.

Linder Myers

Phoenix House Cross

Street M2 4TF. T:0161-832-6972. General solicitor practice.

Livingstone & Co

36 Peter Street. T:0161-834-0611. General solicitor practice.

Lizar R.

2 Woodcote Square Hulme M15 6DZ. T:0161-226-2314. General solicitor practice.

Longsight Law Centre

584 Stockport Road. T:0161-225-5111. General law centre. Legal aid available.

Manchester Clipper

Brazenose Street. T:0161-833-2437. Lesbian and gay friendly barber.

MARC (Manchester Area Resource Centre)

Brownsfield Mill Binns Place 104 Great Ancoats Street M4 5BP. T:0161-236-0350. F:0161-237-1450. Printing and computer equipment services.

Monsalls

212 Chapel Street M36. T:0161-834-0909. Mobile 0860-544633. General solicitor practice which offers 24-hour police call out.

Moreland Skemp Reed and Co

229 Burnage Lane Burnage M19 1FN. T:0161-432-0171. Solictor practice specialising in family law, relationship breakdown, child custody, conveyancing, wills and probate. Accepts legal aid work.

North Manchester Self Advocacy

Portakabin 3 Abraham Moss Centre Crescent Road M8 5UF. T:0161-720-8485. Self-advocacy support service.

Otten and Skemp

339 Palatine Road Northenden. T:0161-945-1431. Solicitor practice specialising in family and matrimonial work, care proceedings, contact orders, co-habitation, property disputes and wills. Accepts legal aid work. Speaks Urdu and Hindi.

Outspoken Productions

Studio 202 Ducie House M1 2JW. T:0161-228-6228. Lesbian and gay radio production company.

Peasgood Walker

937 Rochdale Road M9 1AE. T:0161-205-2772. Solicitor practice specialising in children's cases, residence orders, family law, happy to deal with lesbian custody cases. Accepts legal aid work. Mainly women in the practice.

Platt Halpern

151 Dickenson Road Rusholme M14 5HZ. T:0161-224-2555. Solicitor practice covering family law, residence orders, care proceedings, crime, racial harassment and conveyancing. Accepts legal aid work.

Rhys Vaughan

382 Dickenson Road Longsight. T:0161-224-1439. General solicitor practice.

South Manchester Law Centre

584 Stockport Road M30. T: 0161-225-

5111. Fax: 0161-225-0210. Mon-Wed 10am-1pm (without appointment). Other times by appointment. Law centre covering housing, social security and immigration. Accepts legal aid work. Punjabi spoken. Disabled access.

Stallion Sauna

At the Carlton House Hotel (see above). T:0161-881-4635. Gay sauna.

Thornhill and Brown

78a Dickenson Road Rusholme. T:0161-224-2255. General solicitor practice.

Tib Street Barber

31 Tib Street. Lesbian and gay barber shop.

Transformation

413 Bury Road Prestwich. T:0161-773-2572. Mon - Sat 9am - 8pm. Shop and business that specialises in turning men into beautiful women for TV/TS.

Twigg CR

61 Bridge Street. T:0161-834-1173. Discount designer clothes shop.

Village Bookshop

105/107 Princes Street. T:0161-236-6441. Lesbian and gay bookshop.

Village Cars

T:0161-237-3383. Gay taxi service.

Worden (Dr T)

42 Canal Street. T:0161-237-9490. Medical practice.

Wythenshawe Law Centre

Fernside Road. T:0161-428-5929. General law centre. Legal aid available.

Organisations

AIDSline

T:0161-839-2442. Mon -Fri. Lesbian, gay, straight. Telephone service offering advice, support and counselling to people affected by AIDS / HIV.

Albert Kennedy Trust

25 New Mount Street M4 4DE. T:0161-953-4059. Fax: 0161-953-4001. Mon - Fri 9am-5pm. Lesbian and gay. Provides housing, support and advice for young people who are homeless, or at risk of becoming so, because of their sexuality.

Anchor

Contact via Lesbian and Gay Centre. T:0161-274-3999. Support group for alcoholic gay men. Meets Sun 7pm at the Lesbian and Gay Centre.

BHAF (Black HIV / AIDS Forum)

Zion Community Resource Centre Zion Crescent Hulme M15 5BY. T:0161-226-9145. F:0161-227-9862. Mon - Fri 9am - 5pm. Offers practical and emotional support for anyone affected by HIV / AIDS in black and minority ethnic communities. Also training and information, monitoring service, newsletter.

Black Lesbian Writing Group

c/o Box 26 1 Newton Street M1 1HW. Meets monthly at Frontline Books.

Body Positive North West

3rd Floor Fourways House 18 Tariff Street M1 2EP. T:0161-2327-9717 (helpline with minicom). Helpline Tues Thurs 7pm - 10pm. drop-in Mon - Thurs midday - 5pm, Fri midday -

4pm. Self-help group for people affected by HIV / AIDS. Organises community care, health promotion, aromatherapy, social and support groups, housing and welfare advice, speakers group, newsletter, counselling, massage, hospital visits, social events, legal advice, hairdressing and a bridge club.

Commonword

21 Newton Street. T:0161-236-2773. Gay writers group.

Crisis Centre

T:0161-437-4594. Community based project offering hostel-type housing in Wythenshawe for 16-25 year olds. Accepts referrals from other agencies only.

Disabled Lesbians

Manchester Disablity Forum Cariocca Business Park 2 Hellidon Close Ardwick. T:0161-273-5033. Mincom 0161-273-5083. Support group for disabled lesbians.

Equality Group

P O Box 532 Manchester. T:0161-234-3259. Lesbian and gay campaigning group.

Face to Face

Contact via Switchboard. Provides face-to-face counselling both inside and outside the Lesbian and Gay Centre.

Family Support Group

T:0161-839-2442 (via AIDSline). Mon - Fri 7pm - 10pm. Meets monthly in a safe venue. Support group for families, lovers or friends of people with an AIDS-related illness or who are HIV+ or who have died as the result of an AIDS-related illness.

FFLAG (Families and Friends of Lesbians and Gays)

c/o P O Box 153 M60 1LP. T:0161-628-7621 or 0161-748-3452. Support group for friends and families of lesbians and gays.

Forty Second Street Youth Counselling Service

Ground Floor Lloyds House 22 Lloyd Street M2 5WA. T:0161-832-0170. Youth counselling service for people aged 15-25. Mon 1pm -4pm, Tues Wed Fri 10am - 1pm.

Funeral Officient

Rev P Whiting c/o Lesbian and Gay Centre. T:0161-205-8905. A gay minister of the Metropolitan Community Church available to conduct religious or non-religious ceremonies particularly where a supportive approach to HIV / AIDS is needed.

Gay Bikers MCC

c/o Lesbian and Gay Centre PO Box 153 M60 1LP. Gay. For people who already own a bike or genuinely interested learners.

Gay Cyclists Group

Contact via Lesbian and Gay Centre. Gay social group.

Gay Mens Sub-Committee

Equal Opportunities Unit of Manchester Council. T:0161-234-3259. Committee for gay men's rights and support.

Gay Outdoor Club

T:0161-860-5267. Local branch of the national lesbian and gay organisation for people interested in outdoor sporting and associated activities.

Gay Youth Manchester

c/o Lesbian and Gay Centre. T:0161-274-3814. Meets Tues 7.30pm - 9.30pm and Sat 3pm - 7pm. Gives help, advice and information to people aged 26 or under.

George House Trust

75 Ardwick Green North M12 6FX. T:0161-839-4340. F:0161-839-6540. North West HIV charity offering emotional support, financial support, training and information, campaigning and HIV community care.

Girth and Mirth

T:0161-707-6207. Gay social group for stocky, heavy, chubby men and their friends.

HARPP (HIV Around Postive People)

c/o The Village Charity P O Box 20 M60 1QW. T:0161-237-3131. A support group for carers, partners and relatives and people directly involved with HIV+ people.

HIV Women's Group

T:0161-839-4340. Women only self-help group for all women who are HIV+. Creche available Mon 10am - midday.

Icebreakers

Contact via Switchboard. For people who are coming out or who are new to Manchester. Wed 8.30pm at the Lesbian and Gay Centre.

Isis

Black lesbian support group. Contact via Lesbian and Gay Centre. Meets 1st Monday of the month 7pm - 9pm.

Kenric

BM Kenric London WC1N 3XX. Local branch of this national lesbian social organisation meets Fri at Sapphos (upstairs at The Rembrandt).

Lesbian Foster Carers Group

c/o The Link PO Box 207 M60 1GL. Support group for lesbians who are or would like to be foster or adoptive carers.

Lesbian and Gay Centre

P O Box 153 Manchester M60 1LP. Mon - Sat 10am - 10pm. Sun 1pm - 7pm. T:0161-274-3814 (advice and information line). Centre offering meeting facilities an informal drop-in, counsellors. Snack bar.

Lesbian and Gay Christian Movement

T:0161-969-8008 (Mike). Local branch of a national network.

Lesbian and Gay Disability Forum

Unit 29 Carrioca Enterprise Park 2 Hellidon Close Ardwick M12 4AH. T:0161-273-5033. Minicom 0161-273-5083. Support group for disabled lesbians and gays.

Lesbian and Gay Medical Association

Contact via The Secretary LGMA Lesbian and Gay Centre. Meets 7.30pm last Friday of the month at the Lesbian and Gay Centre.

Lesbian and Gay Switchboard

P O Box 153 Manchester M60 1LP. T:0161-274-3999. Daily 4pm - 10pm. Telephone service offering advice, support and information.

Lesbian and Gay Teachers Support Group

Contact via Switchboard. Lesbian and gay social and support group.

Lesbian and Gay Youth Manchester

Contact via Lesbian and Gay Centre for details. Tues 7pm - 10pm. Sat 3pm - 7pm. Social group 16-25.

Lesbian Link

PO Box 207 M60 1GL. T:0161-236-6205 or 0161-237-5736 (minicom). Mon, Tues and Thurs 6.30pm - 9pm. Telephone service offering advice, counselling and information to lesbians.

Lesbian Sub-Committee

Equal Opportunities Unit of Manchester Council. T:0161-232-3212. Committee for lesbian rights and support.

Lesbians With Children

Meets Sun 2 - 5pm at Rusholme Children's Centre Great Western Street. Contact Lesbian Link for details.

Lifeline Project

101-103 Oldham Street M4 1LW. T:0161-839-2054. F:0161-834-5903. Mon - Fri 9.30am - 5pm. Needle exchange, condoms and lubricant, drop-in, advice, training and support for other professionals, safer sex information.

Lifeshare

Unit 29 23 New Mount Street M4 4DE. T:0161-953-4069. Mon - Fri 10am - 1pm. Lesbian, gay, straight. Offers counselling and help with homelessness and furniture.

Long Yang Club

P O Box 5 Salford M6 5ET. T:0161-431-5445. Gay men's social group for orientals and their admirers.

Manchester Lesbian Families

Trinity House Grove Close Rusholme or via Lesbian and Gay Centre. Meets 1st Sun of every month 1pm - 4pm. Support group for lesbian families.

MASH (Manchester Action on Street Health)

Unit 110 Ducie House 37 Ducie Street M1 2JW. T:0161-228-3433. F:0161-237-9459. A sexual health and HIV prevention project providing a night time service at street level for women and men who work as prostitutes in Manchester.

Mens Bisexual Group

Meets at the Lesbian and Gay Centre 3rd Thurs evening of the month 7.30pm - 10pm.

Men's Room

T:0161-338-6715 Mon, Tues 6pm - 7pm. Support group for gay men (25+) in Tameside. Meet 1st Tues every month.

Moonshine

Social and support group for lesbians with drink problems. Meets 1st Sunday of the month at the Lesbian and Gay Centre.

Network

Contact via the Lesbian and Gay Centre. Lesbian self-insemination group.

Northern Concord

PO Box 258 M60 1LN. Voluntary self-help and social group for TV / TSs and their partners and families.

Oasis

Salvation Army AIDS Care Centre Grosvenor Street Brunswick M13 9UB. T:0161-273-2081. Tues 3.30pm - 9pm. A centre for support and practical health for people affected by HIV.

Open House Project

Project House PO Box 141 M20 8EQ. T:0161-447-3436. F:0161-447-3436. A residential and palliative care centre for people with HIV-related disease.

Parents Group

A group run by and for the parents of lesbians and gays. Meets regularly at the Lesbian and Gay Centre.

Positive Parenting

Box 7 1 Newton Street M1. Meets every other Thursday 7.30, Town Hall, Albert Square. Mixed campaigning group working towards equal rights in adoption and fostering for lesbians and gays.

Quest

Upstairs Hall St Augustines Church Grosvenor Gardens. T:0161-242-9630. Lesbian and gay Catholic group meets 2.15pm - 5.30pm last Sat of the month.

Rape Crisis

PO Box 336 M25. T:0161-834-8784. Tues Fri 2pm - 5pm. Wed, Thurs Sun 6pm - 9pm. Free and confidential service offering support and counselling run by women for women and girls.

Stepping Stones

Lesbian and bisexual social group which meets 2nd and 4th Monday at the Lesbian and Gay Centre.

South Manchester and Trafford Gay Social Group

Contact via Switch-board. Meets Wed 7pm - 11pm. Lesbian and gay social support group.

Superchain

Meets at Cellar Bar, Napoleon's. Friday 9.30pm. Gay men's leather club.

Thirty Plus Group

Contact Lesbian Link. Social group for older lesbians.

Time for Support

c/o 27 Blackfriars Street M3 7AQ. Ecumenical group of Christians who believe God shares the suffering and isolation of people with AIDS-related illnesses.

TORCH (Tackling Oppression by Radical Co-operative Housing)

c/o LYGM P O Box 153 M60 1LP. T:0161-861-0928.

Triangle Club

Pink Directory

c/o Lesbian and Gay Centre PO Box 153 M60 1LP. Social group for deaf or hearing impaired lesbians and gay men. Meets second Sat of each month at Rembrandts.

TV/ TS Line

T:0161-274-3705. Wed 7pm - 10pm, Thurs 7pm - 10pm. Telephone service offering advice, support and information.

Village Charity

PO Box 20 M60 1QW. T:0161-237-3131. Charity which raises funds for HIV prevention projects in the Manchester area. Fundraising shop in Richmond Street.

Women's Aid Centre

PO Box 156 Newton Street M60 1DB. T:0161-839-8574. Mon - Fri 10am - 4pm. Emergency 0161-434-2992. Local branch of a national organisation offering advice and support for women in violent domestic situations

Women's Domestic Violence Helpline

PO Box 156 Newton Street M60 1DB. T:0161-839-8574. Mon - Fri 10am - 4pm. Telephone service offering advice and counselling.

Young Lesbian Group

Contact via Lesbian Link. Young (under 26) lesbian social group which meets Thurs 7pm - 9pm.

Young Survivors Project

T:0161-236-0829 (Manchester Housing Consortium). Referral service for young women (16-25) who have been sexually abused and who have housing and other support needs.

Y-Wait

Collyhurst Adult Community Education Centre Collyhurst Street. T:0161-205-1257. Wed 4pm - 8pm. Doctor and family planning advice available 5pm - 8pm. Young women's advice, information and support group.

Zami

Contact via Lesbian Link. Social and support group for black lesbians under 26 years of age..

Accrington

Dolly Grays

98a Blackburn Road. T: 01254-31924. Sunday 7pm - 11.30pm. Gay club.

Altrincham

Robinson King

298 Hale Road Hale Barns WA15 8SL. T:0161-980-5200. Solicitor practice covering personal injury, civil and ten years' experience of lesbian custody cases. Ask for Jane Robinson.

Birkenhead

ACASIA (AIDS Care and Support in Action)

3 Woodchurch Road Birkenhead L41 2UE. T:0151-652-1980, 0850-032925 (24hr emergency). F:0151-670-1363. Mon - Fri 9am - 5pm (office and drop-in). Counselling and information service. Care and support for individuals, families and partners including hospital and home visits.

David Carr & Roe

34 Hamilton Street. T:0151-647-7401. Solicitor practice covering crime, common law, matrimonial.

Response

Callister Youth Centre 19 Argyle Street L41 1AD. T:0151-647-7762. F:0151-650-1392. Organises HIV education and prevention strategies particularly aimed at young people. Outreach and prevention work, training and group work.

Blackburn

Blackburn & Darwen Young Lesbian Group

T:01454-702064. Saturday 2pm - 5pm. Support, information and social group for young lesbians. Childcare and transport can be provided.

C'est La Vie

11-15 Market Street. T:01254-51442. Sun 8pm - midnight and Tues 9pm - 2am. Lesbian and gay club.

Farleys

1-2 Richmond Terrace BB1 7AT. T:01254-668844. Emergency telephone : 01254-52552. F:01254-693941. Mon - Fri 9am - 5pm, Sat 9.30am - midday. Emergency line operates 24-hours. Solicitor practice covering criminal, civil, matrimonial, conveyancing, wills and probate. Accepts legal aid work. Emergency service. Speaks Spanish, Gujerati, Urdu. Disabled access.

HIV Prevention Team

53 James Street BB1 6BE. T:01254-263525. F:01254-668372. First point of contact for anyone in Blackburn affected by HIV. The unit runs a specific, detached programme aimed at men who have sex with men that offers information, advice, support and free condoms.

Sky High @ Manhattan Heights

Cicilly Lane. T:01254-682241. Third Thurs each month 10pm -2am. Lesbian and gay club.

Wheatsheaf

Mincing Lane. Lesbian and gay pub open usual pub hours.

Women's Support Line

T:01254-702064. Tues and Thurs 4pm - 9pm. Advice line for all women under 25.

Blackpool

Admiral House Hotel

40 Burlington Road FY4 1JU. T:01253-42854. Lesbian and gay hotel.

Amalfi

19-21 Eaves Street FY1 2NH. T:01253-22971. Lesbian, gay straight hotel. Open all year. Car park.

Basil's on the Strand

9 The Strand. T: 01253-298377. Lesbian and gay pub with dance floor. Clone Zone shop in the pub.

Blackhursts

22 Edward Street FY1 1DP. T:01253-293061. Emergency telephone: 0370-304844. F:01253-293519. Mon - Fri 9am - 5pm. Solicitor practice covering all legal services with emphasis on domestic conveyancing, crime and matrimonial.

Accepts legal aid work. Emergency service. Speaks French and German. Disabled access.

Budd and Co.

Phoenix House 283 Church Street FY1 3PG. T:01253-26557 or emergency 391990. F:01253-751055. Mon - Fri 9am-5pm. General law practice. Accepts legal aid work and offers emergency service.

Carrington's Hotel

21 Holmfield Road FY2 9TV. T:01253-28353. Lesbian and gay hotel. Open all year.

Colin's Hotel

9-11 Cocker Street FY1 1SF. T:01253-20541. Lesbian and gay hotel.

Cove Hotel

9 Banks Street FY1 1RN. T:01253-21438. Lesbian and gay hotel. Accepts Visa and Access.

Dudley Hotel

3 Alexander Road. T:01253-346872. Lesbian and gay hotel.Car park.

Edward Hotel

27 Dickson Road FY1 2AT. T:01253-24271. Lesbian and gay hotel.

501 Club

92-94 Talbot Street. T: 01253-26691. Gay club and bistro with occasional cabaret. Mon - Sat midday - 5pm and 7pm - 2am. Sun midday - 2pm and 7pm - 10.30pm.

Flamingo Club

176 Talbot Square FY1 3AZ. T:01253-24901. Lesbian and gay disco, bistro, piano bar and shop. Mon - Sat 9.30pm - 2am and Sun 8.30pm - midnight.

Glenroy Hotel

10 Trafalgar Road FY1 6AW. T:01253-344607. Lesbian and gay hotel. Accepts Access and Visa.

Gynn House Hotel

20 Gynn Avenue North Shore FY1 2LD. T:01253-352285. Lesbian, gay straight hotel. Open all year.

Highlands

45-54 High Street FY1 2BN. T:01253-752264 or 752249. Lesbian and gay bed and breakfast.

Kingston Hotel

12 Cocker Street. T:01253-24929. Lesbian and gay hotel.

HIV Unit

145 Newton Drive FY3 8LZ. T:01253-303326. F:01253-3033626 Co-ordinates HIV prevention and education methods and suuports HIV awareness events and activities.

Lawson & Co

90 Whitegate Drive. T:01253-392444. General solicitor practice.

Longdale Hotel

25 Cocker Street FY1 2BZ. T:01253-21628. Lesbian and gay hotel. Accepts Visa and Access.

Lucy's Bar

Below Rumours Fun Bar, Talbot Square. T:01253-293204. Lesbian and gay disco and cabaret club. Mon - Fri midday - 4pm and 7pm - 1am. Sat midday - 4pm and 7pm - 1am. Sunday midday - 3pm and 7pm - 10.30pm.

Lynton Hotel

53 Holmfield Road FY2 9RY. T:01253-351493. Lesbian, gay straight hotel. Open all year. Car park.

Accepts Visa and Access.

Lynwood Hotel

4 Trafalgar Road FY1 6AW. T:01253-346156. Lesbian and gay hotel. Accepts Access and Visa.

New Haven Guest House

59 High Street North Shore FY1 2BN. T:01253-26898. Lesbian and gay guest house.

Pierrots Guest House

45 High Street. T:01253-28125. Lesbian and gay guest house.

Pennine Hotel

70 Central Drive. T:01253-295205. Lesbian, gay, straight bed and breakfast.

Primrose Hotel

16 Lord Street FY1 2BD. T:01253-22488. Lesbian, gay, straight hotel which is exclusively lesbian and gay on all Bank Holiday and selected weekends. Open all year.

Royale Guest House

18 Regent Road FY1 4LY. T:01253-26623. Lesbian, gay, straight guest house. Open all year. Car park.

Sandolin Guest House

117 High Street FY1 2DW. T:01253-752908. Lesbian and gay hotel.

Sunnyside House

27 Vance Road FY1 4QD. T:01253-23752. Lesbian and gay bed and breakfast. Open all year.

Sunnyside Hotel

16 Charles Street FY1 3HD. T:01253-22983. Lesbian, gay, straight hotel.

Terry's Guest House

7 St Bedes Avenue FY4 1AQ. T:01253-347769. Lesbian, gay, straight guest house. Open all year. Car park.

Trades

51-55 Lord Street FY1 2BJ. T:01253-26401. F:01253-23179. Gay hotel open all year. Accepts Visa, Access.

Tremadoc Hotel

127-129 Dickson Road North Shore FY1 2EU. T:01253-24001. Lesbian and gay hotel offering residential driving courses.

Village Hotel

40 Foxhall Road. T: 01253-27004. Lesbian and gay hotel.

Waterside Hotel

6 Cocker Square FY1 1RX. T:01253-26890. Lesbian, gay, straight hotel.

Winterbourne House

22-26 Clarendon Road FY1 1EF. T: 01253-405613. Lesbian, gay and TV/TS bed and breakfast. Sauna and sun bed. Open Easter - September.

Bolton

Bolton Accommodation Project

8 St Georges Street BL1 2EN. T:01204-362228. Advice, support, accommodation for homeless single, young people aged 16-25.

Church

172 Crook Street. T:01204-21856. Lesbian and gay pub with disco on Fri, Sat and Sun.

Egan J.

13 Mawdsley Street BL1 1JZ. T:01204-

386214. Emergency telephone: 01204 848874. Mon - Fri 9am - 5.30pm. Solicitor practice covering accidents, matrimonial, crime, conveyancing, wills and probate and consumer. Accepts legal aid work. Emergency service. Speaks Gujerati, Spanish, French and German. Disabled access.

Gay News from Bolton

c/o 108 Newport Street BL3 6AB. T:01204-667747. Bi-monthy newsletter dealing with local issues.

Jesse's Disco @ Balmoral Hotel

Bradshawgate. Sun 7.30pm - 10.30pm. Lesbian and gay disco with occasional lesbian only discos.

Lesbian Gay and Bisexual Helpline

c/o 108 Newport Street BL3 6AB. T:01204-373747. F:01204-388982. Thursday 7pm - 10pm. Telephone service offering support, information and advice.

Lesbian Gay and Bisexual Youth Penpals

c/o 108 Newport Street BL3 6AB. T:01204-373747. Youth penpal service for under 18s. Write with s.a.e.

Lesbian Line

T:01204-394610. Thurs 7pm - 9pm. Telephone advice line for lesbians offering advice, support and information.

Star and Garter

11 Bow Street. T:01204-25926. Lesbian and gay pub which has recently been refurbished.

Stephens (Dr. D.)

39 Church Road BL1 6HD. T:01204-842720. Mon - Fri 8.30am - 6.30pm (half day Wed.). Medical practice. Male doctor. NHS only. Bolton FHSA. Disabled access.

Quest

T:01204-72490. Lesbian and gay Catholic social and religious group.

Youth Group Liaison Initiative

c/o 108 Newport Street BL3 6AB. T:01204-373747 or 667747. F:01204-388982. Lesbian, gay and bisexual support group for people under 25.

Burnley

AIDSLINE

The Community Health Council Offices 79 Church Street BB11 1DY. T:0800-220704. Mon - Fri 7pm - 9pm. Helpline, buddying, family support group, face-to-face counselling, outreach, publicity and education.

Donald Race & Newton

4 Nicholas Street BB11 2AG. T: 01282-33241. Mon - Fri 9am - 5pm. Solicitor practice covering criminal, family, employment, consumer, personal injury, conveyancing, commercial and general litigation. Accepts legal aid work. Emergency service. Disabled access.

Red Triangle

St. James's Street. Lesbian, gay, straight cafe.

Bury

HIV /AIDS Information Service

Parsons Lane BL9 0JZ. T:0161-705-3027. F:0161-705-3140. Advice and counselling, information, resources and training for anyone.

Metro Books

34 Market Street. T:0161-761-7584. Mon - Sat 9am-6pm. Lesbian, gay and straight bookshop.

Nero's

Whiteless Street Tossington Road. T:0161-764-2576. Gay sauna with steam room, jacuzzi and food. Mon - Fri and Sun 1pm - midnight. Sat all night.

Carlisle

Citizens Advice Bureau

East Tower Street CA3 8QB. T:01228-591986. Mon - Fri 10am - 4pm, 7.30pm - 11pm. Helpline offering advice for anyone affected by HIV / AIDS.

HIV Support Group

c/o Social Work Department Cumberland Infirmary CA2 7HY. 01228-591986 (helpline). Daily 7.30pm - 11pm. A support group for anyone affected by HIV / AIDS. Offers a befriending and volunteer service.

Chester

Cavendish Hotel

44 Hough Green CH4 8JQ. T:01244-67500. Lesbian, gay, straight hotel.

Connections @ Caverns

39-41 Watergate Street. T: 01244-320619. Mon, Weds, Fri and Sat 9.30pm - 2am, Sun 8.30pm - midnight. Lesbian and gay club with restaurant.

Hungry Pilgrim

41 Watergate Street. T: 01244-320699. Mon - Fri 9.30am - 4.30pm and Sat 9.30am - 5pm. Lesbian and gay vegetarian cafe bar, restaurant.

Icebreakers

c/o Quaker Meeting House Frodsham Street CH1 3LF. T:01244-342066. Meets first and third Thurs 7.30pm - 10pm. Lesbian, gay and bisexual social group for people new to the scene, coming out etc.

Lesbian Gay Bisexual Social Group

c/o Quaker Meeting House Frodsham Street CH1 3LF. T:01244-318931 or 01244-342066. Meets first and third Sun of every month 4pm - 6pm.

Liverpool Arms

79 Northgate Street. T: 01244-310232. Lesbian, gay, straight pub.

Clitheroe

Forbes & Partners

Garter House 28 Castle Street. T:01200-27228. F:01200-28777. General solicitor practice covering adult and juvenile crime, matrimonial, divorce and civil litigation.

Isle of Man

Hoblink

P O Box 45 Ramsay. T:01785-213259. Lesbian, gay, bisexual newsletter, contact service and networking service for pagans, witches and occultists.

Kendal

High Laverock House Hotel

Mealbank LA8 9DJ. T:01539-723082. Lesbian, gay, straight hotel.

Lancaster

Duke's Theatre

Moor Lane LA1 1QD. T:01524-67461. Lesbian, gay, straight theatre, cinema, bar and cafe. Bar open during usual pub hours.

Farmer's Arms

Penny Street LA1 1XT. T:01524-36368. Thurs, Fri evenings bar within pub for lesbians and gay men. Monthly lesbian event.

Gay Men's Social Group

Contact via Switchboard. Meets first Fri of each month.

Gay Outdoor Club

c/o Switchboard. Local branch of national social group which organises lesbian and gay outdoor and associated activities.

Lesbian and Gay Switchboard

78a Penny Street LA1 1XN. T:01524-847437. Thur and Fri 7pm - 9pm. Telephone service offering advice support and information.

Lesbian Line

T:01524-63021. Wed 7pm - 9pm. Advice counselling and support line for lesbians.

Lesbian and Gay Youth Group

Contact via Switchboard. Meets at the Bottle Shop Arts Centre (behind Duke's Theatre) Sun 6.30m - 9.30pm.

Single Step Co-operative

78a Penny Street LA1 1XN. T:01524-63021. Mon - Sat 9.30am - 5pm. Wholefood and environmentally-friendly grocers which also sells alternative literature and gifts.

Wild Disco

Wild, PO Box 11, Lancaster. Lesbian disco held at Farmer's Arms last Fri each month 8.30pm until late.

Leigh

The Lamp Bookshop

22 Church Street. T:01942-606667. Tues - Sat 9.30pm - 5pm (half day on Wed). Stocks lesbian and gay literature and magazines.

Liverpool

Baa Bar

43-45 Fleet Street. T:0151-708-6810. Mon - Sat 9am - 2am, Sun 7pm - midnight. Lesbian, gay, straight restaurant bar serving Spanish food. Live music.

Cafe Tabac

126 Bold Street. T:0151-709-3735. Mon - Sat 9.30am - 11pm, Sun 10.30am - 5pm. Lesbian, gay, straight licensed cafe.

Curzon

8 Temple Lane. T:0151-236-5160. Mon - Thurs 2pm - midnight. Fri and Sat 2pm - 1am. Sun 7pm - 10.30pm. Lesbian and gay members' club.

E. Rex Makin and Co

Whitechapel, Leigh Street L1 1HQ. T:0151-709-4491. General solicitor practice.

Garland's

8 -10 Eberle Street. T:0151-236-3946. Thurs - Sat 9pm - 2am. Lesbian and gay club. Thurs is women only.

Greenbank

332 - 338 Smith Down Road, near Penny Lane. T:0151-734-2378. Lesbian, gay, straight bar with live music.

HIV Counselling and Testing

Fazakerley Hospital Longmore Lane L9 7AL. T:0151-529-3490. Mon - Fri 9am - 5pm. Same day HIV testing and counselling service.

Jody's

27 Stanley Street. T:0151-236-1666. Wed - Sat 10pm - 2am. Lesbian and gay nightclub.

Lesbian and Gay Christian Movement

LGCM Liverpool BM6914 London WC1N 3XX. Lesbian and gay Christian group. Meets fourth Wed each month, social second Tues each month. Bible studies, country rambles, meals and a newsletter.

Lesbian Line

T:0151-708-0234. Tues - Thurs 7pm - 10pm. Advice support and counselling for lesbians.

Lesbian and Gay Youth Group

Contact Merseyside Friend for details. Meets Wed 7.30pm - 9.30pm for people under 25.

Level 3

Victoria Street. Lesbian and gay club on three levels. Bar, disco and food.

Liberal Party Lesbian and Gay Rights Campaign

Liberal Party 41 Sutton Street L13 7EG. T:0151-259-5935 or 01704-500115 (24 hours). Liberal Party network for lesbian and gay rights campaigns.

Lisbon Bar

35 Victoria Street. T:0151-236-1248. Open usual pub hours. Lesbian, gay, straight pub.

Merseyside Friend

36 Bolton Street L3 5LX. T:0151-708-9552. Open 7pm - 10pm daily. Telephone line offering information, support and befriending. Coffee bar and room for hire.

Merseyside Gay Men's Group

PO Box 11, L69 1SN. T:0151-708-9552. Meets first and third Tues each month.

New Manx Hotel

39 Catherine Street L8 7NE. T:0151-708-6171. Lesbian, gay, straight hotel. Open all year. Car park. Accepts Visa and Access.

News from Nowhere

112 Bold Street L1 4HY. T:0151-708-7270. Mon - Sat 9.30am - 5.30pm. Lesbian and bisexual women's collective which stocks lesbian and gay literature and magazines.

OutRage! Merseyside

c/o 12 Cavendish Gardens L8 3TH.

Pink Directory

T:0151-726-1594 (9am - 11pm, answerphone). Lesbian and gay direct action and campaigning group. Meets on last Thurs each month.

Paco's Bar

25 Stanley Street. T:0151-236-9737. Lesbian and gay bar open during usual pub hours.

Reflections

Temple Lane. T:0151-236-3946. Open until 2am daily. Lesbian space open on Tues upstairs. Lesbian and gay bar and disco.

Time Out

30 Highfield Street L3. T:0151-236-6768. Mon - Sat 12.30pm - 11pm. Sun midday - 3pm, 7pm - 10.30pm. Lesbian, gay, bisexual bar.

TV/TS Line

T:0151-709-4745. Fri 7pm - 10pm. Telephone line offering advice support and counselling for TV/ TS.

Urquhart Knight and Broughton

8 Dale Street L2 4TA. T: 0151-236-3355. F:0151-236-4408. Mon - Fri 9.15am - 5.15pm. Solicitor practice covering crime, accident, matrimonial, child care, adoption, landlord and tenant, employment, civil proceedings. Legal aid available. Emergency service.

Vauxhall Community Law Centre

Multi-Services Centre Silvester Street L5 8SE. T:0151-207-3502 or 0151-207-2004. Mon - Thurs 9am - 5pm. Fri 9am - 4.15pm. Law centre covering social security, employment, debt, consumer. Accepts legal aid work.

Macclesfield

Evangelical Fellowship within the Lesbian and Gay Christian Movement

13 Westbrook Drive SK10 3AQ. T:01625-426178. Aims to support evangelical Christians who are lesbian or gay or who are coming to terms with their sexuality and to encourage other evangelical Christians to re-examine their understanding of human sexuality.

Gay and Lesbian Youth at Macclesfield

T:01625-501203. Meets Thurs 7pm - 10pm. Lesbian and gay social group (14-26 years).

Morecambe

Bramar Hotel

22 Clarendon Road. T:01524-417916. Lesbian, gay, straight hotel.

Sandven Holiday Flats

41 Marine Road West. LA3 1BZ. T:01524-418003. Holiday flats available for rent.

Mossley

AIDSline

Mossley Health Centre Market Place Mossley OL5 0HE. T:01457-832222. Mon - Fri 9am - 12.30pm. Telephone service offering advice, support and information to people who are affected by HIV / AIDS.

Nantwich

AIDSLink

Austin House 122 Hospital Street TW5

5RY. T:01270-627666. F:01270-627777. HIV/AIDS information network for Cheshire HIV voluntary organisations and purchasers.

New Brighton

Wirral Peninsula Group

T:0151-6910378 or 0151-6306251. Meets Wed 9pm - 1am at Queen's Royal, Marine Promenade. Gay social group.

Oldham

AIDS Prevention Team

Westhulme Hospital Westhulme Avenue OL1 2PN. T:0161-624-0420 ext. 5597. F:0169-627-8119. Provides advice information and counselling (individual and family). Training and resources. Needle exchange.

Booth and Middleton

366 - 368 Manchester Road Hollingwood OL9 7NS. T:0161-624-5665. F:0161-627-5128. Mon - Fri 9am - 5pm. Solicitor practice covering children's disputes, cohabitation and marriage disputes, personal injury and civil litigation, medical negligence, probate trust, conveyancing, leases, wills, housing problems. Accepts legal aid work. Emergency service. Disabled access.

Dorothy's Nightclub

171 Union Street Rhodes Bank. T:0161-652-5662. Mon - Sat 9pm - 2am, Sun 9pm - 10.30pm. Lesbian and gay nightclub.

Gaslight

24 Lees Road OL4 1JS. T:0161-624-1325. Open usual pub hours. Lesbian and gay club and pub.

Marc the Builder

152 Coalshaw Green Road Chadderton OL9 8JR. T:0161-627-1869. Mobile:0860 443865. F:0161-624-3954. Lesbian and gay friendly builder.

Pennine Sauna

96 Rochdale Road Shaw, nr Oldham. T:01706-842000. Weds midday - 10pm and Sun 2pm - 10pm *North-West England* gay only sauna.

Ormskirk

HEAL (Health Education AIDS Liaison)

PO Box 26 L39 2WE. T:0800-220704. Daily 7pm - 9pm. Telephone service offering advice counselling information and support for people affected by HIV/AIDS. Also coordinates HIV prevention education.

Penrith

Croft House Farm

Crosby Ravenworth near Penrith. T:01931-715286. Lesbian, gay and straight bed and breakfast.

Fawcett Mill Fields

Gaisgill Tebay CA10 3UB. T:015396-24408. Women only holiday accommodation. Open all year.

Shalom

25 Sandgate CA11 7TJ. T:01768-64164. Lesbian, gay, straight bed and breakfast.

Preston

Alibis @ The

Gatsby

Market Street West. T: 01772-252808. Thurs 10pm - 2am. Lesbian and gay club.

Bisexual Group

PO Box 375, Preston PR2 2UP. Bisexual support group.

Calland (Dr V) Singh (Dr H) and Payne (Dr A)

50 Fishergate Hill P4 8DN. T:01772-254484. Ask for Dr Calland. Mon - Fri 8.30am - 5.30pm, Sat 9am - 10am. Male and female medical practice. NHS only. Offers acupuncture. Lancashire FHSA. Disabled access and facilities.

CAST (Community AIDS Support Team)

PO Box 17 PR1 4UG. T:01772-200911. Tues and Thurs 7.30pm - 9.30pm. Telephone service offering advice support and information for people affected by HIV/ AIDS. Drop-in facility offering discussion and support for people who are HIV+ or have an AIDS diagnosis.

Family and Partners Support Group

PO Box 72, Preston PR5 1PH. T:01772-621111. Support group for people who are affected by HIV/ AIDS.

Gay Social Group

PO Box 64. T: 01772-51122. Gay social group which meets regularly.

Gay Women's Group

Contact via Lesbian Line. Meets second and fourth Weds of each month.

HEAL (Health Education AIDS Liaison)

PO Box 137 PR1 8UU. T:01772-555525. Mon 7.30pm - 9.30pm. Telephone service offering information advice and support for people affected by HIV/ AIDS. Operates a buddying scheme and support services for people affected by HIV/AIDS.

Lesbian and Gay Switchboard

T:01772-51122. Tues, Thurs and Fri 7.30pm - 9.30pm. Telephone service offering advice, support, counselling and information.

Lesbian Line

T: 01772-51122. Mon, Wed 8pm - 9.30pm. Telephone service offering advice support and information for lesbians.

Mitre Tavern

North Road. Lesbian and gay pub open usual pub hours.

Social Services Department

166 Tulketh Road Ashton PR2 1ER. T:01772-724431. Social work services for people with HIV/ AIDS.

Trap Door

28 Croft Street. T: 01772-251275. Lesbian and gay pub and disco.

Whittle Robinson & Partners

13 Cross Street PR1 3NH. T:01772-258574. Solicitor practice covering crime, welfare, matrimonial and immigration.

Rochdale

AIDS Helpline

c/o Health Education Unit Penn Street OL16 1HY. T:01706-755024. F:01706-755076. Mon - Fri 9am - 5pm. Telephone advice service offering information, counselling and support for people affected by HIV/AIDS.

AIDS Unit

c/o Health Education Unit Penn Street OL16 1HY. T:01706-755088. F:01706-755076. Offers face-to-face counselling and outreach work for people affected by HIV/AIDS. Health education information available in Urdu and Bengali. Training and education services for voluntary and statutory bodies.

Gay Society

T:01706-359968. Meets Tues 8pm - 11pm. Gay social group.

Lesbian and Gay Action

T:01706-373344. Meets third Mon each month at 7pm at Rochdale Law Centre, Smith Street.

Lesbian and Gay Switchboard

T :01706-59964. Tues 7pm - 9pm. Telephone service offering advice, support, counselling and information.

Penn Street Sauna

1 Penn Street, off Yorkshire Road. T:01706-527786. Open daily midday - 10pm, Sun 2pm - 10pm. Gay sauna.

Runcorn

Halton Men 4 Men

PO Box 97 WA7 2XF. T:01928-580308. Group of gay and bisexual men living and working in area working to increase HIV/AIDS awareness.

Saddleworth

Printers Arms

Oldham Road, Denshaw. Lesbian, gay, straight bar open usual pub hours.

Sale

Social Services

PO Box 16 Warbrick House Washway Road M33 7DJ. T:0161-872-2101 ext. 2493. First point of contact to HIV/AIDS access services. Individual support and counselling for people affetced by HIV/AIDS.

Salford

Casson & Co

3 Bexley Square M3 6DB. T:0161-834-7176. Emergency: 0378-157630 or 0161-795-0731. F:0161-835-3614. Mon - Fri 9.15am - 5.15pm. General solicitor practice specialising in crime, family, personal injury and housing. Accepts Legal Aid work. Emergency service. Speaks Hebrew and French. Disabled access.

HIV Occupational Therapy

Community Disability Services 22 Lane End Eccles M30 OED. T:0161-789-2340. Council and community services provided for people with HIV/AIDS.

Malone C J

72a Broad Street M6 5BZ. T:0161-736-9166. Solicitor practice covering car proceedings, crime, mental health, personal injury, divorce, contact orders, child care, gay related crime.

Salford Law Centre

498 Liverpool Street M6 5QZ. T:0161-736-3116. F:0161-745-9257. Mon - Fri 10am - 1pm and 4pm - 5pm. Law centre covering race and sex discrimination, housing, immigration, law relating to HIV and AIDS, disability rights. Accepts legal aid work. Speaks Punjabi, Urdu and Hindi. Disabled access and facilities.

Salford Women's Centre

89 Rowan Close. T:0161-736-3844. Mon - Fri 9.15am - 4pm. Women's centre offering support, advice and information. Free creche.

St Helens

Gay Contact Group

PO Box 135 St Helens WA10 1JD or contact via Helpline. Social group which meets weekly in various local pubs and which organises events.

Lesbian and Gay Helpline

PO Box 135, St Helens WA10 1JD. T:01744-454823. Mon - Wed 7pm - 9pm. Telephone service offering advice, support, counselling and information.

Southport

AIDSLine

T:01704-531435. Mon - Thurs 9am - 5pm. Telephone service offering support counselling information and advice for people affected by HIV/AIDS.

Gay and Bisexual Men's Health and Social Group

T:01704-531435. Meets Thurs fortnightly. Health and social group for all gay men.

TFG's

Coronation Walk. T:01704-566104 after 1pm or 01704-530114 after 10pm. Weds - Sat 10pm - 2am Sun 8pm - late. Lesbian and gay disco.

Stockport

Adswood Road Surgery

270 Adswood Road SK3 8PN. T:0161-483-5115. Mon, Tues, Wed, Fri 8.30am - 6.30pm, Thurs 8.30am - 12.30pm, Sat 9am - 11.30am. Male and female medical practice. NHS only. Stockport FHSA. Disabled access and facilities.

Lesbian Gay and Bisexual Group

Contact via SMASH. Youth group for those under 26.

Metcalfe Wright and Platt

4 Moorside Road Heaton Moor SK4 4JT. T:0161-432-4325. F:0161-443-1141. Mon - Fri 9am - 5.30pm. Solicitor practice covering conveyancing, wills and probate and litigation. Accepts Legal Aid work.

New Inn

95 Wellington Road South. T:0161-480-4063. Open Mon - Sat 11am - 3pm and 7pm - 11pm, Sun midday - 3pm, 7pm - 10pm. Lesbian and gay pub. Discos on Fri and Sat.

Prague

Turncroft Lane Offerton. T:0161-476-3666. Open Fri and

Sat. Lesbian and gay club.

SMASH

188 Buxton Road SK2 7AE. T:0161-487-2020. Gay men's health project.

Todmorden

Lesbian Information Service

PO Box 8 OL14 5TZ. T:01706-817235. Weds 7pm - 10pm. Telephone advice service for young lesbians.

Pennine Todmorden

1 Longfield Road OL14 6LY. T:01706-817612. Women only bed and breakfast.

Wallasey

Wirral Peninsular Group

c/o 2 Oakland Vale Magazine's Promenade L45 1LQ. T:0151-638-6371 (answerphone). Mon - Fri 10am - 4pm. Lesbian and gay support and social group which holds regular functions. Holds fundraising functions and activities in aid of HIV/AIDS causes and local charities.

Warrington

AIDSline

5 Hanover Street WA1 1LZ. T:01925-417134 or 01925-234990 (minicom). Mon, Wed 7pm - 9pm. Telephone service offering advice, support and information for people affected by HIV/AIDS.

Youth Advice Shop and Travelling Youth Advice

37-39 Buttermarket Street WA1 2LY. T:01925-231880. Drop-in service Mon, Wed, Thurs, Fri 3.30pm - 7pm. An informal drop-in where young people can meet with health workers and youth workers. Travelling youth advice tours places where young people meet.

Restons Linaker and Linaker

8 Suez Street WA1 1EF. T: 01925-34561. Solicitor practice covering crime, accident, injury, employment and property.

Wigan

Cricketer

Keat's Avenue. T:01942-824555. Tues 11pm - 2am. Lesbian and gay pub with cabaret.

HIV/AIDS Helpline

PO Box 138 WN5 OPW. T:01942-221977. Weds 7pm - 10pm. Telephone service offering advice, counselling and information.

Matts Cross Hotel

136 Standishgate. T:01942-41484 or 48180. Open usual pub hours. Lesbian, gay, straight hotel and pub with sauna and disco.

Workington

West Cumbria HIV Counselling and Support Group

c/o Department of GU Medicine Workington Infirmary. T:01900-602244 ext 170.

NORTH-EAST ENGLAND

Sexual Politics

ORDER FORM

To order titles direct from Cassell see the form at the back of the directory : here we list some 30 innovative and acclaimed new books in our Lesbian and Gay Studies, Women on Women and AIDS Awareness series.

PUB QUIZ

Throughout 1995 Cassell and *The Pink Paper* shall be running a nationwide tournament of pub quizzes. If you run a pub and would be interested in taking part, contact Cassell's Sexual Politics Quiz, Villiers House, 41/47 Strand, London WC2N 5JE.

MAKE CASH! HOLD A BOOK PARTY!

If you are interested in hosting a book party for you and your friends contact Cassell's Sexual Politics Book Party, Villiers House, 41/47 Strand, London WC2N 5JE.

MAILING LIST

For regular information about our forthcoming titles, catalogues and news of special offers and book events in your area, fill in the form below and return to Cassell's Sexual Politics Mailing List, Villiers House, 41/47 Strand, London WC2N 5JE. No charge and no obligation.

Please include my details on the Sexual Politics Mailing List for receipt of details of forthcoming titles, news of special offers and of Cassell book events:

Name ....
Address ....
....
....
....

Send to Cassell Sexual Politics Mailing List, Villiers House, 41/47 Strand, London WC2N 5JE.

LEEDS

Hotels, Guest Houses and B&Bs

City Centre Hotel

51a New Briggate LS2 8JD. T:0113-242-9019. Lesbian, gay, straight bed and breakfast. Open all year. Car park.

Crown Hotel

Crown Point Road. T:0113-245-1901. Open usual pub hours. Lesbian, gay, straight hotel and pub.

New Townsman Hotel

35 New Briggate. T:0113-245-5164. Lesbian, gay, straight hotel.

Bars, Clubs, Pubs, Cafes, Restaurants

Boys will be Boys

Exchange Bar Corn Exchange LS1. T:0113-244-5314. Tues 9pm - 1am. Gay club.

Bridge Inn

Call Lane. Lesbian, gay, bisexual and straight pub. Open usual pub hours.

Confetti's

Merrion Street LS1. T:0113-238-0999. First Tues each month, 10pm - 2am. Lesbian, gay, bisexual and straight club.

Engine Room @ Hi-Flyers Nightclub

City Square LS1 (under Queen's Hotel). Weds 9.30pm - 2.30am. Gay club.

Erotica @ Mr. Craig's

51 New Briggate LS1. T:0113-242-2224. Third Tues each month. Lesbian and gay club with cabaret.

Faversham

Springfield Mount L2. T:0113-245-8817. Open usual pub hours. Lesbian, gay, straight pub.

Flesh @ The Music Factory

Call Lane L1. T: 0113-244-9474. Second Tues each month. Lesbian and gay club.

Glamour Pussy @ Warehouse

19-20 Somers Street. T:0113-246-8287. Third Wed each month 10pm - 2am. Lesbian and gay dress up club.

Hollywood Bar

13 Duncan Street. T:0113-245-8845. Lesbian, gay, straight pub open usual pub hours.

Homodisco @ The Music Factory

Call Lane. T:0113-244-9474. Sun 8pm - 10.30pm. Lesbian and gay club.

Jester

Harrogate Road Alwoodley. T:0113-268-2738. Pub hours. Gay and straight pub.

New Penny

Call Lane. T:0113-243-8055. Lesbian, gay, bisexual, straight pub. Open usual pub hours.

Old Red Lion

Meadow Lane L1. T:0113-242-6779. Lesbian, gay, straight pub. Open usual pub hours.

Phoenix (Cosmo's)

Francis Street Chapletown LS7. T:0113-262-4138. Sun 8pm - late. Lesbian gay and straight club.

Primo's 2

Westminster Buildings 41 - 43 New York Street LS2 7BT. T:0113-244-6300. Mon, Wed and Thurs 9pm - 2am, Fri and Sat 9pm - 6am. Third Wed each month is women only. Lesbian, gay and bisexual club.

QC Club @ Rio's

Merrion Centre L1. T:0113-242-9222. Thurs 10pm - 2.30am. Gay men's club.

Shayla's @ Ricky's

Merrion Street L1. Wed 10pm until late. Gay club.

Trash @ The Astoria Ballroom

Roundhay Road L8. T:0113-249-0362. Fri and Sat 10pm - 2.30am. Lesbian, gay straight club.

Vague @ Warehouse

Somers Street. T:0113-246-8287. Sat 10pm- 2.30am. Lesbian, gay, straight, TV/TS club run by Trannies With Attitude.

Businesses

Annares

The Piazza Corn Exchange Call Lane Leeds LS1. T:0113-245-3889. Daily 9am - 5.30pm. Lesbian, gay, straight cafe and delicatessen.

Cohen & Co

3 Park Square LS1 2NE.T:0113-244-0597. F:0113-242-1291. Mon - Fri 9am - 5.30pm. Solicitor practice covering all areas (except corporate), particularly crime, matrimonial, litigation and property related. Accepts Legal Aid. Offers emergency service. Translation for Urdu and most Indian subcontinent languages. Speaks Hebrew.

Craig A

107 Kirkgate Leeds LS1. T:0113-244-4081. General solicitor practice. Lesbian and gay friendly.

Delaney & Co

13 Bond Court LS1 2JZ. T:0113-246-8151. Emergency: 01924-259220. F:0113-243-1342. Mon - Thurs 8.30am-5.15pm, Fri 8.30am - 4.30pm. Solicitor practice specialising in criminal and family law. Accepts Legal Aid. Emergency service offered.

Hurwitz (Dr N A)

Woodsley Health Centre Woodsley Road LS6. T: 0113-244-4831. Lesbian and gay friendly doctor.

Lotus Book Shop

10 The Crescent Hyde Park Corner LS6 2NW. T:0113-274-2055. Mon - Sat 9.30am - 5.30pm. Stocks lesbian gay and feminist books.

Organisations

ACT UP ! (AIDS Coalition to Unleash Power)

PO Box 293 50 Call Lane LS1 6DT. T:0113-262-0293. F:0113-231-0604. Meets fortnightly at 50 Call Lane. Lesbian, gay, straight campaigning group.

Bisexual Group

Contact Switchboard for details. Meets Mon at The Old Red Lion. Support and social group for bisexuals.

Black Community AIDS Team

T:0113-242-3100. Mon 9.30am - 4pm. Confidential advice to all black people on

AIDS issues.

FFLAG (Families and Friends of Lesbians and Gays)

c/o Parents Friend. T:0113-267-4627. Daily 7.30pm - 11pm. Campaigning group for parents interested in equality issues for lesbians, gay men and bisexuals.

Gay Community

PO Box 1 Unit 1A Middleton Road Morley LS27 8BB. Meets Fri 7.45pm at the Swarthmore Centre Woodhouse. Gay social group.

Gay Men's Dance Group

Yorkshire Dance Centre St Peter's Square LS9 8AH. T:0113-244-4209. Mon 8pm - 9.30pm. Informal dance group of mixed abilities. All gay men welcome.

Gay Outdoor Club

Contact Switchboard for details. Local branch of the national lesbian and gay social group for people interested in outdoor sports and associated activities.

Gay Workers in Education

Meets Old Red Lion first Mon each month at 8pm. Networking and social organisation for lesbians and gay men working in education.

Lesbian Line

c/o Leeds Lesbian and Gay Switchboard. PO Box HH29 LS8 2UA. T:0113-245-3588. Tues 7.30pm - 9.30pm. Telephone advice information support and counselling service for lesbians.

Lesbian and Gay Christian Movement

Contact Switchboard for details. Local branch of national lesbian and gay Christian movement.

Lesbian and Gay Switchboard

PO Box HH29 LS8 2UA. T:0113-245-3588. Daily 7pm - 10pm except Tues. Telephone service offering advice support and counselling for lesbians, gay men and bisexuals.

Lesbian and Gay Theatre Group

Portland Centre. Meets Tues 7.30pm. *North-East England* Lesbian and gay theatre group which stages regular shows. No previous experience required.

Leeds General Infirmary and St. James' Hospital Health Workers

Contact via Switchboard. Support group for lesbian and gay health workers in both hospitals.

Line Dancing Women

Meets at Methodist Mission Hall Wood Lee Road L6. Contact Switchboard for further details. Lesbian social group which meets for regular line dancing sessions.

Lola Walking Group

T:01423-870829. Lesbian social group organising monthly walks (7-12 miles) in the Yorkshire Dales and in North Yorkshire

Older Lesbian Association

c/o Switchboard. T:0113-245-3588. Meets regularly for socials and support.

Parent's Friend

Pink Directory

c/o Voluntary Action Leeds Stringer House 34 Lupton Street Hunslet LS10 2QW. T:0113-267-4627. Daily 7.30pm - 11pm. Helpline and support group for parents finding their child/ children is lesbian, gay or bisexual. Registered charity.

PASTELS (Partners and Spouses Telephone Support)

c/o Voluntary Action Leeds, Stringer House, 34 Lupton Street Hunslet LS10 2GW. T:0113-267-4627. Daily 7.30pm - 11pm. Telephone support service for those finding their partner, wife, husband is lesbian, gay or bisexual.

Survivors

Contact via Switchboard for details. Support group for victims of gay rape.

TV Social Group

Contact via Switchboard. Meets first and third Thurs each month at 8pm at Social Services Centre Woodhouse Lane.

Yorkshire Gay Bridge Club

PO Box HH29 Leeds LS8 2UE. T:0113-269-7081. Lesbian and gay social group which meets to play bridge.

West Yorkshire Gay Naturists - Ganymede

Box No.2 Unit 1a Middleton Road Morley LS27 8BB. Gay and bisexual men's naturist group which meets regularly for trips and social.

Appleton - Le - Moors

Dweldapilton Moor Hotel

Appleton - Le - Moors YO6 6TF. T:017515-227. Lesbian, gay, straight hotel.

Barnsley

Charlie's Bar

Sheffield Road. T:01226-282149. Pub which is lesbian and gay on Tues and Thurs.

Connections

c/o MIND Dove House Sheffield Road S70 1JH. T:01226-730703. Thurs 7pm - 10pm Sun 3pm - 8pm. Lesbian, gay, bisexual self-help group and helpline.

Greenhouse Health Club

56 Sheffield Road S70 1HS. T:01226-731305. Open daily 1pm - 11pm. Gay sauna.

Toby Jug

Doncaster Road. T:01226-294719. Lesbian and gay pub on Sun evenings.

Batley

The George

Wellington Street. T:01924-472892. Lesbian, gay, straight pub. Open usual pub hours.

Bradford

Bavaria Tavern

Heaton Road. T:01274-487681. Mon - Thurs 7pm - 11pm, Fri and Sat midday - 11pm. Sun usual pub hours. Lesbian pub and disco.

Bradford Friend

c/o Council for Voluntary Services 19-25 Sundbridge Road BD1 2AY. T:01274-723802. Mon and Weds 6.30pm - 8.45pm. Telephone service offering information support and advice for lesbians, gay and bisexual men and women.

Bradford Law Centre

31 Manor Row BD1 4PS. T:01274-306617. F:01274-390939. Mon 10am-1pm, Tues 10am-4pm, Thurs 10am - 4pm. Law centre covering immigration, employment and discrimination, housing benefits, and judicial review. Accepts Legal Aid work. Speaks Urdu and Hindi. Disabled access.

Bradford Lesbian and Gay Youth

c/o 19-25 Sunbridge Road BD1 2AY. T:01274-395815. 24-hour answerphone. Meets once a month on Sat. Lesbian and gay youth social group for all under 25s.

Caligula's

7 Barry Street BD1. T:01274-731606. Mon, Tues 9pm-12.30am, Weds - Sat 9pm - 2am, Sun 9pm - midnight. Lesbian, gay, straight club with cabaret.

Checkpoint

Contact via Lesbian Line T:01274-305525. Alternate Fri lesbian disco.

Chivers Walsh Smith

Broadway House 9 Bank Street BD1 1HN. T:01274-740077. Emergency:0831-485450. F:01274-740442. Mon - Fri 9am - 5.30pm. Solicitor practice covering child care, adoption, crime, civil, conveyancing and probate, employment, mental health, benefits advice and matrimonial. Accepts Legal Aid work. Emergency service. Speaks Urdu.

Club 0898

Midland Hotel Forster Square. T:0831-230778. Sun 9pm - late. Lesbian and gay club.

Friends of Dorothy VW Club

T:01274-674907. Club for gay VW owners and enthusiasts.

Gay Community Group

c/o CVS First Floor 19-25 Sunbridge Road BD1 2AY. Lesbian and gay social group.

Meets Thurs 7.30pm.

Gordons Wright and Wright

14 Piccadilly BD1 3LX. T:01274-733771. F:01274-728346. Mon - Fri 9am - 5.30pm. Solicitor practice covering all areas of commercial and personal law except crime and immigration. Accepts Legal Aid. Speaks French. Disabled access.

LAGPAN (Lesbian and Gay Postal Action Network)

24 Briggs Street Queensbury BD13 2EW. T:01274-883845 (Dr Austin Allen). A campaign group for lesbian and gay equality which lobbies individuals and organisations by letter.

Lesbian and Gay Switchboard

31 Manor Road BD1 4PS. T:01274-722206. Tues and Thurs-Sat 7.30pm - 9.30pm. Telephone service offering advice support and information to all lesbians and gay men.

Lesbian Line

Pink Directory
T:01274-305525. Thurs 7pm - 9pm with 24-hour answerphone. Telephone service offering advice support and counselling for lesbians.

Lesbian Line Social

Bavaria Tavern Heaton Road. Meets Tues evening. Contact Lesbian Line for further details.

Lesbian Walking Group

Meets fortnightly for 6-8 mile walks in the Yorkshire Dales. Usually Sat sometimes Sun. Contact Lesbian Line for details.

Lesbians with Children

Meets at Bradford Resource Centre last Sun of each month. Social and support group for lesbians with children. Contact Lesbian Line for details.

Nancy's Tea Dance

Queen's Hall. Lesbian and gay tea dance. Meets first Sun each month 1pm - 5pm with lessons at 12.

Pennine AIDS Link

4 Duke Street BD1 3QR. T:01274-734354. F:01274-732939. Aims to provide services for people affected by HIV, create a positive climate and be an integral part of developing HIV policies and good practice in Bradford. Drop-in, therapy, education and advice.

Splinter's

T:01274-601677. Social group for lesbian and gay MENSA members.

Sun Hotel

124 Sunbridge Road. T:01274-73722. Open daily 2pm - 11pm. Lesbian, gay, straight bar and hotel.

TV Social Group

Caligula's 7 Barry Street. T:01274-731606. First Tues each month 9pm - 2am. TV social and disco.

Brighouse

Hair Pieces for TVs

T:01484-714053 (ask for Tina). Private studio which makes hair pieces for TVs.

Castleford

Hartley & Worstenholme

20 Bank Street WF10 1JD. T:01977-553721. F:01977-603105. Mon - Fri 9am - 5pm. General solicitor practice. Accepts Legal Aid work. Emergency service. Speaks French, Chinese and Ukranian. Disabled access.

Chester-le-Street

AIDSline

T:0191-388-9830. Mon - Fri 9.30am - 4pm. Telephone service offering advice, support and information to people affected by HIV / AIDS.

Young Gay Men's Project

Health Centre Newcastle Road DH3 3UR. T:0191-388-6084 or 0850-122987. F:0191-387-1942. Work with young gay men on sexual health issues.

Cramlington

A & M Guest House

36 Minting Place

NE23 6AX. T:01670-715132. Mobile 0860-437157. Lesbian, gay straight guest house. Open all year. Accepts Visa, Access.

Darlington

Gay Community Service

T:01325-365725. Wed and Sat 7pm - 10pm. Offers support and advice to men who have sex with men, especially young gay men who are 26 or under.

Dewsbury

KAR (Kirklees AIDS Response)

33 Wellington Road WF13 1HN. T:01924-454421. Drop-in Fri 10am - 6pm. Offers face-to-face counselling, buddying and other practical help for people living with AIDS or HIV-related illnesses.

Doncaster

Body Heat @ Ritzy

Silver Street.T:01623-748235. Second Tues each month. Lesbian and gay disco.

Lesbian Group

c/o Women's Centre 21 Cleveland Street DN1 3EH. Lesbian social group.

Network

T:01302-341010. Lesbian and gay workers' support group which has regular social meetings.

Palace

North Bridge Road. T:01302-361803. Mon, Tues, Wed 8pm - midnight, Thurs - Sat 8pm - 2am, Sun 8pm - midnight. Lesbian and gay club with karaoke night.

Vine Hotel

Kelhan Street Balby Street. T:01302-364096. Open usual pub hours. Lesbian, gay, straight pub.

Durham

Alleycats Book Co-op

28b Sutton Street DH1 4BW. T:0191-386-1296. Lesbian and gay section.

Body Positive

Wilton House Milburngate Bridge DH1 5XZ. T:0191-383-1625. F:0191-384-7293. Self-help, support, advice and information to people throughout the County Durham area directly affected by HIV / AIDS.

North Durham Young Gay and Bisexual Men's Project

T:0191-388-6084 or 0850-122987. Offers support, information advice and help to young gay and bisexual men on issues that affect them.

Gateshead

Gay and Bisexual Men's Project and Advisory Group

T:0191-491-3372. Meets every two months to advise about the health requirements and needs of gay men in Gateshead.

Gay Men's Project

Whinney House Resource Centre Durham Road Low Fell NE9 5AR. T:0191-491-3372. Aims to meet the health needs of gay and bisexual men by sponsoring a number of initiatives in the district.

Guisborough

Lesbian and Gay

Christian Movement

38 St.Leonards Road TS14 8BU. T:01287-632404 daily. Local branch of national lesbian and gay Christian organisation.

Halifax

Brody's

Bull Green. Meets Wed 8pm - 9.30pm. Lesbian and gay social group which meets weekly.

Calderdale Women's Aid

PO Box 66. T:01422-351498. Women's refuge which has drop-in Thurs 10am-midday. Advice and support for women suffering domestic violence.

Citizens Advice Bureau

37 Harrison Road HX1 2AF. T:01422-342917. Mon Tues Fri 10pm - 4pm Wed 10am - 1pm. Thurs 10am - 7pm. General advice agency. Disabled access.

Gay Group

c/o Citizen's Advice Bureau 37 Harrison Road. T:01422-375307. Meets Weds at 8pm. Lesbian and gay social group which meets at Crown and Anchor pub.

Guy's for Guys

T:01422-342219. Escort agency for gay men.

Muir Hewitt

Queens Road Mills Gibbett Street HX1 4LR. T:01422-347377. Tues-Sat 10am-5pm. Lesbian and gay friendly art deco original ceramics.

Wilkinson Woodward & Ludlam

11 Fountain Street HX1 1LU. T:01422-340711. F:01422-330417. Mon - Fri 9am - 5.30pm. Solicitor practice which specialises in criminal, matrimonial, property, civil, accident, employment, wills and welfare. Accepts Legal Aid work. Speaks French.

Harrogate

Barber Robinson

Queensgate House 23 North Park Road HG1 5PF. T:01423-566611. F:01423-508836. Mon - Fri 9am - 5.30pm. General solicitor practice which specialises in conveyancing, probate, tax and litigation. Accepts Legal Aid work. Disabled access.

Bedrock @ The Zoo

Station Parade. T:01423-503294. Thurs 10pm - 2am. Lesbian and gay club.

Dungeon @ The Cellar Bar

Off Parliament Street. T:01423-524629. Sun 7pm - late. Gay men's disco bar.

Hale's

1 Crescent Road. T:01423-569861. Open usual pub hours. Lesbian, gay, straight bar.

Oakwood Hotel

Valley Drive. Open usual pub hours. Lesbian gay straight pub.

Reach Out Yorkshire

T:01423-564749. Daily 7pm - 10pm. Telephone helpline which offers support information and advice for lesbians and gay men.

Slosh

PO Box 73 Harrogate HG1 4TS. Fetish

group for gay men who enjoy slapstick.

Hartlepool

Hartlepool Happy Hours

T:01642-363514 or 01429-222999. Mon 7pm - 9pm and Thurs 2pm - 4pm. Drop-in for lesbians, gays and bisexuals in Hartle-pool.

Hartlepool Law Centre

The People's Centre Raby Road TS24 8LA. T:01429-861333. F:01429-862787. Mon - Fri 10am - 3pm. Law centre offering general legal advice. Accepts Legal Aid work.

Haworth

Old Silent Inn

Stanbury near Haworth. T:01535-42503. Lesbian, gay, straight hotel.

Ye Sleeping House

8 Main Street. T:01535-645992. Lesbian, gay, straight hotel.

Hebden Bridge

Bookcase

29 Market Street. T:01422-845353. Stocks lesbian and gay books and magazines.

Horton-in-Ribblesdale

Women's Holiday Centre

The Old Vicarage Horton near Settle BD24 0HD. T:01729-860207. Women only holiday house that welcomes lesbians. Male children wel-come up to10 years-old. Car park.

Houghton-le-Spring

Ruby's @ The Market Tavern

T:0191-512-0270. Daily 7pm - late. Lesbian, gay, straight bar and club with party nights on Wed and Sat.

Huddersfield

Bereavement Support

c/o Community Health Council 12 New North Parade HD1 5JP. T:01484-544676. Mon - Thurs 9am - 5pm, Fri 9am-4pm. Lesbian and gay bereavement support group.

Greyhound Hotel

16 Manchester Road. T:01484-420742. Opens usual pub hours. Lesbian and gay pub and hotel.

Lesbian and Gay Social Group

c/o KCVS 12 St. George's Square HD1 1JF. T:01484-538070. Contact Switchboard for further details. Lesbian and gay social group which meets regularly.

Lesbian and Gay Switchboard

c/o KCVS 12 St. George's Square HD1 1JF. T:01484-538070. Tues 7pm-9pm, Sun 6pm - 9pm. Lesbian and gay telephone service which offers advice support and information for lesbians and gay men.

Marshall Mills & Sykes

14 High Street HD1 2HA. T:01484-423434. F:01484-516621. General solicitor practice which specialises in litigation, domestic conveyancing, wills, probate and trusts, company and com-mercial. Accepts Legal Aid work. Speaks Ukranian.

Will arrange home visits for disabled clients.

MESMOP

1 Estate Buildings 11 Railway Street HD1 1JY. T: 01484-435005. Sexual health information for gay and bisexual men.

Tullie Woodward & Co

Bradford and Bingley House 16/18 Cloth Hall Street HD1 2EQ. T:01484-530297. Emergency: 01484-612317. F:01484-510055. Mon - Fri 9am - 5.30pm. General solicitor practice which specialises in crime, matrimonial, conveyancing, probate and wills and common law. Accepts Legal Aid work. Emergency service.

Unit 51 Addiction Agency

24 Westgate HD1 1NU. T:01484-510826. Support and advice agency for all with alcohol or drug problems.

Women's Social Group

c/o KCVS 12 St. George's Square HD1 1JF. Contact Switchboard for details. Lesbian social group.

Hull

AIDS Action North Humberside

Cornerhouse 29 Percy Street HU2 8HL. T:01482-27044. F:01482-27044. Mon - Fri 9am - 5pm. Voluntary non-medical HIV /AIDS agency for North Humberside offering care and support to people directly affected by HIV. Also training and education, outreach, counselling, helpline.

Alexandra Palace Hotel

69 Hessle Road. T:01482-27455. Fri, Sat, Sun open until 12.30am. Lesbian gay bisexual straight disco. Also offers bed and breakfast accommodation.

Body Positive

PO Box 304 HU3 2YX. T:01482-581101. Mon, Thurs 7pm - 9pm (Helpline). Office hours Mon - Fri 10am - 4pm. Support and social group offering aromatherapy, acupuncture, massage and social outings. Telephone service offering advice, information and support.

Caesar's Palace

114-116 George Street. T:01482-225533. Thurs 10pm - 2am. Lesbian, gay, straight club.

Earl de Grey

7 Castle Street. T:01482-24989. Sun and Mon lesbian and gay pub. Rest of the week is lesbian and gay friendly pub offering bed and breakfast accommodation.

Friend

c/o CVS 29 Anlaby Road HU1 2PG. T:01482-443333. Mon and Thurs 8pm - 10pm and Sat 7pm - 9pm. Telephone service offering advice support and information to lesbians and gay men.

Gay Men's Group

c/o CVS 29 Anlaby Road HU1 2PG. T:01482-443333. Meets at Lonsdale Community Centre on Sun 7pm - 9pm. Gay men's social group.

Ivesons

19 Bowlalley Lane

HU1 1YL. T:01482-26511. Emergency: 01482-640510. F:01482-228008. Mon - Fri 9am - 5.15pm. General solicitor practice. Accepts Legal Aid work . Speaks French and Dutch.

Juice @ The Room

82-84 George Street. T:01482-23154. Second Tues each month 10pm - 2am. Lesbian and gay club.

Lesbian Disco

Contact Friend for details. Meets monthly at Lonsdale Community Centre. Disco for all lesbians.

Lesbian and Gay Christian Movement

T:01482-587033. Local branch of national lesbian and gay Christian movement.

Lesbian Line

PO Box 26 Hull HU1 2RX. T:01482-214331. Mon 7pm - 9pm. 24 hour answerphone. Telephone service offering advice information and support for lesbians.

Page One Books

9 Princess Avenue. T:01482-41925. Book shop which stocks lesbian and gay books.

Polar Bear

229 Spring Bank. T:01482-23959. Pub which is lesbian and gay on Fri.

St. George's Hotel

St. George's Road. T:01482-219780. Open usual pub hours. Lesbian, gay, straight, bisexual pub with drag nights on Weds and Sats.

Stimulation @ Tower Night Club

Anlaby Road. T:01482-23121. Tues fortnightly 10pm - 2am. Lesbian and gay club.

Vauxhall Tavern

1 Hessle Road. T:01482-20340. Open usual pub hours. Gay and straight pub.

Youth Group

c/o CVS 29 Anlaby Road. T:01482-443333. Sun 3pm - 5pm. Lesbian and gay youth group which offers support and social meetings.

Keighley

Airedale AIDS North-East England Advice Line

c/o Department of Genito-Urinary Medicine, Airedale General Hospital Eastburn BD20 6TD. T:01535-656256. Mon - Fri 9am - 4pm. Telephone service offering information support and advice for people affected by HIV/AIDS.

Luddenfoot

The Cottage Brearley Old Hall. T:01422-884046. Lesbian, gay, straight hotel.

Middlesborough

Cleveland AIDS Support

63 Kings Road North Ormesby TS3 6EP. T:01642-254598. F:01624-244558. Mon - Fri 9am - 6pm. Offers support for people living with HIV/AIDS and their partners, families and carers. Befriending, education and information offered as well as complementary therapies.

Friend

T:01642-248888. Tues and Fri 7pm - 9.30pm. Telephone service offering advice, support and information to lesbians, gay men and bisexuals.

Friend Drop-In

Meets second Saturday of the month. 3pm - 5pm. Contact Friend for details.

Lesbian Line Teesside

T:01642-217955. Mon 8pm - 10pm. Telephone service offering advice, support and information to lesbians.

Married Men's Group

T:01642-311241. Meets fortnightly on Tuesdays. Advice, information and support.

Middlesborough Law Centre

St Mary's Centre 82/ 90 Corporation Road TS1 2RB. T:01642-223813. Mon - Fri 9.30am - 11.30am. Law centre which provides legal advice, representation for social security and mental health tribunals. Advice on immigration, housing, criminal injuries and employment. Disabled access.

Paradise

Newport Road 53 Newport Road. T:01642-244149. Wed Fri Sat 10pm - 2am. Lesbian, gay club.

State 52 @ Cassidy's Club

Grange Road. T:01642-244149. Nightly 7pm - 11pm. Lesbian, gay, straight bar, disco, restaurant.

Newcastle-upon-Tyne

ACET (AIDS Care Education and Training)

PO Box 1QN NE99 1QN. T:0191-273-5200. F:0191-273-5277. Local branch of national Christian AIDS charity offering practical home based help for people affected by HIV/ AIDS.

Body Positive

12 Princess Square NE1 8EG. T:0191-232-2855. F:0191-222-0514. Mon -Fri 10am - 7pm. Drop-in Tues & Thurs 10am - 5pm. Offers information, advice and support on all aspects of HIV. Volunteer service for domestic tasks, counselling and complementary medicine.

Cheviot View Hotel

194 Station Road Wallsend. T:0191-262-0125. Gay bed and breakfast.

COMBINE

NEBG PO Box 1JR NE99 1JR. Meets third Mon of each month at 8pm. Call MESMAC for venue details. Support and social group for bisexual women and men.

Courtyard

2 Scotswood Road. T:0191-232-2037. Open usual pub hours. Lesbian and gay pub. Lesbian disco upstairs every Tues.

Cruise @ Bliss

Market Street. Tues 9.30pm - 2am. Lesbian and gay club.

Friend

T:0191-261-8555. Mon - Fri 7pm - 10pm. Telephone service offering advice, information and support.

Friend Drop-In

T:0191-261-8555. Sat 1pm - 4pm. Social group for lesbians and gay men. Children welcome.

Friend Men's

Group

T:0191-261-8555. Tues 7.30pm - 9pm. Support group for men coming to terms with their sexuality. Open to all ages.

GMT (Gay Men Tyneside)

T:0191-233-1333. Meets Wed evenings. Social group which offers an alternative to the commercial scene.

Gay Outdoor Club

c/o GOC PO Box 24 Minehead Avon TA24 8YZ. Local branch of national organisation which arranges regular walks, swims and other outdoor pursuits.

Gay Youthline

T:0191-233-1551. Thurs 3.30pm - 5.30pm. Telephone service offering advice, support and information for gay and bisexual men under 26.

GETOUTS (Gays Enjoying Themselves Outside The Scene)

T:0191-233-1333. Ask for Andrew. Interest and activity group for lesbians, gays and bisexuals who seek an alternative to the commercial scene.

Gray & Co

56 Westgate Road NE1 5XU. T:0191-232-9547. Emergency: 0191-222-0830. F:0191-230-4149. Mon - Fri 9am - 5pm. General solicitor practice. Accepts Legal Aid work. Emergency service. Speaks Urdu, Hindi and Punjabi. Disabled access.

Heaven Cafe

Pink Lane. T:0191-232-9648. Open all day Sun and late during week. Lesbian, gay, straight cafe and art gallery.

Heaven's Above

T:0191-232-2037. Mon - Sat 3pm - 11pm. Sun pub hours. Lesbian and gay bar above The Courtyard.

Henry's Bar

Upstairs at the Barking Dog Marlborough Crescent. Open usual pub hours. Lesbian and gay pub. Women only bar upstairs on Mon, Wed, Sun.

Lesbian and Gay Alcoholics Anonymous

c/o MESMAC 7 Drury Lane NE1 1HL. T:0191-233-1333. Sat 7pm - 8.30pm. Support group for lesbian and gay people with drink related problems.

Lesbian and Gay Police Monitoring Group

Freepost P O Box 1XD NE99 2RP. Monitoring and campaigning group.

Lesbian Line

PO Box 1HT NE99 1HT. T:0191-261-2277. Tues 7pm - 10pm. 24hr answerphone and minicom. Telephone service offering advice information and support for lesbians

Married Men's Drop-In

T:0191-233-1333. Support group for married men which offers confidential support and advice.

MESMAC Tyneside (Men who have Sex with men - action in the community)

7 Drury Lane NE1 1HL. T:0191-233-1333. Minicom. Campaigning information and outreach group who work with groups and individuals to increase positive choices around safer sex. General support and advice to gay and bisexual men.

Metropolitan Community Church

St James United Reform Church Northumberland Road. T:0191-526-0974. Sun 7.30pm evening service. Offers fortnightly discussion groups.

Newcastle Young Lesbian Group

T:0191-261-2277. Mon 6pm - 7pm for information. Meets Wed 7.30pm - 9.30pm. Social and support group for women under 25 who are lesbian or who think they may be.

Phillips & Co

86 Pilgrim Street NE1 6SR. T:0191-232-8451. F:0191-232-7664. Mon - Fri 9am - 5pm. General solicitor practice. Accepts Legal Aid work. Emergency service. Speaks French and German. Home visits arranged for disabled clients.

Powerhouse

Blenheim Street. T:0191-261-4507. Mon, Thurs, Fri and Sat 9pm - 1am, Sun 7pm - 10.30pm. Lesbian and gay club. Women's bar on Thurs, men only bar on Sun. Third Weds of each month women's club night, first Weds each month men's club night.

Rockies

78 Scotswood Road. T:0191-232-6536. Open pub hours. Gay bar and disco.

Rockshots

Waterloo Street. T:0191-232-9648. Mon, Wed 11pm - 2am, Sat 11pm - 3am. Lesbian and gay club.

SIDA Centre

12 Princess Square NE1 8EG. T:0191-232-2855. F:0191-222-0514. Mon - Fri 10am - 7pm., Sat 10am - 4pm. Resource centre providing information and services on sexual health. Library, educational outreach project, safer sex training courses, space available for community groups to meet.

String's

29 Blenheim Street. T:0191-232-3530. Open usual pub hours. Lesbian and gay pub and disco.

Survivors Group

T:0191-233-1333. Meets fortnightly. Support group for gay and bisexual men who have been sexually abused or raped.

Stars and Moon Group

T:0191-233-1333. Minicom 5. Group for deaf lesbians and gay men.

Stratford Lodge Guest House

T:0191-265-6395 or 0831-879182. Lesbian and gay guest house. Open all year. Residents car park. Accepts Visa and Access. Will also supply a chauffeur driven Rolls Royce!

Tyneside Young Gay Men's Group

T:0191-233-1333. Tues 7.15pm - 9pm. Group for gay men aged 25 and under offering support and social activities.

Village

Sunderland Street (next to Powerhouse). Open usual pub hours. Lesbian and gay pub.

West City Gay Group

T:0191-273-6747. Lesbian, gay and bisexual social group which meets once a month, Thurs afternoons.

Women for Women

PO Box 1JR NE99 1JR. Meets at 7 Drury Lane Fri 7.30pm - 9.30pm. Social for all lesbians and bisexual women.

Northallerton

Dales Information and Support Line

T:01677-424665. Weds 7pm -9.30pm. Telephone service which offers support information and advice for lesbians and gay men.

Gay Men's Support Group

T: 01677-424665. Gay men's group which meets weekly for social occasions.

HARCAS (Hambleton & Richmondshire Community Addiction Services)

c/o Zetland Street Centre Zetland Street DL6 1ND. T:01609-780486. Mon and Weds - Fri 9am - 5pm. Tues 9am - 5pm and 6pm - 8pm. Offers information on safer sex and safer drug use. Counselling information and support available.

North Shields

Long & Purves

29 Northumberland Square NE30 1EW. T:0191-259-5199. Emergency :0191-251-2100. F:0191-296-2300. Mon - Fri 9am - 5pm. General solicitor practice which specialises in crime, matrimonial, personal injury and welfare. Accepts Legal Aid work. Emergency service.

Pontefract

DASH Line

Southmoor House Southmoor Road Hemsworth WF9 4SQ T:01977-790999 (staffed 24 hours). Offers information on safer sex and safer drug use. Operates a drop-in service.

Hartley and Worstenholme

Gillygate Chambers WF8 1PQ. T:01977-793496. Emergency: 01977-780115 F:01977-600343. Mon- Fri 9am - 5pm. General solicitor practice. Accepts Legal Aid work. Emergency service. Speaks French.

Richmond

Northallerton and Dales HIV Awareness Group

Cherry Tree Cottage Colburn Village DL9 4PE. T: 01748-833135. Education care counselling and information to increase awareness about HIV/AIDS. Also runs Alverton Holiday Respite Scheme which organises breaks for people affected by HIV/AIDS.

Rotherham

Brynes (Dr R M)

Woodstock Bower Kimberwoth Road S61 1AD. T:01709-561442. Male doctor's practice. Mon - Fri

8.30pm - 6pm. NHS only. Offers acupuncture. Rotherham FHSA. Disabled access.

Rothergays

c/o CVS (Council for Voluntary Services) 5 Moorgate Road S60 2EN. T:01709-820304. Mon and Weds 7pm - 10pm. Telephone service offering advice information and support to lesbians and gay men.

Scarborough

Cambridge Centre

1 Westbourne Grove YO11 2DJ. T:01723-500600. Mon 10am-1pm, Weds 2pm - 4pm, Thurs 7pm - 9pm Helpline during these office hours. Drop-in Mon -Fri 9am - 4pm. Operates a needle exchange, drop-in, information, advice and support on HIV/AIDS issues via the Helpline.

Drabble & Co

50 Albemarle Crescent YO11 1XZ. T:01723-367121. Emergency 01723-862048. F:01723-500374. Mon - Fri 9am - 5.30pm. General solicitor practice. Accepts Legal Aid. Emergency service.

Interludes

32 Princess Street. T:01723-360513. (Contact Ian or Rob). Lesbian, gay, straight hotel.

Yorkshire Coast Gay Men and Women's Group

T:01723-362205. Meets second Thurs each month. Regular social events for lesbians and gay men.

Scunthorpe

Body Positive

22 Laneham Street DN15 6PB. T:01724-289440. Mon, Wed, Fri 11am - 3pm. Self-help group for people affected by HIV/AIDS meets first and last Thurs each month 7pm - 9pm. Administers Tom Johnson Trust Fund which is a hardship fund.

Ebb and Flow

22 Laneham Street DN15 6PB. T:01724-289292 (Helpline) Mon - Fri 10am - 5pm. Drop-in Mon 11am - 2pm. Women's Health Information Service Sat 11am - 2pm. Telephone service offering information advice and counselling to people affected by HIV/AIDS. Befriending information and counselling via drop-in.

Gay Helpline

T:01724-271661. Wed and Fri 7pm - 9pm. Telephone service which offers advice, information and counselling.

Gay Men and Women's Group

T:01724-845155. Mon 7.30pm - 9.30pm. Lesbian and gay social group.

Lesbian and Gay Youth Group

T:01724-845155. Tues 7.30pm - 9.30pm. Lesbian and gay support and social group for people under 26.

Selby

HIV/AIDS Counselling and Testing Service

Raincliffe Street Clinic. T:01904-454042. Mon 2pm - 4pm. Testing and counselling for those with concerns around HIV.

Sheffield

AIDSline

PO Box 816 S1 4JS. T:0800-844344. Tues, Weds, Thurs 8pm - 10pm. Telephone service offering information advice and counselling for people affected by HIV/AIDS.

A Touch of Class

218 Middlewood Road Hillsborough S6. At weekends operates as gay sauna.

Albert Inn

Sutherland Street. T: 0114-272-3569. Open usual pub hours. Lesbian and gay pub with discos at weekends and a stripper on Sundays.

Ambling Dykes

Contact Lesbian Line for details. Informal group which meets monthly for walks up to 4 miles.

Body Positive

PO Box 816 S1 4JS. T:0114-278-8025. Self-help group for people affected by HIV/AIDS. Organises hospital visits and has weekly meetings which are occasionally open to carers and partners.

Bulldog

387 Attercliffe Road. T:0114-244-2180. Open usual pub hours. Gay men's pub. Sunday has strippers.

Cavalier's @ Norfolk Arms

208 Saville Street East. T:0114-278-0383. Mon - Sat 8pm - midnight, Sun 8pm - 10.30pm. Lesbian and gay club.

Centre for HIV and Sexual Health

22 Collegiate Crescent S10 2BA. T:0114-267-8806. Produces a range of literature and health promotion materials and young people's video. Outreach for gay men, prostitutes, youth workers and young people. Have produced lesbian safer sex material.

Club (formerly Rockie's)

429 Effingham Road. T:0114-244-0110. Weds - Sat 10pm - 2am, Sun 10pm - 1am. Lesbian and gay club.

Club Mimosa

T:0114-258-1238. Call Lesbian Line for further details. Third Sat of each month 9pm - 2am. Lesbian club.

Cossack Hotel

45 Howard Street. T:0114-272-2889. Open usual pub hours. Lesbian and gay pub.

Delicious @ Cuba

Rear of Kiki's Charter Square. T:0114-275-4500. Fri 10pm - 2am. Lesbian and gay club.

Gay Phone

c/o MIND 57 Wostenholme Road. T:0114-258-8199. Mon & Wed 7.30pm - 9.30pm. Telephone service, offering advice, information and support.

Gay Phone Socials

Contact Gay Phone for details. Alternate Mon 8pm - 10pm. Lesbian and gay social group.

Harlequin @ Isabella's

Eyre Street. T:0114-265-0082. Thurs 11pm - 2am. Lesbian and gay club.

Hiking Dykes

Contact Lesbian Line for details. Organises walks in the Peak

District every 2-3 weeks up to 12 miles. Weekend and week long trips further afield. Quarterly meetings and newletter.

Howell & Co

42 Spital Hill S4 7LG. T:0114-249-6666. F:0114-250-0656. Mon - Fri 8.30am - 6pm. General solicitor practice specialising in criminal, family, civil, immigration, welfare, conveyancing and education. Accepts Legal Aid work. Emergency service. Speaks Punjabi, Urdu and Spanish.

Lesbian Line

T:0114-258-1238. Thurs 7pm - 10pm. Telephone service offering advice information and support for lesbians.

Lesbian and Gay Youth Group

PO Box 425 Sheffield S1 3UX. T:0114-258-8199. Meets regularly for social and support for lesbians and gay men under 26. Contact Gay Phone for further details.

Liberation

The Park, Sheffield University Students Union Western Bank. Third Sat each month 10pm - 2am. Lesbian and gay disco.

MSC Hallamshire

c/o The Albert Inn Sutherland Street S4 7WG. T:01709-550858. Meets first and third Sat each month. Gay men's leather fetish club.

Norrie Bowler & Wrigley

11/12 East Parade S1 2ET. T:0114-276-6166. Emergency service: 0114-273-0636 ext 21. F:0114-273-9311. Mon - Fri 9am - 5.30pm. General solicitor practice specialising in crime, matrimonial, personal injury, conveyancing and debt. Accepts Legal Aid work. Emergency service. Speaks Urdu, Punjabi and some Arabic. Disabled access.

Partners Group

c/o Voluntary AIDS Liaison Group. PO Box 816 S1 4JS. Meets alternate Weds 7.30pm - 9.30pm. Support group for partners and family of those affected by HIV/AIDS.

PRAIS (Prostitutes Rights and Information Group)

22 Collegiate Crescent S10 2BA. T:0114-267-8806. F:0114-267-8808. Street based health work which provides advice information and support, condoms and referrals.

Queen's Hotel

85 Scotland Street. T:0114-272-6909. Open Sun- Thurs 7pm -11pm, Fri and Sat 7pm - 12.30am. Lesbian and gay pub, club and hotel.

Rose's

29 Roundell Street S9 3LE. T:0114-261-9444. Mon - Fri 9am - 10pm. Support group for TVs. Publishes TV *Repartee* magazine.

SHIELD (Sheffield AIDS Support Group)

PO Box 816 S1 4JS. T:0114-278-7916. Offers buddying service and support group, individual support and counselling service.

Shout!

T:0114-258-8199.

Group which promotes sexual health for all bisexual and gay men.

SYHALG (South Yorkshire HIV/ AIDS Liaison Group)

PO Box 816 S1 4JS. T:0114-275-5500. Co-ordinates the work of the Sheffield voluntary AIDS groups providing premises, office space, meeting rooms and training.

Triangle Travel

The Leadmill S1. T: 0114-272-2990. Open every day of week.Lesbian gay straight travel agent. Specialises in trips (groups or individuals) to Mardi Gras, Boston Women's Music Festival, as well as packages throughout the world.

Women's Cultural Club

Grinders Hill Paternoster Row. T:0114-272-1866. Lesbian and straight women's bar and cafe.

Stockton-on-Tees

Health Advice Centre

29-31 Yarm Lane TS18 3DT. T:01642-607313. Drop-in, Mon, Wed, Thurs, Fri 9.30am - 4.30pm, Tues 9.30am - 7.30pm. Offers health information and advice, safer sex advice, safer drug use, free condoms, HIV counselling and testing service, Hepatitis B testing.

Stockton Law Centre

76 Norton Road TS18 2DE. T:01642-605060. F:01642-618616. Mon - Fri 10am - 3pm. Law centre offering general legal advice. Accepts Legal Aid. Disabled access.

Sunderland

Ben Hoare Bell & Co

52 Frederick Street SR1 1NF. T:0191-565-3112. F:0191-510-9122. Mon - Fri 9am - 5.30pm. General solicitor practice specialising in crime, family, accident, welfare, landlord and tenant and mental health issues. Accepts Legal Aid work. Emergency service. Speaks French and Spanish.

Cellar Bar

Mowbray Park Hotel. Tues and Fri. Open usual pub hours. Gay bar. Contact Newcastle Friend or MESMAC for details.

Lesbian and Gay Young People's Group

T:0191-565-7905. Mon or Thurs 7pm - 9pm. Meets in the centre of Sunderland and offers support to lesbian and gay young people (16-25) in a relaxed and informal atmosphere.

Wear Body Positive

Ford and Pennywell Advice Centre 468 Hilton Road SL4 8LB. T:0191-565-5033. F:0191-5510-2599. Self-help group for people affected by HIV/AIDS. Groups include HIV+ only, women's group, alternative therapies, lesbian, gay and bisexual support group, married men's support group, art workshop, vreative writing, drama group, quilt group/Names Project.

Wakefield

Begin Learning and Living

H Gwynne Jones Centre Stanley Royd Aberford Road WF1 4DG. T:01924-364144. Group of people who voluntarily provide workshops on HIV related issues, befriending service, practical help, legal issues, relaxation and massage, equipment loan, training visits for community groups, fundraising.

Bourbon Street Night Club

Radcliffe Place. T:01924-360147. Tues 11pm - 2am. Gay club.

Catteralls

15 King Street WF1 2SL. T:01924-291122. F:01924-290953. Mon - Fri 9am - 5.15pm. General solicitor practice. Accepts Legal Aid work. Offers emergency service.

Coach Inn

281 Doncaster Road. Usual pub hours. Lesbian and gay pub.

Dolphin

6 Lower Warrengate. T:01924-201705. Open usual pub hours. Gay pub with Sunday cabaret.

HIV Counselling and Support Service

H Gwynne Jones Centre Stanley Royd Aberford Road WF1 4DG. T:01924-364144. Mon - Fri 9.30am - 4.30pm. Counselling service for people affected by HIV/AIDS. Support for carers and health care workers.

Nightlife Entertainments

PO Box 91 WF1 5YU. T:01924-384084. Mon - Fri 10am - 8pm. Professional mobile entertainments for gay organisations.

Switalski Jones

19 Wood Street WF1 2EL. T:01924-290029. Mon - Fri 9am - 5pm. General solicitor practice.

Whitley Bay

Lindisfarne Hotel

11 Holly Avenue. T:0191-251-3954. Lesbian, gay, straight hotel.

Seaham Hotel

The Promenade. T:0191-251-3727. Lesbian, gay, straight hotel. Open all year.

York

Blue Star

1 Victoria Street off Nunnery Lane YO2 1LZ. T:01904-624901. Tues - Fri 10am - 5pm. Bookshop which stocks lesbian and gay books, magazines and videos.

Body Positive

7 Bell View Court Byland Avenue YO3 9BG. T:01904-671631 or out of office hours 0374-229133. Self-help group for people affected by HIV/AIDS.

Bull Lodge

37 Bull Lane Lawrence Street YO1 3EN. T:01904-415522. Lesbian, gay, straight bed and breakfast.

Chimneys Guest House

18 Bootham Crescent. T:01904-644334. Lesbian, gay, straight guest house.

Churchill Hotel

65 Bootham. T:01904-644456. Lesbian, gay, straight bed and breakfast.

Dairy Guest House

3 Scarcroft Road. T:01902-639637. Lesbian, gay, straight bed and breakfast.

Fantasy Island @ Tofts Night Club

3/5 Toft Green Micklegate. T:01904-620203. Mon 10pm - 2am. Lesbian, gay club.

Gay Gardeners Contact Group

GGCG P O Box 284 YO1 1TX. Social group for gay men interested in gardening.

Gay Group

Friends Meeting House Friargate off Clifford Street YO1 1EX. T:01904-671945 or 01904-626790. Mon 8pm onwards. Social group for gay men.

Guppys

The Old Brit Nunnery Lane. T:01904-646812. Fortnightly discos. Call Lesbian Line for details. Lesbian disco.

Harrowell Shaftoe

1 St Saviourgate YO1 2NQ. T:01904-620331. Emergency: 01904-426303. F:01904-655855. Mon - Fri 9am - 5pm. General solicitor practice which specialises in crime, matrimonial, welfare, property, civil litigation, personal injury and medical negligence. Accepts Legal Aid work. Emergency service.

Lesbian Group

PO Box 225 YO1 1AA. T:01904-646812. Last Friday of the month. Lesbian social group.

Lesbian Line

PO Box 225 YO1 1AA. T:01904-646812. Fri 7pm - 9pm. 24-hour answerphone. Telephone service offering advice, support and counselling to lesbians.

Milk and Honey

York Arts Centre Micklegate. T:01904-642582. First Fri of the month 9pm - 2am. Lesbian, gay, straight club.

One in Ten Project

c/o Community House 10 Priory Street YO1 1EZ. T:01904-612629. Mon 7pm - 9pm. Lesbian, gay, bisexual youth group.

Pauleda House Hotel

123 Clifton YO3 6BL. T:01904-634745. Lesbian, gay, straight hotel.

Positive Advocacy

7 Bell View Court Byland Avenue YO3 9BG. T:01904-611304 or Crisis Line 0374- 229133. Independent organisation which represents and uphold rights of people living with HIV/AIDS.

White Horse

Bootham. T:01904-623778. Lesbian and gay bed and breakfast.

YAA

PO Box 318 YO3 4XY. T:01904-639595. Thurs 3pm - 7pm. Telephone service offering advice support and information to people affected by HIV/AIDS.

York Arms

26 High Petergate. Open usual pub hours. Lesbian, gay, straight pub.

Sexual Politics

ORDER FORM

To order titles direct from Cassell see the form at the back of the directory : here we list some 30 innovative and acclaimed new books in our Lesbian and Gay Studies, Women on Women and AIDS Awareness series.

PUB QUIZ

Throughout 1995 Cassell and *The Pink Paper* shall be running a nationwide tournament of pub quizzes. If you run a pub and would be interested in taking part, contact Cassell's Sexual Politics Quiz, Villiers House, 41/47 Strand, London WC2N 5JE.

MAKE CASH! HOLD A BOOK PARTY!

If you are interested in hosting a book party for you and your friends contact Cassell's Sexual Politics Book Party, Villiers House, 41/47 Strand, London WC2N 5JE.

MAILING LIST

For regular information about our forthcoming titles, catalogues and news of special offers and book events in your area, fill in the form below and return to Cassell's Sexual Politics Mailing List, Villiers House, 41/47 Strand, London WC2N 5JE. No charge and no obligation.

Please include my details on the Sexual Politics Mailing List for receipt of details of forthcoming titles, news of special offers and of Cassell book events:

Name ....

Address ....

....

....

....

Send to Cassell Sexual Politics Mailing List, Villiers House, 41/47 Strand, London WC2N 5JE.

WALES

Clwyd

Buck Farm

Hanmer. T:019487-4339. Lesbian, gay, straight guest house and restaurant which has organic food, caters for vegetarians and vegans.

Cheshire and North Wales Gay Social Group

T:01978-291008 (Nigel). Meets alternative Tues in private homes.

Clwyd Lesbian and Gay Local Government Group

Contact via Gwynedd Lesbian Line. Meets the 1st Wed night every month.

Watkin - Jones (Dr T)

Pierce Street Queensferry CH5 1SY. T:01244-813440. Mon - Fri 8.30am - 6pm. Sat 9am - noon. Medical practice. Male doctor. NHS only except in emergencies. Offers acupuncture and lesbian, gay and bisexual related psychotherapy. Clwyd FHSA. Disabled access and facilities.

Ysbyty Glan Clwyd

GUM Department Bodelwyddan LL18 5UJ. T:01745-583910. Specialised HIV/AIDS care is provided on Ward 11.

Rhyl

Westminster Hotel Cellar Bar

East Parade Rhyl. Lesbian, gay, straight bar.

Wrexham

Wrexham Dental Centre Grove Park Road LL11 1DY. T:01978-262050. Mon - Fri 9am-4.30pm. Dental treatment for people with HIV/AIDS.

Dyfed

Brynerw

Near Llandovery. T:01559-20729 Lesbian, gay, straight bed and breakfast in a 17th century country house.

CYLCH

PO Box 23 Aberystwyth. T:01222-499593 (Chris). Welsh-speaking lesbian and gay social group.

Dyfed Diners

Gay monthly dining club. T:01239-79633 (Godwin).

Fountain

Trefechan. Tues only. Open usual pub hours. Lesbian, gay, straight pub one night of the week.

Friendly Rivals

Heol Beiliglas Swiss Valley Llanelli. T:01554-757838. Lesbian, gay, straight pub. Gay night every Sun.

Georges Inn

Haverfordwest. Lesbian, gay, straight pub and restaurant.

Lesbian and Gay Line

P O Box 23 Aberystwyth SY23 1AA. T:01970-615076. Tues 6pm - 8pm. Telephone service offering advice, support and counselling to lesbians and gay men.

Lesbian and Gay Society

PO Box 23 Aberystwyth. Meets every Sat at 2.30pm in Room 3 The Liberal Club 32 North Parade. Social group.

Non's Place

40 Church Street

Pembroke Dock. T:01646-684398. Lesbian and straight women's bed and breakfast.

Torch Theatre Bar

The Torch Theatre Bar St Peter's Road Milford Haven. Lesbian, gay, straight bar.

White D.H.

15 Williams Terrace Bury Port. T:01554-833210 after 6pm. Private qualified counsellor who also teaches counselling skills.

Glamorgan

Cardiff

AIDS Helpline

T:01222-223443. Mon - Fri 7pm - 1pm. Telephone service offering advice, support and information to people affected by HIV and AIDS.

Beaufort House

20 Plasturton Gardens. T:01222-237003. Lesbian, gay, straight bed and breakfast.

Club X

39 Charles Street. T:01222-645721. Weds-Sat 10pm-2am. Lesbian and gay club.

Courtfield Hotel

101 Cathedral Road CF1 9PH. T:01222-227701. AA two star. Lesbian, gay straight. Open all year. Accepts Visa, Access, AMEX, Diners Club.

CYLCH

Contact via Cardiff Friend. Lesbian and gay Welsh-speaking social group.

Dragons Club

The Secretary 147 Coed Y Gores Llandedryn Cardiff. Lesbian and gay deaf social group. Meets at the Exit Bar at 9pm, 1st Sat of the month.

Exit Bar

48 Charles Street. Mon & Tues midnight - 2am, Wed - Sat midday - midnight. Sun midday - 3pm, 7pm - 10.30pm. Lesbian, gay, straight bar with cabaret and various entertainments.

Friend

P O Box 479 Cardiff CF1 8YJ. T:01222 - 340101. Tues - Sat 8pm - 10pm. Lesbian, gay, bisexual, straight. Information, counselling and befriending for lesbians, gays and bisexuals or those in contact with them..

Gay Christian Movement

P O Box 479 Cardiff CF1 8YJ or via Cardiff Friend. Meets at the Courtfield Hotel 101 Cathedral Road, 1st Friday of the month at 8pm.

Gay Social Group

Contact via Cardiff Friend. Meets at the Courtfield Hotel, 101 Cathedral Road on the 4th Fri of each month.

Girth and Mirth of Wales

T:01222-472583 (Phillip or Tony). Gay social group for larger-than-life people and those interested in them.

Hermer and Evans

10 St Andrew's Crescent CF1 3DD. T:01222-387766 or 224009. Emergency:01222-482054. Mon - Fri 9am - 6pm. Small general family solicitor practice. Accepts legal aid work. Emergency service. Speaks Welsh.

King's Cross

Hays Bridge Road. Open usual pub hours. Lesbian and gay pub.

Lesbian Line

CLLC P O Box 87 Cardiff CF1 3YZ. T:01222-374051. Tues 8pm - 10pm. Telephone service offering advice, information and support to lesbians.

Lesbian and Gay Youth Group

Contact via Cardiff Friend. Meets every other week. Sun 6.30pm - 8.30pm. Organises social activities for young (16-25) lesbians and gay men.

Locker Room

50 Charles Street. T:01222-220388. Sun - Fri, 1pm - midnight. Sat 1pm - 8pm. Gay sauna and health club.

Oasis Salvation Army AIDS Care Centre

Walker Road Splott CF2 2EG. T:01222-451693. Mon 10am - 4pm. Drop-in for those affected by HIV/ AIDS. Offers confidential support.

Older Bolder

Contact via Cardiff Lesbian Line. A group for lesbians over 35.

Riverside Hotel

53-59 Despenser Street. T:01222-378866. Lesbian, gay, straight pub.

Scene @ Riverside Hotel

Corner of Despenser Street, Taff Embankment. T:01222-378866. Wed - Sun. Gay bar with cabaret.

Short (Christopher)

3rd Floor USDAW Building 42 Charles Street CF1 4EE. T:01222-232657. Emergency:01446-742402. F:01222-342612. Mon - Fri 9am - 5pm. Solicitor practice covering criminal law, immigration, matrimonial, conveyancing, personal injury, employment law, probate and welfare benefits. Accepts legal aid work. Emergency service. Arranges home visits for disabled clients.

Triangle Housing Association

P O Box 479 Cardiff CF1 8YJ. T:01222-666662. An organisation which provides accommodation for lesbians and gays in need or in danger. Keeps lists of currently available lesbian and gay accommodation on offer by other landlords.

Women's Disco

Contact via Cardiff Lesbian Line. Monthly at the Star Centre, Splott 9pm - 1am.

Youthlink Wales

91a Cardiff Road Caerphilly CH8 1FQ. T:01222-885711. F:01222-888727. Supports and develops young people's initiatives throughout Wales aiming to prevent the spread of HIV and substance abuse.

Pontypridd

Bronyna

Mersey Street LL49 9UB. T:01766-512792. Lesbian, gay, straight bed and breakfast. Open all year.

Lan Farm

Grangwen Pontypridd. T:01443-403606. Lesbian and gay guest house and bed and breakfast. Open all year. Car park. Does not accept credit cards.

Mid-Glamorgan AIDSLine

PO Box 24 Pontypridd CF37 1YF. T:01443-486254. Tues, Thurs 7pm-9pm. Telephone service offering advice support and information for people affected by HIV/ AIDS.

Swansea

AIDSline

T:01792-456303. Thurs 3pm - 8pm. Telephone service offering advice, counselling and information to people affected by HIV and AIDS.

Citizens Advice Bureau Lesbian and Gay Helpline

T:01792-652902. Tues 6pm - 9pm. Telephone service offering advice, counselling and information.

Champers

210 High Street. T:01792-655622. Open usual pub hours.Lesbian, gay, straight bar.

Chatthams

The Grand Hotel High Street (opposite the railway station). T:01792-650641. Lesbian, gay, straight bar in hotel. Open usual pub hours.

Lesbian, Gay and Bisexual Switchboard

P O Box 348 SA1 1XE. T:01792-301855. Tues 7pm - 9pm. Telephone service offering advice, counselling and information.

Lesbian and Gay Christian Movement

T:01554-63210 (David after 6pm). Christian social and religious group for lesbians and gay men.

Lesbian Line

c/o The Women's Centre 228 High Street. T:01792-651995. Wed 7pm - 9pm. Telephone service offering advice, counselling and information for lesbians.

Palace Club

High Street (near the railway station). T:01792-466632. Mon, Thurs Fri Sat 9pm - 2am. Lesbian and gay club. Also has a women only night.

SWISH (South Wales Immune Deficiency Self-Help)

PO Box 507 Pontardawe SA6 5YA. T:01792-772007. Wed 2pm-5pm. Telephone line offering information, advice and support for people affected by HIV/AIDS. Also has drop-in centre (Wed 10am-5pm), a hardship fund, closed support groups, a library of HIV/AIDS resources, offers complementary therapies, diet and nutrition workshops, multi-gym, pool table and social events.

Women's Centre

228 High Street. Community centre for all women. Offers information and support.

Gwent

AIDSLine

c/o GUM Department Royal Gwent Hospital Newport NP2 2UB. T:01633-841901 Mon-Fri 7am-4.30pm. Telephone service offering information advice and support for people affected by HIV/AIDS. GUM Department also runs a coffee and condom van which travels throughout the entire county one evening each week offering health care and education.

Greenhouse Health Club

24 Church Street. T:01633-221172. Mon - Fri 1pm - 11pm. Sat open all night. Sun 2pm - 11pm. Gay sauna and steam room, sun beds, jacuzzi, TV lounge, refreshments and meals.

Gwynedd

Broadway Boulevard

Mostyn Broadway Llandudno. T:01492-879614. Mon fortnightly 8.30pm - 12.30pm. Lesbian and gay club.

Garth Hotel

Bangor. Lesbian, gay, straight pub. Fri evenings.

Gay Line

c/o Greenhouse 1 Trevelyan Bangor Gwynedd. T:01248-351263. Fri 7pm - 9pm and 24-hour answerphone service. Telephone service offering advice, counselling and information to gay men.

Gwynedd Drugs Advisory Service

3 Llys Gwynedd LL57 1DT. T:01248-351829. F:01248-371248. Supplies information on safer sex, safer drug use, needle exchange, counselling.

Gwynedd Healthy Sexuality Outreach Project

Health Promotion Unit Traeth Laffan Bryn y Neuadd Llanfairfechan LL57 2EN. T:01248-351149. F:01248-371034. Outreach project targeting gay men to promote safer sex.

Kenric Group North Wales

Contact via Gwynedd Lesbian Line. Lesbian social group which organises parties, meetings, trips to clubs etc.

Lesbian and Gay Line

T:01248-351263. Fri 7pm-9pm. Telephone service offering advice, support and information for lesbians and gay men.

Lesbian Line

c/o Greenhouse 1 Trevelyan Bangor Gwynedd. T:01248-351263. Tues 7pm - 9pm and 24-hour answerphone. Telephone service offering advice, counselling and information to lesbians.

Platform 3

The Station Colwyn Bay. Thurs evenings. Lesbian, gay, straight pub.

Youth Group

Contact via Gwynedd Lesbian Line or Gay Line. Lesbian and gay social group.

Powys

Powys AIDSline Services

P O Box 24 Llandrindod Wells LD1 6RD. T:01597-824200. Wed, Sat 8pm - 10.30pm. Telephone service offering advice, counselling, support and information to people affected by HIV /AIDS.

MIDLANDS

Sexual Politics

ORDER FORM

To order titles direct from Cassell see the form at the back of the directory : here we list some 30 innovative and acclaimed new books in our Lesbian and Gay Studies, Women on Women and AIDS Awareness series.

PUB QUIZ

Throughout 1995 Cassell and *The Pink Paper* shall be running a nationwide tournament of pub quizzes. If you run a pub and would be interested in taking part, contact Cassell's Sexual Politics Quiz, Villiers House, 41/47 Strand, London WC2N 5JE.

MAKE CASH! HOLD A BOOK PARTY!

If you are interested in hosting a book party for you and your friends contact Cassell's Sexual Politics Book Party, Villiers House, 41/47 Strand, London WC2N 5JE.

MAILING LIST

For regular information about our forthcoming titles, catalogues and news of special offers and book events in your area, fill in the form below and return to Cassell's Sexual Politics Mailing List, Villiers House, 41/47 Strand, London WC2N 5JE. No charge and no obligation.

Please include my details on the Sexual Politics Mailing List for receipt of details of forthcoming titles, news of special offers and of Cassell book events:

Name ....
Address ....
....
....
....

Send to Cassell Sexual Politics Mailing List, Villiers House, 41/47 Strand, London WC2N 5JE.

BIRMINGHAM

Hotels, Guest Houses and B&Bs

Fountain Inn

102 Wrentham Street. T:0121-622-1452. Lesbian and gay bed and breakfast above a pub. Open all year. Car park. Accepts Visa, Access, AMEX.

Oak Leaves Guest House

Gibson Drive Handsworth Wood. T:0121-551-6510. Lesbian and gay guest house. Open all year. Accepts Access and Visa.

Village Inn

152 Hurst Street. T:0121-622-6742. Lesbian and gay guest house. Open all year. Car park. Accepts Visa and Access.

Bars, Clubs, Pubs, Cafes, Restaurants

Fountain Inn

102 Wrentham Street. T:0121-622-1452. Mon - Fri midday - 3pm, 6pm - 11pm. Sat midday - 3pm, 7pm - 11pm, Sun midday - 3pm, 7pm - 10.30pm. Lesbian and gay pub.

Fox

17 Lower Essex Street. T:0121-622-1210. Mon - Sat midday - 3pm, 6pm - 11pm. Sun 7pm - 10.30pm. Lesbian pub.

Jester

Bristol Street. T:0121-643-0155. Mon - Fri midday - 11pm, Sat 11.30am - 11pm. Sun midday - 3pm. Gay pub.

Jug

27 Water Street. T:0121-233-2906. Mon - Sat 10pm - 2.30am. Lesbian and gay club.

Nightingale

40 Thorp Street. T:0121-622-1718. Mon - Thurs 10pm - 2am, Fri & Sat 9pm - 2am. Sun 9pm - midnight. Lesbian and gay club. Separate women-only level on Sat.

Partners

Hurst Street. T:0121-622-4710. Mon - Thurs 3pm - 11pm. Fri & Sat 1pm - 11pm. Sun 12.30pm - 3pm, 7pm - 10.30pm. Lesbian and gay bar.

Peacocks

Bull Ring Centre Smallbrook Queensway. T:0121-643-3127. Mon - Sat 1pm - 11pm. Sun midday - 3pm, 7pm - 10.30pm. Lesbian and gay bar.

Route 66

139/147 Hurst Street. T:0121-622-3366. Mon - Sat midday - 3pm, 5pm - 11pm. Sun midday - 3pm, 7pm - 10.30pm. Gay bar. Disabled access and toilet.

Tin Tin's

308 Bull Ring Centre Queensway. T:0121-643-4129. Lesbian, gay, straight club.

Village Inn

152 Hurst Street. T:121-622-4742. Mon - Sat midday - 11pm. Sun midday - 3pm, 7pm - 10.30pm. Lesbian and gay bar.

Businesses

Adie Evans and Walker

4 Temple Row. T:0121-236-8166. General solicitor practice which has extensive experience of cottaging cases.

Clone Zone

42 Bristol Street. T:0121-666-6640.

Pink Directory

Mon - Sat 11am - 6pm. Stocks, literature, magazines, cards, clothes, sex toys for lesbians and gay men.

Driving Instructor

T:0121-778-5524. (Robric). Free pick-up service and progress reports.

Interior Decoration

T:0121-565-2144 (Shaun). Decorating company which is lesbian and gay friendly.

Loading Bay Records

586 Bristol Road Selly Oak. T:0121-472-2463. Stocks Hi-NRG / disco records.

Shakespeares

10 Bennett Hill B2 5RS. T:0121-632-4199. F:0121-643-3109. Mon - Fri 8.30am - 6pm. Solicitor practice covering all areas of English and European law. Accepts Legal Aid work Speaks French, German and Spanish. Disabled access.

Transformation

62/64 Oxhill Road Handsworth Wood. T:0121-554-2429. Stocks clothes for TV/ TSs.

Young and Lee

432 Stratford Road Spark Hill. T:0121-772-5012, 0121-200-2717 ext 248 (emergency). Solicitor practice specialising in crime, child care, family, conveyancing, mental health, wills and probate, civil litigation and welfare benefits. Accepts Legal Aid work. Speaks Punjabi, Urdu, Gujerati, Hindi. Disabled access.

Organisations

Adullam Homes Housing Association

11 Park Avenue Hockley B18 5ND. T:0121-551-5030. F:0121-554-9715. Self-contained flats and house for people living with HIV/ AIDS. Services include practical and emotional support, care at home and social events.

AIDS Lifeline and Counselling Centre

T:0121-440-0034. Mon - Fri 10am - 4pm. Telephone service offering advice, information, and counselling to people affected by HIV. Face-to-face counselling, community training and support, produces a twice monthly bulletin.

AIDSline West Midlands

T:0121-622-1511. Mon - Fri 7.30pm - 10pm. Telephone service offering advice, information and counselling to people affected by HIV/AIDS.

Aquarius

Pebble Mill House 236 Bristol Road B5 7SL. T:0121-471-1361. F:0121-472-8350. Mon - Fri 9.30am - 5.30pm. Lesbian, gay, straight residential and day individual and group counselling programme for men and women with alcohol problems.

Body Positive

47 George Street Hockley B3 1QA. T;0121-212-3636. Wed 8pm - 10pm, Thurs midday - 2pm, 7pm - 9pm. Self-help group for those

affected by HIV. Hospital and home visits , day centre advocacy and information, library for people living with HIV/AIDS. HIV+ women's group, a support group for partners, families and carers, complementary therapies.

Boot Women

Contact via Switchboard. Lesbian group which organises country walks and hikes.

BTM

Barry Tomes 98 Lower Beeches Road Northfield B31 5JS. T:0121-475-9335. F:0121-476-9224. Daily 10am - 6pm (24-hour answerphone). Lesbian, gay, straight artist management agency.

Central Rainbow

PO Box 4036 Kings Norton B30 1AT. Lesbian and gay deaf and hearing impaired support and social group. Meets third Sat of the month 8.30pm at The Jester.

Contact Project

PO Box 5332 B5 4AY. T:0121-622-5332. Telephone line operates Mon - Thurs 1pm - 5pm. Project operates a telephone line for victims of gay bashing, a system for anonymous reporting of anti-gay incidents, police and courts assistance service.

Dental Hospital

Dept of Restorative Dentistry St Chad's Queensway B4 6NN. T:0121-236-8611. Dental treatment for people with HIV/ AIDS. Appointments necessary.

Freshwinds Charitable Trust

Freshwinds House 13 Gravelly Hill North Erdington B23 6BT. T:0121-350-8423. Spiritually directed, holistic health agency which includes services for people affected by HIV/ AIDS. Counselling, psychotherapy and complementary therapies.

Friend West Midlands

PO Box 2405 B5 4AJ. T:0121-622-6351. Befriending and counselling organsiation. Telephone line operates nightly 7.30pm - 9.30pm. Also has a drop-in nightly 7.30pm - 9.30pm at 37 Thorpe Street B5.

Friend Women's Social Group

Contact via Friend. Informal social group for lesbians which meets on Tuesday evenings.

Gay Alcoholics Group

St John Fischer Church West Heath . T:0121-475-3904. Lesbian and gay alcoholism support group.

Gay Football Supporters Network

Birmingham branch meets at The Fountain on Mon evenings when live football is broadcast.

Gay Outdoor Club

T:0121-420-2694 (Gordon) or 0121-779-2402 (Andy). Local branch of the Gay Outdoor Club which organises outdoor sporting and associated events.

Gay Sign Group

T:0121-643-7974 (Zak). Lesbian, gay and bisexual group

which teaches basic sign language.

Gay Swimming Group

T:0121-455-6623 (Oliver). Gay. Meets Mon 6.30pm - 7.30pm at Tudor Grange Baths in Solihull.

Henrietta's Out!

Contact via Switchboard. Lesbian social group that organises regular events

ID (In Distress)

c/o Birmingham Citizen Advocacy Southside Sparkwood B12 8LF. Support and advocacy for lesbian and gay people with mental health problems.

LESBEWELL

PO Box 4048 Moseley B13 8DP. Campaigning and social group for lesbian health issues.

Lesbian, Gay and Bisexual Youth Group

Contact via Switchboard. Youth (under 26) group which meets every Sat .

Lesbian and Gay Christian Movement

PO Box 59 Wolverhampton WV4 5TR. T:0121-515-4131 (John) or 01527-63976 (David). Meets Sat 2pm, Friends Meeting House George Road Fiveways Edgbaston.

Lesbian and Gay Switchboard

PO Box 3626 B5 4GL. T:0121-622-6589. Daily 7pm - 10pm. Telephone service offering advice, information and counselling.

Lesbian Line

Dept LL PO Box 2405 B5 4AY. T:0121-622-6536. Mon - Fri 7.30pm - 9.30pm. Telephone service offering advice, information and counselling to lesbians.

LIB (Lesbians in Birmingham)

Contact via Switchboard. Young lesbian social group which meets on the first three Fri of each month.

Long Yang Club

T:0121-745-1071. South East Asian social group.

Midland Link MSC

MSC 20 Mapperley Gardens Moseley B13 8RN. Gay leather social group which meets at The Fountain on the first and third Sun of the month at 8.30pm.

Out and About Gay Men's Outreach Project

4th Floor Smithfield House Digbeth B5 6BS. T:0121-622-1941. F:0121-622-3616. Safer sex and health education project for gay men.

Pride Place

Suite 1 Waverley Court 26 Wake Green Road Moseley B13 9PA. T:0121-449-0525 or 0121-350-0526. Private residential home for young gay people in the care system (by self-referral).

Police Liaison Group

Co-ordinated by the Contact Project. Lesbian and gay. Meets first Thurs of the month at Peacocks at 7.30pm. Consultative meetings between the lesbian and gay community and representatives of the West Midlands police.

Positively Close

T:0121-622-6496. Last Mon of the month. 8pm - 10pm. Telephone service offering information and support to friends and relatives of people with HIV.

Quest

T:0121-454-8431 (Carl). Lesbian and gay Catholic social group which meets weekly on Tues evenings at various venues.

Safe Project

Lancaster Street Clinic 90 Lancaster Street B4 7AR. T:0121-359-6989. Outreach work with sex workers. Well-women clinic on Mon afternoons.

SPYCE

Lesbian, gay, bisexual black social group which meets on first Wed of the month at The Village Inn. Call Switchboard for details.

St Michael's TV/ TS Centre

55 Powke Lane Blackheath. Social group for cross-dressers, TVs and people with gender concerns. Can be contacted via St Michael's Helpline.

St Michael's TV/ TS Helpline

T:0121-559-3181. Tues - Thurs & Sat 7pm - 10pm. Telephone service offering advice, information and counselling to TV/ TSs.

Victim Support Group

Contact via Switchboard or Contact. Gay support group for victims of homophobic violence.

Writers' Group

T:0121-427-8153 (Howard). Gay social and mutual interest group for writers.

Zami

Contact via Switchboard. Support, information and counselling for black lesbians.

Bedworth

Lesbian and Gay Advice Line

Bedworth CAB High Street Warwicks CV12 8NG. T:01203-640710. Wed 6pm - 8pm. Telephone service offering advice, information and counselling to lesbians and gay men.

Bromsgrove

North East Worcestershire Community Drug Team

165a Birmingham Road B61 0DJ. T:01527-831593. Offers HIV testing, counselling, advice on safer sex, free condoms.

Cheltenham

County HIV/AIDS Counselling and Support Service

Cheltenham General Hospital Sandford Road GL53 7AN. T:01242-274285. Mon - Fri 9am - 5pm. HIV testing and counselling service. HIV+ and relatives and carers support groups.

Gloucestershire AIDSline

PO Box 122 GL53 7NH. T:01285-653477. Offers one-to-one befriending and hardship grants. Telephone service is currently under review.

Isbourne House

Castle Street Winchcombe. T:01242-602281. Lesbian and gay bed and breakfast seven miles from Cheltenham.

Phoenix

Andover Road Tivoli. T:01242-529417. Open usual pub hours. Gay pub.

Racecourse Disco

T:01452-502412 (Mervyn). Lesbian and gay disco held monthly at The Insurance Suite Cheltenham Racecourse.

Coventry

Body Positive

T:01203-229292. Lesbian, gay, straight self-help group for those affected by HIV.

Buddies Group

T:01203-229292. Local buddying service which provides practical and emotional support for people with HIV/ AIDS.

Friend

PO Box 8 CV1 2LD. T:01203-714199. Lesbian and gay befriending and counselling organisation. Operates a telephone counselling, information and support line Wed & Fri 7.30pm - 9.30pm.

GHASP (Gay Health and Sex Promotion)

Contact via MESMEN. Gay and bisexual men's group promoting health and community issues.

GYGL (Godiva Young Lesbians and Gays)

12 Park Road CV1 2LD. T:01203-717166 (lesbian), 01203-224090 (gay). Youth group for under 23s which meets on Mon.

HIV Network

12 Park Road CV1 2LD. T:01203-229292. Co-ordinates voluntary HIV/AIDS groups in Warwickshire.

Indulgence @ Brown's

Lower Precinct. Second Tues of the month 9.30pm - 1am. Lesbian and gay disco.

Lesbian and Gay Dining Group

PO Box 130 CV4 9TN. Lesbian and gay dining and social group for 21-40 year olds.

Lesbian Line

12 Park Road CV1 2LD. T:01203-717166. Wed 7pm - 9.30pm. Telephone service offering advice support and counselling to lesbians.

McGuigans

Swanswell Street. T:01203-222536. Mon -Wed 11am - 11pm. Thurs- Sat 11am - 1am. Sun 11am - 3pm, 7pm - 11pm. Gay pub.

MESMEN

12 Park Road CV1 2LD. T:01203-224090. Gay and bisexual men's project.

Paul's Night @ Bobby's Club

25 The Burgess. T:01203-338533. Mon 9.30pm - 2am. Lesbian, gay, straight club.

Wedge Co-operative Bookshop

13 High Street. Stocks lesbian and gay literature and magazines.

Dudley

Dudley HIV/AIDS Support Group

13 Lower High Street Stourbridge DY8 1TA. T:01384-

444300. Tues 7pm - 9pm. Telephone service offering advice, support and counselling for people with HIV/AIDS. Also has meetings every Mon, Tues, Thurs 7pm - 9pm.

Gloucester

Crackers

Burton Way. Mon 9.30pm - 2.30am. Lesbian and gay club.

Elmbridge Guest House

59 Elmbridge Road GL2 0NX. T:01452-414421. Lesbian and gay guest house.

Friend

PO Box 23 GL1 1YW. T:01452-306800. Mon and Thurs 7pm - 10pm. Telephone service offering advice, support and counselling to lesbians and gay men. Lesbian callers only on Thurs.

Gay Community

Contact via Friend. Lesbian and gay social group. Meets Thurs 8pm and holds occasional discos.

Health Promotion Gloucester

Gloucestershire Royal Hospital Great Western Road GL1 3NN. T:01452-394597. Training and education to promote safer sex. Produced video for young people about HIV called *Groping in the Dark*.

Yew Tree Cottage

Bradley Hill Soudley GL14 2QU. T:01594-824823. Lesbian and gay bed and breakfast 15 miles from Gloucester. Also runs de-stressing breaks, including walking, writing, aromatherapy courses in the Forest of Dean.

Henley-in-Arden

Ashleigh House

Whitely Hill B95 5DL. T:015642-2315. Lesbian, gay, straight bed and breakfast one mile from A34 near Coventry, Warwick and Stratford.

Hereford

HIV/AIDS Advice and Helpline

c/o Saint Guthlac Clinic Hereford County Hospital Union Walk HR1 2ER. T:01432-278787. Mon - Thurs 8.30am - 2.30pm. Wed evening 7.30pm - 9.30pm. Telephone service offering advice, counselling and information to people with HIV/AIDS.

Kenilworth

Gay and Lesbian Humanist Association

34 Spring Lane CB8 2HB. T:01926-58450. Promotes lesbian, gay and bisexual human rights and a humanist approach to sex and morality. Provides information on HIV/AIDS and humanist (non-religious) funeral ceremonies throughout UK.

Kidderminster

KGMG

KGMG PO Box 149 or via Hereford and Worcester Switchboard (*see Worcester*). Gay health and social group. Meets the first and third Wed each month.

Leamington Spa

Dorothy's @ Hobnobs

Augusta Place. T:01203-714950.

Pink Directory

Fourth Fri each month 8pm. Lesbian disco.

Women's Resource and Information Centre

Bath Place. Tues and Thurs 1.30pm-4.30pm. Social and support group for lesbians. Also organises occasional women only discos.

Ludlow

Border Women

Also known as Offa's Dykes! PO Box 42 Ludlow or via Hereford and Worcester Switchboard (see Worcester). Network for lesbians in the rural areas of Hereford, Shropshire, Worcester and Powys. Meets first Sat each month at Women's Centre, Ludlow.

Nuneaton

Harcourt

Princess Street. T:01203-386585. Gay, straight pub. Lounge bar is a gay meeting point Sat 8pm.

Oldbury

Unity Centre for HIV and Sexual Health

6 Unity Place B69 4DB. T:0121-544-3737. Mon - Thurs 9am - 5pm, Fri 9am-4.30pm. Offers sexual health information, counselling, advice, free condoms. Drop-in Mon 4pm-7pm. Has a gay men's health and outreach worker.

Oxford

Body Positive

Ebor House 5 Blue Boor House OX1 4EZ. T:01865-204606. Mon - Fri 10am-5pm. Self-help group for people with HIV/AIDS. Offers befriending, outreach work, social events, fundraising and financial assistance. Drop-in.

Corruption @ Arena

100 Oxford Road. T:01865-240519. Monthly lesbian and gay disco.

Friend

c/o Box F The Inner Bookshop 111 Magdalene Road OX4 1RQ. T:01865-726893. Tues, Wed, Fri 7pm - 9pm. Telephone service offering advice, support and information to lesbians, gay men and bisexuals.

Inner Bookshop

111 Magdalen Road OX4 1RQ. T:01865-245301. Mon - Sat 10am-5.30pm. Stocks lesbian and gay literature and magazines.

Jolly Farmer's

Paradise Street OX1 1LD. T: 01865-793759. Open usual pub hours. Lesbian and gay pub.

Lesbian and Gay Centre

Northgate Hall St. Michael's Street OX1 2BU. T:01865-200030. Fri 7.30pm-11.30pm women's evening, Sat midday - 4pm drop-in and 8pm-11.30pm mixed disco, Sun midday-4pm drop-in and 8pm-11pm mixed bar.

Lesbian and Gay Switchboard

PO Box 7 Standlake OX8 7GG. T:01865-793999. Tues-Thurs 7pm-9pm. First ever switchboard in UK. Telephone service offering advice information and counselling for lesbians and gay men.

Lesbian Line

T:01865-242333. Wed 7pm-10pm. Telephone service offering advice support and information to lesbians.

OXAIDS

43 Pembroke Street OX1 1BP. T:0800-393999. T:01865-200282 (gay men's line). Mon - Fri 6.30pm-8.30pm for helpline. Telephone helpline offering advice support and counselling for people affected by HIV/ AIDS. Respite care scheme. Runs support groups, offers financial assistance and buddy groups.

Oxford Student Lesbian and Gay Society

Student Union New Barnet House Little Clarendon Street OX1 2HU. T:01865-27077. Meets Thurs 8pm at Wadham College, Parks Road. Lesbian and gay group which offers social and support meetings.

Oxford University Student Lesbian and Gay Committee

Meets every Thurs in term time at 1pm at Oxford University Student Union, Meeting Room, Little Clarendon Street. Campaigning organisation for lesbian, gay and bisexual students.

Pink Times

PO Box 28 34 Cowley Road. Lesbian and gay magazine which holds regular meetings. All welcome.

Redditch

Kyngfisher Gay Group

Contact via Hereford and Worcester Switchboard (see Worcester listing). Lesbian and gay social group which meets each Wed 8pm-11pm.

Rugby

AIDS Helpline

Orchard Centre for Community Health Lower Hillmorton CV21 3SR. T:01788-555102. Mon-Fri 9am-5pm. Telephone service offering counselling, information and advice for people affected by HIV/AIDS. Also offers face-to-face counselling.

Shrewsbury

AIDS Helpline

c/o Royal Shrewsbury Hospital Dept GU Medicine Mytton Oak Road SY3 8XF. T:01743-261113. Mon 9am-midday, 2pm-5pm, Wed 9am-midday, Thurs 1pm-5pm. Telephone service offering advice, information and support for people affected by HIV/ AIDS. Face-to-face counselling available.

Body Positive

PO Box 241 SY1 4UA. T:01743-350075. Mon 10am-4pm. Offers help, advice, information and support for people affected by HIV/ AIDS. Weekly support meetings for HIV+ people.

Gay Group

Contact via Shropshire Switchboard (see Telford listing). Gay social group.

Gay Mesmen's Health Project

The Reilly Centre Unit 3 1a Wyle COP SY1 1UT. T:01743-344179. Tues 10.30am-4pm. Offers advice, information and support for gay men on all sexual health matters.

Stoke-on-Trent

Bisexual Group

Contact via North Staffordshire Switchboard. Meets for Tues each month at The Observatory Hillcrest Street Hanley.

Body Positive

T:01782-201251. Mon, Tues, Wed, Fri 10am-5.30pm. Thurs 10am-5.30pm, 7pm-9.30pm. Telephone service offering advice, information and support for people affected by HIV/AIDS. Self-help advice group has weekly meetings for people who are HIV+.

Cactus Bookshop

2b Hope Street Hanley. T:01782-744740. Stocks lesbian and gay books.

Hollybush

Keelings Road Northwood. Open usual pub hours. Lesbian, gay, straight bar.

Lesbian Social Group

Contact via North Staffordshire Switchboard. Meets first and third Mon each month at The Observatory Hillcrest Street Hanley.

Mates

Hillcrest Street Hanley. Mon-Thurs 7pm-2am. Fri, Sat 7pm-11pm, Sun 7pm-10.30pm. Gay club.

North Staffordshire Lesbian and Gay Switchboard

PO Box 1 46 Marsh Street Hanley. T:01782-266998. Mon, Wed, Fri 8pm-10pm. Telephone service offering information, advice and support to lesbians and gay men.

The Observatory

Hillcrest Street Hanley. Open usual pub hours. Lesbian, gay, straight pub.

Staffordshire Buddies

PO Box 474 Hanley ST1 5BZ. T:01782-201251. Mon, Tues, Weds, Fri 10am-5.30pm. Thurs 10am-5.30pm, 7pm-9.30pm. One-to-one befriending and practical emotional support for people with HIV/AIDS. Hardship fund, quarterly newsletter.

Three Tuns

Bucknall New Road Hanley. T:01782-213408. Open usual pub hours. Gay pub.

TORCH

PO Box 671 Stoke-on-Trent ST4 7QS or via North Staffordshire Switchboard. Gay social group that meets Tues 8pm at Hollybush.

Stratford-upon-Avon

Queen's Head

Ely Street. T:01789-204914. Open usual pub hours. Lesbian, gay, straight pub.

Tamworth

Premier Health Community Nursing

Tamworth Health Centre Upper Gungate B79 7EA. T:01827-308810 ext. 8622. Co-ordinates community nursing care for people with HIV/AIDS in south east Staffordshire.

Telford

Dining Group

Contact via Shropshire Switchboard.

Gay social group which meets monthly on Wed in local restaurants.

OLGA

PO Box 41 Wellington or via Shropshire Switchboard. T:01743-249888. Lesbian and gay campaigning group.

Shropshire AIDSLine

T:01743-261113. Mon, Wed morning and Thurs afternoon. Telephone service offering advice, support and information to people affected by HIV/AIDS.

Shropshire Lesbian and Gay Switchboard

PO Box 41 Wellington. T:01743-232292. Tues and Fri 8pm-10pm. Telephone service offering advice, support and information to lesbians and gay men.

Transvestite Group

Contact via Shropshire Switchboard. TV support and social group.

Wild Women

Contact via Shropshire Switchboard. Lesbian social group which organises walks for lesbians.

Youth in the Pink

PO Box 130 Wellington or via Shropshire Switchboard. Lesbian and gay youth social and support group. Meets Mon 7.30pm - 10pm, Wed - Fri 10am - midday.

Walsall

AIDSLine

T:01922-644853. Mon 9am-11.30am, Tues 1pm - 7pm, Wed 9am - 3pm, Thurs 9am - midday and Fri 9am - midday and 1.30pm - 4.30pm. Telephone service offering advice, support and information to people affected by HIV/AIDS.

Gay Men's Health Project

T:01922-613141. Information, support and health education group.

Golden Lion/ Monroes

Birchill Street. T:01922-32429. Mon - Sat 7.30pm - 2am. Lesbian and gay pub and club.

Greenhouse

47a Picturedrome Way Darlaston. T:0121-5686126. Mon - Sat midday - 4am and Sun noon-11pm. Gay sauna, gym and cafe.

PROGRESS

PO Box 31 Aldridge Walsall WS9 8RH. Gay and straight. Contact, advice and support initiative aimed at men with penis size or testicular related worries.

Warwick

Antelope

Birmingham Road Saltisford. Open daily 11am-11pm. Gay pub.

Wolverhampton

Fattie Arbuckle's

Showell Road. T:01902-773669. Thurs 9am-2am. Gay cabaret and club.

Gavan's

The Dorchester Summer Row. T:01902-716676. Gay club open Sat only.

Gay Men's Group

Contact via West Midlands Switchboard (see Birmingham listing). Gay social group which meets every second Sun of month.

Greyhound

Bond Street. T:01902-20916. Open usual pub hours. Lesbian, gay, straight pub.

Harp

Lower Walsall Street. T:01902-451136. Open usual pub hours. Lesbian, gay, straight pub.

Lesbian Group

Contact via West Midland Switchboard (see Birmingham listings). Meets Tues evenings at Greyhound. Lesbian social group.

Lesbian, Gay and Bisexual Youth Group

Contact via West Midlands Switchboard (see Birmingham listing). Youth (under 21) social group which meets at 1pm - 4pm each Sat.

Married Gay Men

Contact via West Midlands Switchboard (see Birmingham listings). Support group for gay men who are married, separated or divorced. Meets first Tues of each month.

Out and About

Sheldon/Langley Ward The Royal Hospital Cleveland Road WV2 1BT. T:01902-644853. HIV prevention project working with gay men.

Outset

16a Temple Street WV2 4AN. T:01902-20940. Job placement scheme which helps people with HIV/AIDS to return to or enter employment.

Raffles's Europa

47 Thornley Street. T:01902-711657. Tues - Sun 7.30pm-11pm. Gay bar and club.

Reach

Temple Street. T:01902-25702. Mon, Wed, Thurs 6pm-8.45pm. Fri 2pm-6pm. HIV/AIDS community support group which operates a drop-in.

Sunbeam

Penn Road . Open usual pub hours. Pub which is popular with lesbians.

White Hart

66 Worcester Street. T:01902-21701. Open usual pub hours. Gay bar.

Worcester

Foundation

PO Box 225 WR5 3QZ. T: 01905-763973. Practical and emotional support to all people affected by HIV/AIDS. Offers counselling, buddy service, safer sex information and legal and benefits advice.

Hereford and Worcester Switchboard

PO Box 156 WR5 1BP. T:01905-723097. Tues - Thurs 7.30pm-10.30pm. Telephone service offering, advice, information and support to lesbians and gay men.

HIV and Sexual Education Unit

Worcester Royal Infirmary Castle Street WR1 3AS. T:01905-22957. Counselling, support and prevention project for all people affected by HIV/AIDS. Two gay men's outreach workers.

Images

The Butts. First Tues each month. Gay club. Contact via Switchboard.

EAST ENGLAND

Sexual Politics

ORDER FORM

To order titles direct from Cassell see the form at the back of the directory : here we list some 30 innovative and acclaimed new books in our Lesbian and Gay Studies, Women on Women and AIDS Awareness series.

PUB QUIZ

Throughout 1995 Cassell and *The Pink Paper* shall be running a nationwide tournament of pub quizzes. If you run a pub and would be interested in taking part, contact Cassell's Sexual Politics Quiz, Villiers House, 41/47 Strand, London WC2N 5JE.

MAKE CASH! HOLD A BOOK PARTY!

If you are interested in hosting a book party for you and your friends contact Cassell's Sexual Politics Book Party, Villiers House, 41/47 Strand, London WC2N 5JE.

MAILING LIST

For regular information about our forthcoming titles, catalogues and news of special offers and book events in your area, fill in the form below and return to Cassell's Sexual Politics Mailing List, Villiers House, 41/47 Strand, London WC2N 5JE. No charge and no obligation.

Please include my details on the Sexual Politics Mailing List for receipt of details of forthcoming titles, news of special offers and of Cassell book events:

Name ....
Address ....
....
....
....

Send to Cassell Sexual Politics Mailing List, Villiers House, 41/47 Strand, London WC2N 5JE.

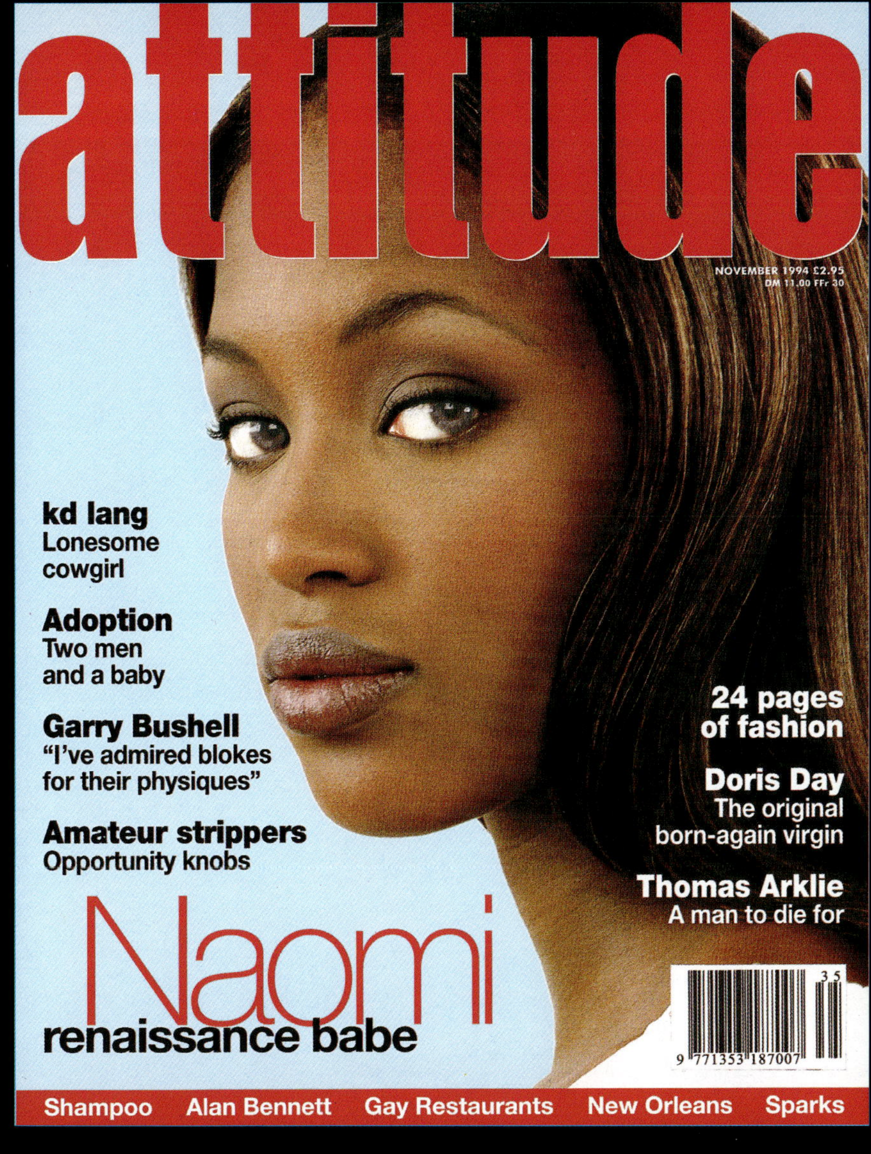

ON SALE LAST THURSDAY OF

EVERY MONTH

Fighting AIDS

Fighting to prevent

Fighting for our rights as gay men

HIV transmission

Fighting AIDS

Fighting for proper serv

Fighting to prevent HIV transmission

ices for gay men with HIV

Fighting to prevent HIV transmission

JOIN THE FIGHT, PHONE OR WRITE GAY MEN FIGHTING AIDS

UNIT 42, EUROLINK CENTRE, 49 EFFRA ROAD, LONDON SW2 1BZ
PHONE 071 738 6872 FAX 071 738 1740

GMFA

Fighting for our rights as gay men

Fighting AIDS

Fighting for proper services for gay men with HIV

Alfreton

Derbyshire and North Staffs Lesbian and Gay Christian Movement

P O Box 16 Somercotes DE55 7SA. T:01773-607577. Phone at any reasonable time. Exists to support lesbian, gay and bisexual Christians through social events and caring friendship.

Belper

Derby Gay Youth

PO Box 20 DE56 1ZY. Support group for lesbians and gay men under 26.

Pyms

The Triangle 131 Bridge Street. T:01773-822307. F:01773-826518. Mon - Fri 9am - 5pm. General solicitor practice which specialises in convey-ancing, company, probate, divorce, accident and debt collection. Legal Aid accepted.

Boston

AIDS Helpline

Pilgrim Hospital Sibsey Road PE21 9QS. T:01205-354462. Mon Thurs Fri 9.30am - 10.30am. Telephone service offering advice information and counselling to people affected by HIV / AIDS.

Burton-on-Trent

Goodger Auden

2-4 Lichfield Street DE14 3RB. T:01283-535448. General solicitor practice which offers criminal advice. Emergency service offered. Legal Aid available.

Bury St Edmunds

Bury Buddy Service

c/o Health Promotion Unit Hospital Road IP33 3NR. T:01284-725333 ext. 248. F:01284-769942. Practical support and assistance for people affected by HIV/ AIDS. Buddy services available for anyone who is HIV+, their partners or family.

Bury Gay Befriending Group

PO Box 61 IP33. Befriending group for lesbians and gay men in the area.

MESMAC Project

c/o Health Promotion Unit Hospital Road IP33 3NR. T:01284-725333 x 2408. Aims to establish a local community initiative which explores the needs of men who have sex with men in relation to safer sex.

Partridge & Wilson

88 Guildhall Street IP33 1PT. T:01284-762281. General solicitor practice which is lesbian and gay friendly.

West Suffolk AIDSline

18 St John's Street IP33 1SJ. T:01284-761216. F:01284-725512. Mon - Fri 9am - 5pm. Tel-ephone service offering advice, counselling and information. Face-to-face counselling also available.

West Suffolk AIDS Resource Centre

18 St. Johns Street IP33 1SJ. T:01284-762377. Mon - Fri 9am - 5pm. Library open to professionals,

counsellors and the public concerned with HIV/AIDS.

Cambridge

AIDS Helpline

T:0800-697697. F:01223-359857. Tues, Weds 7.30pm-10pm and Sat mid-day-2pm. Telephone advice line which offers support, information and counselling for those affected by HIV/AIDS. Also buddying, health education outreach group, self-support group for people who are HIV+; training offered.

Burleigh Arms

9-11 Newmarket Road. T:01223-316881. Open usual pub hours. Lesbian, gay, straight pub.

Cambridge Gay Group

T:01223-246031. Thurs evenings. Gay social group organised by Friend.

Cambridge Friend

129 Coldham's Lane. T:01223-246031. Weds 6.30pm-9.30pm. Telephone service offering support, information and advice.

Cambridge Lesbian Gay and Bisexual Group

T:01223-333313. Tues 8pm-10pm. University social group which welcomes non-students.

C.H.E. (Campaign for Homosexual Equality)

Llandaff Chambers 2 Regent Street CB3 1AX. Campaigning group for lesbian and gay equality.

Dot Cotton Club

The Junction Clifton Road. T:01223-412600. Lesbian and gay monthly discos. Call for dates.

Gay Outdoor Club

T: 01223-893419. Local branch of national organisation for those lesbians and gays interested in outdoor sports and associated activities.

Graduates Plus

Keynes House Trumpungton Street. Lesbian and gay group for graduates. Call Cambridge Friend for further details.

Lesbian and Gay Christian Group

T:01223-666137. Local branch of national organisation for lesbian and gay Christians.

Lesbian Line

T:01223-311753. Fri 7pm - 10pm. Telephone service offering advice support and information to lesbians.

Lesbian Social Group

T:01223-246031. Meets first and third Thurs each month at Women's Resource Centre Hooper Street 7.30pm. Social and support group for lesbians.

Male Eros

T:01638-743655 or 01638-741149. Weekly meetings for gay computer enthusiasts.

Palmer Wheeldon

Daedulus House Station Road CB1 2RE. T:01223-355933. General solicitor practice. Speaks Polish, Punjabi and Urdu. Disabled access.

Rape Crisis

Box R 12 Mill Road

CB1 2AZ. T:01223-358314. Wed 7pm - 10pm, Sat 11am - 5pm. Telephone service for lesbians and straight women which offers advice, information and support to women who have experienced rape or sexual assault or sexual abuse as children.

Sex(you)ality Group

c/o Centre 33 Clarendon Street. T:01223-316488. Lesbian and gay youth group for under 25s.

SHAGM (Sexual Health and Gay Men)

The Shed Addenbrooke's Hospital Hills Road CB2 2QQ. T:01223-216865. F:01223-216868. Sexual health projects for gay and bisexual men and other men who have sex with men.

Sister Act

PO Box 294 CB4 2XR. Social club for lesbians and bisexual women. Weekly events and monthly newsletter.

Chesterfield

CASH (Community Action on Sexual Health)

4 Rose Hill S40 1LW. T:01246-559431 (answerphone). A project aimed at addressing the sexual health needs of men who have sex with men. Advice, information, support, one-to-one counselling, training around sexual health.

Cutts Shiers

Embassy House Soresby Street. T:01246-237231. F:01246-235946. General solicitor practice which specialises in litigation, personal injury, debt, civil disputes, employment, conveyancing, family law and children's issues. Legal Aid is available. Disabled access.

Gay Community Group

PO Box 23 S40 1FH. Meets second and fourth Tues at 8.30pm at Marsden's bar. Lesbian and gay social group.

HAND (HIV and AIDS in North Derbyshire)

4 Rose Hill S40 1LW. T:01246-550550. Sun 7pm - 9pm. Telephone service offering help, advice and support to people living with and affected by HIV infection.

Lesbian Social Group - Cloot

PO Box 22 S40 2NZ. Meets each Tues at Marsden's. Lesbian social and support group.

Manhattan

50 Saltergate. T:01246-232042. Mon - Sun 8pm -late. Lesbian, gay, straight pub.

Marsden's

13 Marsden Street, off Saltergate. T:01246-232618. Mon - Fri 1pm - 3pm and 7pm - 11pm. Sat 7pm - 11pm, Sun 7pm - 10.30pm. Gay run pub which caters for lesbians, gay men and straights.

Corby

Bodywise

Stuart Road Clinic Stuart Road NN17 1RJ. T:01536-400030. Mon 4pm - 6pm. HIV counselling and testing by a doctor and a nurse. Information on safer sex and safer drug use. Bodywise is also held in other locations and has a mobile trainer unit to take to rural areas where services are not normally available.

Derby

AIDSline

c/o South Derbyshire Health Authority AIDS Liaison Unit 27 Normanton Road DE1 2GJ. T:0800-622738. Mon 7pm - 9pm. Thurs 2pm - 4pm, 7pm - 9pm. Telephone service offering information, support and advice for people affected by HIV / AIDS.

Body Positive

P O Box 124 DE1 9NZ. T:01332-292129. F:01332-292129. Office hours Tues 10.30am - 1.30pm. Thurs 11.30am - 4.30pm. Socials Tue 7pm - 10pm (HIV+ only), Thurs 7pm - 10pm (friends, patients and carers), Sat 10.30am - 2.30pm. A support group offering practical and emotional support for anyone affected / infected by HIV / AIDS.

Curzons

25 Curzon Street DE1 1LN. T:01332-363739. F:01332-343960. Wed- Sun 10pm - 2am. Lesbian, gay, straight club.

Derby Gay Group

T: 01332-664234. Meets Thurs evenings. Lesbian and gay social group.

Freddy's Bar

101 Curzon Street. T:01332-204290. Open usual pub hours. Lesbian, gay, straight pub.

Friend

T:01332-349333. Weds 7pm -10pm. Telephone advice line offering support information and counselling to lesbians and gay men.

Goodger Auden

10 Gower Street DE1 1RW. T:01332-349843.Emergency:01332-518197. F:01332-363039. Mon - Fri 9am - 5pm. General solicitor practice which covers all aspects of law except criminal. Emergency service offered. Legal Aid available. Speaks Spanish.

Lesbian and Gay Christian Movement

PO Box 16 Somercoates DE5 7SA. T:01773-607577. Local group of national movement for lesbian and gay Christians.

Lesbian Line

T:01332-41411. Weds 7pm - 9pm. Telephone service offering support information and advice for lesbians.

Men's Sexual Health Project

P O Box 185 DE1 2YN. T:01332-203868 (minicom). Office hours. A developmental outreach project exploring the needs of gay men.

Ruby's at the Gallery

130 Green Lane. T:01332-368652. Mon - Thurs 8pm - 11pm, Fri and Sun open pub hours, Sat 11am -11pm. Lesbian, gay and straight pub.

Women's Centre

135 Green Lane. T:01322-41633. Organises lesbian social and support events.

Great Yarmouth

Formby's Restaurant

43 King Street. T:01493-844744. Tues 12-3pm, Wed - Sat 12-3pm and 7pm - 10pm, Sun 1pm -5pm. 300-year-old gay owned restaurant.

Kings Wine Bar

42 Kings Street. T:01493-855374. Open usual pub hours. Back bar is lesbian and gay. Discos at weekends.

Grimsby

AIDSLine

c/o 138 Scartho Road DN33 2AX. T:01472-240840. Mon and Thurs 7.30 pm - 9.30pm Tues 11am - 3pm. Telephone service offering advice information and support for people affected by HIV/ AIDS. Offers befriending and one-to-one support training.

Butler's

Strand Street. Mon 8pm until late. Lesbian and gay club.

Foreman & Co

Riverhead Chambers 6 New Street DN31 1HJ. T:01472-350881. Emergency: 01652-658393. Mon - Fri 8.45am - 5.15pm. Criminal law practice. Accepts Legal Aid work. Emergency service. Disabled access.

Gay Helpline

T: 01472-251818. Tues and Thurs 7pm - 9pm. Telephone service offering advice support and information for lesbians and gay men.

Gay Men's and Women's Group

c/o 14 Town Hall Street DN13 1HN. T:01472-251818. Lesbian and gay group which meets weekly.

Mincerz

Cleethorpes Road. T:01472-242484. Lesbian and gay club. Third Mon each month.

Tokyo Jo's

Cleethorpes Road. T:01472-242484. Alternate Sat. Lesbian and gay club. (Follow signs for private party).

Huntingdon

HIV Support Team

Newtown Centre Nursey Road PE18 6RJ. T:01480-415333 (24 hour answerphone). Mon - Fri 9am - 5pm. Telephone service offering advice support and counselling for people affected by HIV/ AIDS.

Ipswich

AIDS Helpline

PO Box 57 IP1 3ER. T:01473-232007. Tues and Fri 7.30pm - 10pm. Telephone service offering advice support and information for people affected by HIV/ AIDS.

Country Friends

Contact via Suffolk Switchboard. Lesbian and gay social group covering Suffolk, Norfolk and Cambridgeshire.

Ipswich Area Gay Group

PO Box 63 IP4 2RB. Thurs 8pm at Olive Tree. Social and befriending group for gay men.

Lesbian Group

PO Box 129 IP1 2PL. Social group for lesbians with regular newsletter.

Olive Leaf

St.Helens Street. T:01473-258633. Open usual pub hours. Lesbian and gay bar. Discos Mon, Thurs, Fri and Sat.

Relax and Glow

Martleshan Heath. T:01473-626010. Gay sauna.

Suffolk Lesbian and Gay Switchboard

T: 01473-232212. Tues and Sat 7.30pm - 10pm. Telephone service offering information, advice and support for lesbians and gay men.

Kettering

AIDS Counselling Clinic

Kettering General Hospital Department of GU Medicine Rothwell Road NN16 8UZ. T:01536-410699. F:01536-492223. Weds 2pm - 4.30pm. Offers HIV testing and counselling.

King's Lynn

EAST

11 Portland Street PE30 1PY. T:01553-776655. Weds Sun 7pm - 10pm. Telephone service offering advice information and counselling for people affected by HIV/ AIDS. Buddy scheme and befriending service for people with HIV/AIDS, their family, partners and friends.

KLOUT

PO Box 40 PE32 1HF. T:01553-630012. First and third Thurs of each month at Quaker's, Bridge Street. Lesbian, gay and bisexual social group.

Ward Gethin

11-12 Tuesday Market Place PE20 1JT. T:01553-773456. Emergency: 0860-634055. General solicitor practice. Offers Legal Aid. Emergency service available. French and Spanish spoken. Disabled access.

Leicester

AIDSLine

Leicester Royal Infirmary Department of GU Medicine Informary Close LE1 5WW. T:0116-254-3899. Mon - Fri 9am - 5pm. Telephone service offering advice information and support for people affected by HIV/ AIDS.

Bossa

110 Granby Street. T:0116-275-5400. Lesbian, gay, straight cafe specialising in Mexican food.

Blackthorne Books

70 High Street. Stocks lesbian and gay books and magazines.

Coffee Randall Warnock

25/27 Upper King Street LE1 6XF. T:0116-277-2870. F:0116-247-1097. General solicitor practice. Legal Aid available. Emergency service. Gujerati spoken. Disabled access.

Crown

24 Dryden Street. T:0116-251-0785. Open usual pub hours. Lesbian, gay, straight pub.

Dover Castle

34 Dover Street (off Granby Street). Open usual pub hours. Lesbian, gay, straight pub which has discos on Wed, Fri, Sat and Sun.

FFLAG (Friends

and Family of Lesbians and Gay Men)

T:0116-270-8331 or 0116-235-9774. Local branch of national organisation offering support information and advice for family and friends of lesbians and gay men.

Gay Group

T:0116-276-5931. Gay social group which meets weekly.

GHQ

Madison's Complex Humberstone Gate. T:0116-251-5528. Mon - Sat 9pm - 2am. Lesbian, gay, straight club.

Gay Outdoor Club

T:0116-281-1138. Local branch of national group which meets for sporting and other related activities.

Helsinki Bar

92 Rutland Street. T:0116-262-9604. Mon - Fri 5pm - 11pm, Sat 11am - 11pm, Sun 7pm - 10.30pm. Lesbian, gay, straight bar.

Highfields & Belgrave Community Law Centre

6 Seymour Street LE2 OLB. T:0116-253-2928. F:0116-253-8894. Mon - Thurs 10am - 1pm and 2pm - 5pm, Fri 10am - midday. General law centre which offers advice on social security, employment, immigration, nationality, housing and general lesbian and gay issues. Legal Aid available. Speaks Gujerati and Urdu.

LASS (Leicester AIDS Support Services)

c/o Leicester CVS 29 New Walk LE1 6TE. T:0116-255-9995. Organisation which offers support advice and information for those affected by HIV/AIDS.

Leicester Lesbian and Gay Communities Resource Centre

45 King Street LE1 6RN. T:0116-254-7412. Lesbian and gay centre. Groups meeting regularly at the centre include bisexual group, First Out (for lesbians and gay men under 21), SHAKTI (social group for South East Asian lesbians and gay men), Black Lesbian and Gay Group, Newcomers Group, Gay Group, Leicester Universities Lesbian Gay and Bisexual Group and Leicester Lesbian Gay and Bisexual Communities Police Consultative Forum.

Leicester Lesbian and Gay Coffee Bar

45 King Street LE1 6RN. T:0116-254-7412. Wed midday - 2pm (women only), Thurs midday - 2pm (lesbians and gay men), Fri midday - 2pm (lesbians and gay men), Sat 10.30am - 5pm (lesbians and gay men). Lesbian and gay coffee bar.

Leicester Place

24 Dryden Street (off Lee Circle). T:0116-251-0785. Open usual pub hours. Lesbian, gay, straight pub. Disco Mon - Sat 10pm - midnight.

Lesbian and Gay Action

25 Walton Street LE3 ODX. T:0116-253-3436. Campaigning group for lesbian and gay equality.

Lesbian and Gay Line

T:0116- 255-0667. Mon - Fri 7.30pm - 10pm. Telephone service offering advice, information and support to lesbians and gay men. Female staff only on Tues.

Luxor

57 Welford Street. T:0116-255-6815. Mon - Sat 7pm - 11pm. Lesbian, gay, straight cafe and bar.

Magazine

Newark Street. T:0116-254-0523. Lesbian, gay, straight pub. Women only nights alternate Wed.

Men's Sexual Health Project

45 King Street LE1 6RN. T:0116-254-1747. Mon - Fri 7.30pm - 10pm. Drop-in and telephone service offering advice, support and information for gay and bisexual men. Free condoms, lubricant and dental dams on request.

Open Door

117 Granby Street. T: 0116-254-2225. Mon - Fri 10am - 6pm. Advice and counselling for lesbians and gay men under 26.

Parent's Group

Town Hall. Contact Lesbian and Gay Line for further details. Meet third Wed each month at 7.30pm.

Pineapple Inn

27 Burleys Way. T:0116-262-3384. Mon - Sat 11am - 3pm and 7pm - 11pm. Gay run lesbian, gay, straight pub. Discos at weekends.

Rapture @ The Asylum

Percy Gee Building Leicester University. T:0116-255-0667. Monthly lesbian, gay and bisexual club night for students.

Trade

45 King Street LE1 6RN. T: 0116-254-7412.Voluntary group who offer outreach work to scene providing safer sex information.

Lincoln

Lesbian and Gay Switchboard

PO Box 99 LN4 5SD. T:01522-535553. Thurs 7pm - 10pm, Sun 7pm - 10pm. Telephone service offering advice information and support for lesbians, gay men and bisexuals.

Loughborough

Women's Amblers

T:01509-213894. Meets first Sun of every month to amble 3-4 miles.

Women's Bar @ Labour Club

T:0116-223-5610. First and third Tues each month 8.30pm onwards. Lesbian and straight women's social club.

Mansfield

Limited Editions @ The Yard

61 West Gate. T:01602-22230. Fourth Mon each month, 9pm-2am. Lesbian and gay club.

Mansfield Lesbian and Gay Youth Group

c/o Bob, Information Shop Mansfield Library West Gate NG18. T:01623-657077. Social and support group for young lesbians and gay men in area.

Mildenhall

Dog and Partridge

Newmarket Road Barton Mills. T:01638-712761. Open usual pub hours. Lesbian, gay, straight pub.

Northampton

AIDSLine

c/o AIDS Unit Northampton General Hospital Billing Road NN1 5BD. T:01604-28999. Mon - Fri 9am - 6pm. Telephone service offering advice support and information for people affected by HIV/AIDS.

Lesbian and Gay Switchboard

3-7 Hazlewood Road. T:01604-39722. Tues 7.30pm - 9.30pm. Telephone service offering advice information and support for lesbians, gay men and bisexuals.

Lesbian Line

3-7 Hazlewood Road. T:01604-39723. Tues 7pm - 9.30pm. Telephone service offering advice information and support for lesbians. Organises monthly disco.

Sinatra's

76 Regent Square. Open usual pub hours. Lesbian and gay bar, restaurant and cafe.

Norwich

ACT UP (AIDS Coalition to Unleash Power)

PO Box 73 NR3 1QD. T:01603-631007. F:01603-666879. Direct action and campaigning group against HIV/AIDS discrimination.

AIDSLine

c/o Health Education Unit 36 Unthank Road NR2 2RB. T:01603-615816. Thurs 8pm - 10pm and Sat 11am - 3pm. Telephone service offering advice information and counselling for people affected HIV/AIDS. Offers buddying service, face-to-face befriending, speakers, bereavement counselling and community education.

Attic

14-16 Lower Goat Lane. T:01603-666802. Usual pub hours. Wine bar that is lesbian and gay on Sun 8pm-11.30pm.

Bookmark

83 Unthank Road NR2 2PE. T:01603-762855. Stocks lesbian and gay literature and magazines.

Friend

T:01603-628055. Fri 7pm - 9pm. Information counselling and befriending. Monthly socials and coffee evening.

Gay Men's Health Project

42-46 Bethel Street NR2 1NR. T:01603-627514. F:01603-666879. Wed 3pm - 7pm. Offers telephone information, drop-in, free condoms and lubricant, confidential advice.

Lesbian Line

T:01603-628055. Tues 7pm - 9pm. Telephone service offering advice information and support for lesbians.

Loft

80 Rose Lane. T:01603-623559. Lesbian and gay club.

Lord Raglan

30 Bishop's Bridge Road. T:01603-623304. Mon - Sat

midday - 2pm, 7pm - 11pm. Sun midday - 3pm, 7pm -10.30pm. Lesbian and gay pub.

Lord Rosebery

Rosebery Road. T:01603-486161. Open usual pub hours. Lesbian, gay, straight pub.

Norfolk Lesbian and Gay Line

T:01603-592505. Mon 8pm - 10pm. Telephone service offering information advice and support for lesbians, gay men and bisexuals.

Partridge and Wilson

25 St.John Maddermarket NR2 1DN. T:01603-617826. General solicitor practice.

Positive People

36 Unthank Road NR2 2RB. T:01603-760667. Sun 2pm - 7pm. Support group for people who are HIV+ offering refreshments, information and entertainment.

Social Services HIV/AIDS Team

County Hall Martineau Lane NR1 2DH. T:01603-223011. F:01603-222479. Coordinates social services available for people with HIV/AIDS.

Nottingham

Admiral Duncan

74 Lower Parliament Street. T:0115-950-2727. Sun - Wed 8pm -11pm, Thur-Sat 8pm - 1.30am. Pub for gay men.

AIDS Bereavement Project

PO Box 16 North PDO NG5 2AX. T:0115-962-0920. 24-hour advice and information on palliative care and funeral arrangements.

Bathley Guest House

101 Bathley Street The Meadows NG2 2EE. T:0115-986-2463. Gay run guest house for gay men. Open all year.

Black Lesbian Group

c/o Women's Centre 30 Chaucer Street.Telephone Lesbian Line for details. Meets at Women's Centre first Fri each month 8pm. Social and support group for all lesbian women of colour.

Boulevard Hotel Lesbian Disco

Boulevard Function Suite Hartley Road Radford. T:0115-978-7014. Every Fri 8.30pm - late. Lesbian disco.

Cello's @ The Old Vic

Flechergate. Contact Lesbian Line for dates. Monthly lesbian disco.

Chameleon Group

Wollaton Grange Community Centre Tremayne Road Bilborough. T:0115-928-9479. Meets Thurs 8pm - 10pm. Support and social group for TVs.

Coach House

53a Woodthorpe Drive NG5 4GY. T:0115-960-5436. Lesbian and gay hotel.

Eastern Rainbow

Minicom (Pat):01623-662585 or minicom (Kev):0115-927-9704. Support and social group for deaf lesbians and gay men.

Edward Carpenter Trust/ Community

c/o Outright PO Box 4 West PDO NG7 2DJ. T:0115-978-0124. National organisation which arranges personal growth residential weekends for gay and bisexual men.

Expose Theatre Group

T:0115-952-6146. Lesbian and gay theatre group that welcomes writers, performers and anyone who wants to get involved.

Foresters

St. Ann's Street. T:0115-958-0432. Open usual pub hours. Lesbian pub. Discos Thurs and Sun.

Friend

c/o CVS 31a Mansfield Road NG1. T:0115-947-4717. Tues 7pm - 10pm. Telephone service offering advice support and information to lesbians and gay men. One-to-one contact.

Gatsby's

Huntingdon Street. T:0115-950-5323. Open usual pub hours. Lesbian and gay pub.

Gay Bikers Motorcycle Club

GBMC c/o Nottingham Switchboard 33 Mansfield Road NG1 3FF. Group for lesbian and gay motorbyke enthusiasts. Arranges outings and events.

GLYP (Gay and Lesbian Young People)

Telephone Nottingham Switchboard for details of meetings. Thurs 8pm - 10pm. Weekly social meetings for lesbians and gay men under 26.

GAI Project

The Health Shop Broad Street Hockley. T:0115-947-5414. Gay run organisation which offers support, information and advice on HIV/AIDS.

Health Shop

Broad Street Hockley NG1 3AL. T:0115-947-5414. Advice, information and support on sexual health, drugs and HIV/AIDS. Provide free condoms and safer sex advice, HIV testing and counselling, Hepatitis B testing and vaccination. Operates drop-in for people who are HIV+ Tues 2pm - 4pm.

Hiking Dykes

Call Lesbian Line or write c/o Lesbian Centre, Women's Centre 30 Chaucer Street NG1 5LP. T:0115-941-1475. Walking group for lesbians. Meets on the third Sun of each month.

Lesbian Centre

Women's Centre 30 Chaucer Street NG1 5LP. T:0115-941-1475. Social and support groups including monthly disco for lesbians.

Lesbian and Gay Christian Movement

T:0115-925-5514. Local branch of national organisation for lesbian, gay and bisexual Christians.

Lesbians and Gays in MSF

T:0115-269-3909. Support and campaigning section of Manufacturing Science and Finance Union for lesbians, gay men and bisexuals.

Lesbian Line

T:0115-941-0652. Mon and Wed 7pm - 9pm. Telephone service offering advice support and information to lesbians.

Lesbian Workers in Homelessness and Housing

Lesbian Centre. Meets first Mon each month 3pm -5pm. Support and information group for all lesbians working in housing/ homelessness organisations.

Male Survivors of Sexual Abuse

T:0115-969-1212. Informal support group for male survivors of childhood sexual abuse.

Metropolitan Community Church

Queens Walk Community Centre Queens Walk. Sun 11.30am. T:0115-975-0031. Church for lesbians, gay men and bisexuals.

Mushroom Bookshop

10-12 Heathcote Street NG1 3AA. T:0115-958-2506. F:0115-959-0971. Mon - Sat 10am - 6pm. Lesbian, gay, straight bookshop.

Nero's

22 St. James Street. T:0115-941-0037. Wed-Sat 10pm - 2am. Lesbian and gay club.

Nottingham Bisexual Group

Room 3 International Community Centre 61b Mansfield Road. Meets second and fourth Thurs each month. Support and activist group for all bisexuals.

Nottingham Bisexual Women's Group

Women's Centre 30 Chaucer Street NG1 5LP. T:0115-941-1475 Mon - Fri 10am -4pm. Group meets third Tues each month. Support and activist group for bisexual women.

Notts Central Hotel

Station Road Sutton in Ashfield. T:01623-552373. Gay run guest house.

Nottingham Lesbian and Gay Switchboard

33 Mansfield Road NG1 3FF. T:0115-941-1454. Mon - Fri 7pm - 10pm. Telephone service which offers information, advice and support for lesbians and gay men.

Nottinghamshire Lesbian Gay and Bisexual Youth Coalition

c/o Information Shop 24-32 Carlton Street. Group which organises social and educational events for lesbians, gay men and bisexuals under 26.

Nottingham Trent University Lesbian Gay and Bisexual Group

Conference Room Byron Building Shakespeare Street. Mon 8pm during term time. Lesbian, gay and bisexual group which organises speakers and discussions. Open to non-students.

Out of the Closet

Base 51. Thurs 2pm - 4pm. Advice support and social group for young gay and bisexual men.

Out House Project

Box 11 118 Mansfield Road NG1 3HL. Group setting up a lesbian, gay and bisexual centre in Nottingham.

OutRage! Nottingham

PO Box Q 15 Goosegate NG1 1FE. Non-violent direct action group for lesbians, gay men and bisexuals.

Outright

Naff Co-operative Ltd. PO Box 4 West PDO NG7 2DJ. Free community newspaper for lesbians and gay men with local listings.

Parents Enquiry

T:0115-921-1302. Local branch of national organisation offering support for parents of lesbians and gay men.

Pink Chalk

ICC 61b Mansfield Road. T:0115-958-5814. Social and support group for lesbians, gay men and bisexuals working in education.

Pink Ink

Box 28 Mushroom Books 10-12 Heathcote Street NG1 3AA. Lesbian and gay writing group which meets regularly to share ideas and arrange readings.

Pink Pathfinders

T:0115-967-8134. Group which organises walks in Peak District for lesbians and gay men.

Positive Support

PO Box 135 NG3 5PS. T:0115-942-5133. 24-hour helpline. Provides practical, emotional and social support for carers of people with HIV/AIDS.

Revolution @ MGM

Greyfriar Gate. T:0115-958-0555. First Mon each month. 9pm - 2am. Lesbian and gay club.

Sharp & Partners

6 Weekday Cross NG1 2GF. T:0115-9580381. Emergency :01345-333111. F:0115-9584851. Mon - Fri 9am-5pm. General solicitor practice. Legal Aid available. Speaks French, German, Polish and Gujerati. Disabled access.

Soho Books

147 Radford Road. T:0115-978-3567. Stocks lesbian and gay books and magazines.

Stonewall Breaks

c/o Outright PO Box 4 West PDO NG7 2DJ. T:0115-978-0124. Group which organises residential weekends away for gay and bisexual men.

Triangles/Forest Tavern

North Sherwood Street. Open usual pub hours. Mainly lesbian pub.

Tutti Frutti @ The Garage

41 St.Mary's Gate Lace Market. Second Mon each month. 10pm - 2am. Lesbian and gay club.

UNISON Lesbian and Gay Group

T:0115-945-2764 (Pam Burrows) or 01623-443751 (Karen). Support and campaigning section in UNISON (health workers union).

University of Nottingham Lesbian Gay and Bisexual Society

Room C50 First Floor Portland Building. Tues 7.30pm during term time. Social and support group for lesbians, gay men and bisexuals. Open to non-students.

University of Nottingham Phoneline

T:0115-951-4999.

Mon 8pm - 10pm during term time. Telephone service offering advice support and information for lesbian, gay and bisexual students and non-students. Always staffed by a man and woman.

Viva @ Rockaderos

Huntingdon Street. T:0115-970-8451. Third Fri each month. Lesbian and gay club.

WAG (Women are Gorgeous)

c/o Nottingham Women's Centre 30 Chaucer Street NG1 5LP. T:0115-947-0602. Meets Fri 7.30pm - late at Women's Centre. Social and support group open to all women questioning their sexuality.

Women's Centre

30 Chaucer Street NG1 5LP. Lesbian and straight women's centre. Support, advice and information to all women.

Women's Centre Disco

30 Chaucer Street. First Sat each month. 9pm - late.

Young Lesbian Group

Base 51 51 Glasshouse Street NG1. T:0115-952-5040. Support and social group for young lesbians.

Peterborough

AIDS Helpline

PO Box 142 P1 1AA. T:01733-62334. Tues, Thurs 7.30pm - 9.30pm. Telephone service offering information advice and counselling for people affected by HIV/AIDS. Buddy group and family support.

Friend

PO Box 209 PE1 3EL. T:01733-61499. Tues and Thurs 7.30pm - 9.30pm. Telephone service offering information advice and support for lesbians, gay men and bisexuals.

Wonderland Nightclub

The Gallery Towler Street off Buley Road. T:01733-53331. Second and fourth Fri each month 9pm - 1.30pm. Lesbian and gay club.

Wortley Almshouse

Westgate. Open usual pub hours. Lesbian, gay, straight pub.

Wyman and Abbott

35 Priestgate PE1 1JR. T:01733-64131. General solicitor practice.

Retford

North Notts Gay Advice

c/o BCVS Retford Action Centre 24a The Square. T:01777-709650 (during office hours 9.30am-4pm). Advice offered by local gay men.

Spalding

Redwood Lodge

Dogdrove Holbeach Grove PE12 OSA. Lesbian and gay residential home for elderly people.

Wells

Three Horseshoes

Greek Street. T:01328-710547. Open pub hours. Bed and breakfast open all year. Lesbian and gay pub and bed and breakfast.

SOUTH WEST ENGLAND

Sexual Politics

ORDER FORM

To order titles direct from Cassell see the form at the back of the directory : here we list some 30 innovative and acclaimed new books in our Lesbian and Gay Studies, Women on Women and AIDS Awareness series.

PUB QUIZ

Throughout 1995 Cassell and *The Pink Paper* shall be running a nationwide tournament of pub quizzes. If you run a pub and would be interested in taking part, contact Cassell's Sexual Politics Quiz, Villiers House, 41/47 Strand, London WC2N 5JE.

MAKE CASH! HOLD A BOOK PARTY!

If you are interested in hosting a book party for you and your friends contact Cassell's Sexual Politics Book Party, Villiers House, 41/47 Strand, London WC2N 5JE.

MAILING LIST

For regular information about our forthcoming titles, catalogues and news of special offers and book events in your area, fill in the form below and return to Cassell's Sexual Politics Mailing List, Villiers House, 41/47 Strand, London WC2N 5JE. No charge and no obligation.

Please include my details on the Sexual Politics Mailing List for receipt of details of forthcoming titles, news of special offers and of Cassell book events:

Name ....

Address ....

....

....

....

Send to Cassell Sexual Politics Mailing List, Villiers House, 41/47 Strand, London WC2N 5JE.

Andover

Talbot Walker

16 Bridge Street Andover SP1 1BZ. T:01264-363354 and 01264-324311 (emergency). F:01264-333325. Mon - Fri 9am - 1pm, 2.15pm - 5.30pm. Solicitor practice covering crime, matrimonial, family, children, conveyancing, personal injury, litigation, employment. Accepts Legal Aid work. Emergency service. Disabled access.

Barnstaple

Action Against AIDS

Barum House The Square EX32 8LS. T:01271-24555. Mon, Wed, Fri 7pm - 9pm (24-hour answerphone). Drop-in and helpline. Also organises befriending and buddying, education, outreach. Acts as an information and advice centre.

North Devon Lesbian and Gay Switchboard

P O Box 13 Barnstaple Devon EX31 7YU. T:01271-321111. Thurs and Sun 7pm - 9pm. Lesbian, gay, TV. Provides focus and support for the lesbian and gay community. Gives information on matters of sexual health. Compiles lists of gay friendly and exclusive businesses in Cornwall, Devon , Somerset and Dorset.

Quay Centre

Beachcroft House Litchdon Street EX32 8ND. T:01271-44454. Drop-in Mon - Fri 1pm - 4pm. Safer sex and safer drug information, free condoms, parents support groups, seminars, home visits, needle exchange.

SHOUT! (She's and He's OUT)

Dave, Jim and Caron P O Box 21 Barnstaple EX31 3YU. Social group for lesbians and gay men meeting regularly in Barnstaple creating and uniting the local lesbian and gay community.

Basingstoke

Talbot Walker

64 New Road Basingstoke. T:01256-332404. F:01264-333325. Mon - Fri 9am - 1pm, 2.15pm - 5.30pm. Solictor practice covering crime, matrimonial, family, children, conveyancing, personal injury, litigation, employment. Accepts legal aid work.

Bath

Aled Richards Trust

Hetling House BA1 1SH. T:01225-444347 (office), 01272-553555 (helpline). Thu 2.30pm - 4.30pm (office). Tues - Fri 1pm - 4pm, Mon - Fri 7pm - 9pm (helpline). HIV/AIDS-related support charity. Helpline, buddying, home care, complimentary therapies, drop-in, counselling, support groups, health education and training, gay men's project, black communities project, HIV information service.

Gay West

PO Box 586 Bath Avon BA1 2YQ. T:01272-225396 (Sue) or 01272-776033 (Jon or Andy). Lesbian and gay. Social group with regular meetings and events.

Kennard Hotel

11 Henrietta Street Bath BA2 6LL (Richard Ambler). T:01225-310472. F:01225-460054. Lesbian, gay, straight. Open all year. Accepts Visa, Access, AMEX, Diners Club

Bournemouth

Bakers Arms

77 Commercial Road Bournemouth BH2 5RT. T:01202-555506. F:01202-555506. Mon - Sat 11am - 11pm. Sun midday - 3pm, 7pm - 10.30pm. Lesbian and gay pub with two floors and two bars. Regular cabaret.

Bondi Hotel

Colin or Murray 43 St Michaels Road Bournemouth BH2 5DP. T:01202-554893. Lesbian and gay guest house. Open all year. Accepts Visa and Access.

Bournemouth MSC

BLMSC PO Box 316 Bournemouth BH1 4HL. Gay leather, rubber, uniform club meets Fri at The Triangle Club.

Cerebus

25 The Triangle Bournemouth. T:01202-290529. Lesbian, gay, straight shop. Sells magazines, books, sex toys etc.

Chelsea Hotel

1 Windsor Road Boscombe Bournemouth. T:01202-398838 / 531451. Lesbian and gay hotel.

Climax @ The Boscombe Academy

570 Christchurch Road Bournemouth. T:01202-422690. Gay club. First Sun of the month and bank holidays.

Creffield Hotel

7 Cambridge Road Bournemouth BH2 6AE. T:01202-317900 (Roger). Gay hotel.

Crescent Lodge Hotel

9 The Crescent Boscombe Bournemouth BH1 4EX. T:01202-397741 (Patrick or Malcolm). Lesbian, gay, straight hotel.

Dorset Dykes

c/o Dorset Lesbian and Gay Helpline. Lesbian social group.

Dorset Lesbian and Gay Helpline

PO Box 316 Bournemouth BH1 4HL. T:01202-318822. Mon - Fri 7.30pm - 10.30pm (24-hour answerphone). Telephone service offering advice, support and information.

Double Four Hotel

44-46 St Michaels Road Westcliff Bournemouth BH2 5DY. T:01202-555950 / 292274. Lesbian, gay hotel. Residents parking. Accepts Visa, Access, AMEX, Diners Club.

Gay Outdoor Club

T:01929-462519. Dorset branch of the GOC. Lesbian and gay social group for those interested in outdoor sporting and associated activities.

Grange

24 Leicester Road Branksome Park Bournemouth. T:01202-760278 (Chris). Gay private house accommodation. Open all year (except Xmas and

New Year). Accepts Visa and Access.

Hedley Hotel

125 West Hill Road Westcliff Bournemouth BH2 5PH (Steve or Marcus). T:01202-317168 or 551351. Lesbian, gay, straight hotel. Open all year. Accepts Visa, Access.

Legends

53 Bourne Avenue Bournemouth. T:01202-310100. Lesbian, gay, straight cafe and bar.

Metropolitan Community Church of Bournemouth

Rev Neil G Thomas Hannington Road Pokesdown Bournemouth. T:01202-430888 (24-hour). Lesbian, gay, straight. Worshipping Christian community with a special ministry for lesbians and gay men.

Norwich House

30 Norwich Avenue Bournemouth BH2 5TH. T:01202-553985. Lesbian and gay guest house. Open all year.

Orchard Hotel

15 Alundale Road Bournemouth BH4 8HX. T:01202-767767. Gay hotel. Open all year. Accepts Visa, Access.

Queens Hotel

14 Queens Road Westbourne Bournemouth. T:01202-764416. Large lesbian and gay bar - three separate bars, one is non-smoking. Women only area on Thurs night.

Revival @ Hot House

142 Holdenhurst Road Bournemouth. Tues fortnightly 8.30pm - 1am. Details via Dorset Helpline. Lesbian club.

St Germaine Hotel

24 Derby Road Bournemouth. T:01202-557923. Gay hotel. Open all year. Car park.

Splash @ The Palace

Hinton Road. Sun 8pm - midnight. T:01202-554034. Gay club.

Triangle Club

Keith Smith 30 The Triangle Bournemouth BH2 5SE. T:01202-297607. Mon - Sat 9.30pm - 2am. Lesbian and gay members club.

Walker (Harold G) and Co

Office Chambers Lansdowne House Christchurch Road Bournemouth BH1 3JT. T:01202-555691. F:01202-294118. Mon - Fri 9am - 5pm. Solicitor practice. Accepts Legal Aid work. Partial disabled access - will arrange home visits.

Bridgwater

The Old Vicarage Hotel

45-51 St Marys Street Bridgwater. T:01278-458891. Lesbian, gay, straight hotel.

Bristol

Aled Richards Trust

Queen Anne House 8-140 West Street Old Market BS2 0BH. T:0117-955-1000 (office), 0117-955-3355 (helpline). F:0117-954-1200. Mon, Wed, Thurs 7pm - 9pm, Tues, Fri 1pm - 4pm, 7pm - 9pm. HIV/AIDS-related charity. Helpline, buddying service, home care, complementary therapy, drop-in, counselling, education and training, gay men's project, black community project, HIV information service.

Cafe de Daphne

12 York Road Montpelier. T:0117-942-6799. Lesbian run cafe.

Charlotte Keel Health Centre

Seymour Road BS5 0UA. T:0117-951-2244. Mon - Fri 9am - 7pm (5pm Wed). Medical practice. Male and female doctors. NHS only. Avon FHSA. Disabled access and facilities.

Club 49

20 Christmas Steps Bristol. T:0117-921-1189. Thurs - Sat 9pm - late. Lesbian and gay club.

Dykes Walking Group

T:0117-963-2593. Meets once a month for a 2-3 hour walk with a pub or cafe stop.

Elephant

St Nicholas Street Bristol. T:0117-949-9901. Mon - Sat open all day. Sun midday - 3pm, 7pm - 10.30pm. Lesbian and gay pub.

Excess Motorcycle Club

P O Box 685 BS99 1YY. Gay men. Social group for bikers with fetish interests.

Feminist Archive

Trinity Road Library Trinity Road Bristol BS2 0NW. T:0117-935-0025. Wed 2pm - 7.30pm. Women only. Collection point for women's history, particularly women's movement since 60's. Holds periodicals, tapes, posters, badges etc for women to study. Range of materials in other languages.

Formby (Dr G), Page (Dr M), Welsh (Dr M), Mutch (Dr H), Ronson (Dr M)

1-3 Lewis Road Bishopsmouth BS13 7JD. T:0117-964-2211. Mon - Fri 8.30am - 1pm, 1.45pm - 7.30pm. Medical practice. Male and female doctors. NHS only. Avon FHSA. Disabled access and facilities.

Fussell Wright and Co

59 Queen Charlotte Street BS1 4HL. T:0117-927-9117. F:0117-921-4177. Mon - Fri 9am - 5.30pm. Solicitor practice covering general areas. Accepts Legal Aid work. Speaks some French. Disabled access.

Greenleaf Bookshop

82 Colston Street BS1 5BB. Stocks lesbian and gay literature and magazines.

Griffin

Colston Street Bristol. T:0117-927-2421. Open usual pub hours. Lesbian and gay pub.

Hint of Pink

The Tudor Suite Parkside Hotel Brislington. Fortnightly lesbian / women only disco on Sat.

Lesbian and Gay Christian Movement

T:0117-973-2936. Provides mutual support for lesbian and gay Christians and seeks full recognition in churches for gay people.

Lesbian and Gay

Switchboard (BLAGS)

The Yard 8 Sommerville Road Bishopston Bristol BS7 9AA. T:0117-942-0842 and 942-5927. Mon - Sat 7.30pm - 10.30pm. Women available on Wed. Minicom. Telephone service offering advice, counselling and information.

Lesbian Line

T:0117-929-0855. Thurs 7.30pm - 10pm. Telephone service offering advice, counselling and information to lesbians. Also co-ordinates various social, support group activities in the area.

Queens Shilling

9 Frogmore Street BS1 5NA (Robin). T:0117-926-4342. Mon - Fri 6pm - 11pm. Sat 7pm - 11pm. Sun midday - 3pm, 7pm - 10.30pm. Lesbian and gay pub.

Red Admiral Project

30 Frogmore Street BS1 5NA. T:0117-925-9348. Provides a free and specialist counselling service for people affected by HIV and AIDS.

Women's Centre

82 Colston Street BS1 5BB. T:0117-929-3575 (24hr answerphone). Mon - Fri 10.30am - 2pm. Advice and information, counselling referral service, information on solicitors, refuges, library, drop-in, meeting space and a book shop for lesbian and straight women.

Camborne

Lesbian and Gay Switchboard

P O Box 23 Camborne TR14 8YA. T:01209-31449. Mon & Fri 8pm - 11pm. Telephone service offering advice, support and information.

Independent Cornish Triangle

P O Box 17 TR14 8XG. T:01209-712912. Lesbian and gay monthly newsletter.

Exeter

Acorn

Magdalen Street Exeter. T:01392-210352. Mon 7pm - 11pm, Tues - Sat 11.30am - 3pm, 7pm - 11pm. Sun midday - 3pm, 7pm - 10.30pm. Lesbian and gay pub (mainly lesbian).

AIDSline

P O Box 77 Exeter EX1 2UN. T:01392-411600. Mon - Fri 7pm - 10pm. Telephone service offering advice, information and support for people affected by HIV and AIDS.

Boxes

35/37 The Quay Exeter. T:01803-313960 (Craig) for details. Tues 9pm - 1am. Lesbian and gay club.

Devon HIV and AIDS Association

Palace Gate House Palace Gate EX1 1HX. T:01392-494441. Support centre for people affected by HIV / AIDS. Offers complementary therapies and other support services.

EAGLES (Exeter Lesbian and Gay Social Group)

P O Box 94 Exeter EX2 4YX. Meets Wed 8.30pm at The Loft.

Lesbian and Gay Switchboard

Pink Directory

PO Box 178 Exeter EX4 1GY. T:01392-422016. Mon 7.30pm - 10pm. Telephone service offering advice, support and information.

Loft @ Bart's Tavern

53 Bartholomew Street West. T:01392-422083. Mon - Thurs 8pm - midnight. Fri and Sat 9pm - 1am. Sun midday - 3pm, 7pm- 10.30pm. Gay pub and club.

Man to Man Project

HIV / AIDS Unit Dean Clarke House Southerhay Exeter EX1 1PQ (Alan Crabbe). T:01392-406147 or F:01392-70910. Mon - Fri 10.30am - 5pm. The project is run by gay men for gay and bisexual men. The project offers confidential advice, support and training on all matters of sexual health.

Stones

Northernhay Place Exeter EX4 3QQ. T:01392-51501. F:01392-57007. 9am - 5.15pm. Solicitor practice covering matrimonial, criminal, civil, conveyancing, probate, holiday travel, child, wills, commercial, tax and insolvency. Accepts legal aid work. Speaks French, German and Spanish. Disabled access.

Isle of Wight

Island Lesbian and Gay Group

P O Box 4 Ventnor PO38 1PQ. T:01983-523123. Call Wed and Sun 7.30pm - 10pm. Lesbian and gay social group. Meets regularly on second Thurs of each month.

Isle of Wight Gay Social Group

Pebbles Avenue Road Wroxall nr Ventnor PO32 6AA. T:01983-854355. Call 7pm - 10pm any evening. Lesbian, gay social group which arranges different events, parties, discos and meetings.

Isle of Wight Health Commission

T:01983-526011 ext 289. Co-ordinates health education in response to HIV/ AIDS on the Isle of Wight.

Minehead

Gay Outdoor Club

P O Box 24 Minehead TA24 8YZ. Lesbian, gay. National office of the Gay Outdoor Club. Also organises outdoor sporting and associated events for lesbians and gay men in Somerset.

New Forest

New Forest 30+ Walking Group

T:01590-23828. Lesbian walking group which meets on the last Sunday in every month for 4-5 mile walks with pubs in the middle!

Okehampton

Tor Down House

Belstone Okehampton Devon EX20 1QY (Russell). T:01837-840731. Lesbian and gay guest house on Dartmoor.

Paignton

Sea Sand and Safer Sex Project

Department of Public Health Parkfield House 38 Esplanade Road TQ3 2NH. T:01803-524500.

F:01803-558086. HIV/AIDS prevention project.

Par

Lesbian and Gay Christian Movement

180 Old Roseyon Road PL24 2LN. T:01726-817944. Support for others struggling with their faith and sexuality. General care for the lesbian and gay community.

Penzance

Acorn

Contact Lesbian Line for details. Lesbian social group. Fortnightly discos on Sun.

Capistrano

1 Chy-an-Dour Square Penzance TR18 3LW (Sylvia). T:01736-64189. Daily 10am - 10pm. Lesbian guest house.

Lesbian Line

P O Box 41 Penzance. T:01736-753709. Thurs 8pm - 10pm. Telephone service offering advice, support and information to lesbians.

Perranporth

Rainbow Club

Angela Mallard Maggie Holdsworth Jill Kaptein Andy Walker. Ponsmere Valley Budnick Perranporth TR6 0BX. T:01637-850403 (club) or 01872-572987 or 01736-850894. Wed Fri Sat 8pm - midnight. Lesbian, gay nightclub (also welcomes straights) with special boys and girls nights once monthly. Also arranges functions nights with late extensions.

Plymouth

Alcoholics Anonymous Lesbian and Gay Group

The Monastery Stott Close off Pike Road Efford. T:01822-614995 (Brian). Wed 7.30pm. Lesbian and gay support group. Phone for pre-meeting briefing.

Devon HIV & AIDS Association

c/o ABC Centre Freedom Fields Hospital PL4 7JJ. T:01752-834008. Weds 11pm - 5pm, Thurs 9am-6.30pm. Offers a range of complementary health services for those affected by HIV/AIDS.

Eddystone Group

All Saints House Hanwell Street Plymouth PL1 5BW. T:01752-257077. Mon, Wed, Fri 7pm - 9pm. Tues, Thurs 10am - 2pm. Lesbian, gay, straight HIV and AIDS support and education agency.

GNG (Gay Nudists Group) Devon and Cornwall

Don and Dave 16 Carlton Terrace P21 5EA. T:01752-667859. Meets second Tuesday of each month. Provides a roof for like-minded nudists to gather for a chat and a coffee.

In Other Words

72 Mutley Plain PL4 6LF. T:01752-663889. F:01752-252232. Mon - Fri 9am - 6pm, Sat 9am - 5.30pm. Lesbian, gay, straight bookshop with a community noticeboard with a range of lesbian and gay magazines.Also sells jewellery from San Francisco (wholesale and mail order).

Lesbian and Gay Christian Movement

T:01752-606965. Religious group which exists to help those having difficulty reconciling their sexuality and religion.

Lesbian Network

c/o Martins Gate Bretonside Plymouth PL4 0AT. T:01752-603839. Wed midday - 3pm, Thurs 6.30pm - 8.30pm. Telephone service offering advice, support and information to lesbians.

PASG (Plymouth AIDS Support Group)

c/o Department of Genito-Unrinary Medicine Medicine Freedom Fields Hospital PL4 7JJ. T: 01752-229817 or 01822-852209 (emergencies). Face-to-face counselling, family support group and non-specific sexual orientation group, clergy group.

Swallow

59 Breton Side Plymouth. T:01752-251760. Mon - Sat, open all day. Sun pub hours. Gay pub.

Two Ways Guest House

Peter Brooks 234 Saltash Road Keyham Plymouth PL2 2BB. T:01752-569504. Lesbian, gay, straight guest house. Open all year. Does not accept credit cards.

Poole

DASH (Dorset AIDS Support and Help)

16 Clarence Road Lower Parkstone BH14 8AY. T:01202-738720 or 0585-375932. Help and support for people with HIV/AIDS, families and carers. Produces a bi-monthly magazine called *Hand in Hand.*

Dorset Buddy Support Group

PO Box 1409 BH15 4YL. T:01202-667214. 24hour answerphone. Offers practical care and support services to people who are HIV+ or who are affected by HIV/AIDS. Terminal home care, aromatherapy, counselling and hypnotherapy.

Grange

Chris T:01202-760278. Private house accommodation for gay men.

Portsmouth

Buddying Group

Keswick House 45-47 Copnor Road PO3 5AB. T:01705-866860 or 01705-699477 (answerphone). Support and befriending service for people who are HIV+ or who have AIDS diagnoses.

Gay Men's Health Project

Roberts Centre 82 Crasswell Street. T:01705-866301. Thurs 4.30pm - 7.30pm. Gay men's safer sex health promotion project.

Keswick House

45-47 Copnor Road PO3 5AB. T:01705-650704. F:01705-643906. Provides an administrative and training base for organisations involved in support and education in the field of HIV/AIDS.

Lesbian and Gay Switchboard

P O Box 139 SO14 0GZ. T:01705-655077. Wed 7.30pm - 10pm. Telephone service offering advice, support and information principally to lesbians, gay men and bisexuals, although all callers welcome regardless of sexuality. Information and guidance on HIV and safer sex.

Sex Sense

82 Crasswell Street. T:01705-866301. F:01705-866311. Mon 4pm - 6.30pm. Sexual health project for young people. Services include family planning and pre and post test counselling for HIV.

St Ives

Barkers

11 Seaview Terrace St Ives Cornwall TR26 2DH (Monty or John). T:01736-796729. Lesbian and gay guest house. Open all year round.

Ryn Anneth

Southfield Place St Ives Cornwall TR26 1RE (Pete or Don). T:01736-793247. Lesbian and gay guest house. Open all year round.

Salisbury

AIDS Support Group

Catherine Ferguson and Veronica Hatschek c/o 6 Folkestone Road SP2 8JP. T:0860-859956 (call back system - leave message). Lesbian, gay, straight confidential befriending service for people living with HIV / AIDS and their loved ones.

Crown and Anchor

Exeter Street Salisbury. T:01722-327068 (Chris). Thurs - Sun evening.

Gay Group / Disco

Loft, The White Horse Quidhampton nr Salisbury. Gay group meets in this pub each Tuesday 8.30pm. Disco at same venue last Saturday of the month.

Lesbian and Gay Switchboard

T:01722-415051. Wed 7pm - 10pm. Telephone service offering advice, information and support.

Sherborne

Armstrong (Dr P)

The Beeches Oborne Road Sherborne DT9 3RX. T:01935-815109. Male doctor practice. 24hour availability. Private patients only. Offers acupuncture and hypnotherapy. Will arrange home visits.

South Brent

Pinewood Lodge Nursing and Residential Home

Vanessa Stainthorpe-Williams Pinewood Lodge Nursing and Residential Home Didsworthy South Brent Devon TQ10 9EF. T:01364-72420. Lesbian, gay, straight. Residential and nursing home that has five gay staff. Open all year.

Southampton

Carers Support Group

PO Box 130 (Carers) SO9 7UR. T:0860-223747. Group for carers and immediate relatives of people with HIV. Provides support, help and practical advice.

Gay Men's Health Project

Oatlands House Winchester Road SO1 5NB. T:01703-512900. F:01703-

701489. Provides HIV prevention services for gay and bisexual men including events training and outreach work. Aims to establish local groups promoting sexual health of gay and bisexual men.

Groundswell

PO Box 92 SO19 2AA. T: 01703-703388. Practical care for people with HIV/ AIDS.

Lesbian Line

PO Box 139 SO9 7JE. T:01703-405111. Tues and Thurs 7.30pm-10pm. Telephone service offering advice support and information for lesbians.

Mairs (Dr M L)

72 Belmont Road Portswood SO9 1YS. T:01703-554161. Mon - Fri 8.15am - 6.30pm (half day Wed). Female doctor practice. NHS and private patients by appointment. Also offers physiotherapy, homeopathy and counselling. Hampshire FHSA. Disabled access.

Solent Gay Switchboard and AIDSline

PO Box 139 SO9 7JE. T:01703-637363. Mon, Tues, Thurs, Fri 7.30pm -10pm. Telephone service offering advice information and support principally for lesbians, gay men and bisexuals and all people who are affected by HIV/ AIDS.

Swindon

Cricketers

14 Emlyn Square Swindon. T:01793-523780. Mon - Sat midday - 2.30pm, 7pm - 11pm. Sun midday - 3pm, 7pm - 10.30pm. Gay pub.

Gay Community

Box GCO c/o The Cricketers Emlyn Square Swindon. Contact Thamesline Lesbian and Gay Line for details. Gay social group that organises various events.

Gay Outdoor Club

T:01793-770099 (Nigel). Wiltshire, Avon and Gloucestershire branch of the Gay Outdoor Club. Organises outdoor sporting and associated events for lesbians and gay men.

Merchiston Surgery

Highworth Road. T:01793-823307. Mon - Fri 8.30am - 6.30pm. Ask for Dr Nick Theobald. Male and female doctor's practice. NHS only in the main. Wiltshire FHSA. Disabled access.

Thamesdown Community Law Centre

26 Victoria Road Swindon SN1 3AW. T:01793-486926. F:01793-432193. Law centre covering welfare benefits, housing and employment law. Accepts limited legal aid work. Disabled access and will undertake home visits.

Thamesdown Lesbian and Gay Line

P O Box 40 Swindon Wiltshire SN1 3QR. T:01793-644585. Wed Fri 8pm - 10pm. Lesbian, gay, bisexual, straight, telephone service which provides support, information and counselling for anyone experiencing problems in relation to sexuality.

TV Forum

T:01793-420262. Telephone helpline and information service for TVs. Also holds monthly meetings.

Torquay

Body Positive Devon

The Castleton 11 Castle Road TQ1 3BB. T:01803-200222. Self-help group for people affected by HIV/AIDS.

CARD (Community AIDS Relief in Devon)

2 Vaughan Parade TQ2 5EF. T:01803-296221. Provides a wide range of grants for people with AIDS. Plans to support projects for information, education and community care services.

Cliff House Hotel

St Marks Road Torquay TQ1 2EH (Alan or Robbie). T:01803-294656 / 211983. F:01803-211983. Lesbian and gay hotel and bed and breakfast..Open all year. Residents car park. Accepts Visa and Access. Disabled access.

Gowmans

61 Abbey Road Torquay and 65 Hyde Road Paignton. T:01803-559934 and 01803-291133 (emergency). F:01803-528351. Mon - Fri 9am - 5.15pm. Solicitor practice with a complete range of legal services. Accepts legal aid work. Emergency service. Speaks French and Norwegian. Disabled access.

Meadfoot Inn

7 Meadfoot Lane Torquay TQ1 2BW. T:01803-297112. Mon - Sat midday - 4pm, 7pm - 11pm. Sun midday - 3pm, 7pm - 10.30pm. Lesbian and gay pub.

Summerland House Hotel

42 Warren Road Torquay TQ2 5TL. T:01803-297120. Gay (90%) hotel. Open all year. Accepts Visa, Access, AMEX.

TAGS (Torbay AIDS Support Group)

Pandaric Braddens Hill Road West TQ1 1BG. T:01803-299266. Mon - Fri 4pm - 10pm (Helpline). Drop-in centre Mon - Fri 10am - 4pm. Befriending, informal support, laundry service, hospital/home visiting for people who are HIV+ or have AIDS diagnosis.

Truro

CAC (Cornwall AIDS Council)

11 Walsingham Place TR1 2RP. T:01872-225022. Mon - Fri midday - 5pm Helpline.Office Mon and Tues 1pm - 5pm, Weds -Fri 9.30am - 5pm. Helpline, education, counselling, befriending, training, legal advice, transport, special need fund, resource centre.

Cornwall AIDS Helpline

Department of GU Medicine Royal Cornwall Hospital Infirmary Hill TR1 2HZ. T:01872-42520. Mon - Fri 9am - 5pm. Telephone service offering advice support counselling and information for people affected by HIV/AIDS.

Woodbine Villa

Pink Directory

Fare Street Grampound nr Truro TR2 4QP. T:01726-882005. Lesbian and gay bed and breakfast.. Also has a sauna open to the public. Wed - Sun 6pm - 10pm.

Weston-super-mare

Chalet

14 Meadow Street. T:01934-419444. Mon - Sat open all day. Sun midday - 3pm, 7pm - 10.30pm. Lesbian and gay pub.

Lodge

Oxford Street. T:01934-629844. Mon - Wed 8.30pm - 1pm. Thurs - Sat 8.30pm - 2pm. Sun 8pm - midnight. Gay club.

Weymouth

DASH (Dorset AIDS Support and Help)

5 Belle Vue DT4 8DR. T:01305-779224 (office) 01258-456505 (24 hours helpline). Help and support for people with HIV/AIDS, their families and carers, practical help, home and hospital visiting, buddying service.

MSM Dorset

5 Belle Vue DT4 8DR. T:01305-779224. F:01305-766462. Sexual health project for gay and bisexual men. Community based, needs assessment and ongoing outreach work.

Winchester

Help for Health Trust

Highcroft Cottage Romsey Road SO22 5DH. T:0800-665544. F:01962-849079. Health information service providing confidential health information including HIV/AIDS for all.

Yeoford

Pollards

Yeoford Devon EX17 5JD. T:01363-84402 (Martin and Rob). Lesbian and gay guest house.

SOUTH-EAST ENGLAND

Sexual Politics

ORDER FORM

To order titles direct from Cassell see the form at the back of the directory : here we list some 30 innovative and acclaimed new books in our Lesbian and Gay Studies, Women on Women and AIDS Awareness series.

PUB QUIZ

Throughout 1995 Cassell and *The Pink Paper* shall be running a nationwide tournament of pub quizzes. If you run a pub and would be interested in taking part, contact Cassell's Sexual Politics Quiz, Villiers House, 41/47 Strand, London WC2N 5JE.

MAKE CASH! HOLD A BOOK PARTY!

If you are interested in hosting a book party for you and your friends contact Cassell's Sexual Politics Book Party, Villiers House, 41/47 Strand, London WC2N 5JE.

MAILING LIST

For regular information about our forthcoming titles, catalogues and news of special offers and book events in your area, fill in the form below and return to Cassell's Sexual Politics Mailing List, Villiers House, 41/47 Strand, London WC2N 5JE. No charge and no obligation.

Please include my details on the Sexual Politics Mailing List for receipt of details of forthcoming titles, news of special offers and of Cassell book events:

Name ....

Address ....

....

....

....

Send to Cassell Sexual Politics Mailing List, Villiers House, 41/47 Strand, London WC2N 5JE.

Addlestone

Woburn Park Hotel

Station Gate. T:01932-853764. Open usual pub hours. Lesbian and gay pub and hotel with discos.

Basildon

HANCS

P O Box 25 SS16 4AY. T:01268-282134. Advice, information, counselling and support for anyone affected by HIV. Advice on benefits, housing, transport and legal issues. Clinical advice, therapy access, bereavement support.

Bedford

Barley Mow

75 Loyes Road. T:01234-59355. Open usual pub hours. Lesbian and gay pub.

Bedfordshire Lesbian and Gay Helpline

26-28 Bromham Road MK40 2QD. T:01234-218990. Tues 7.30pm - 10pm. Telephone service offering advice, information and counselling.

Matt's Place

8 Lime Street. T:01234-352326. Open evenings. Lesbian gay straight jazz bar and Creole restaurant.

Bognor Regis

TAGS (The Arun Gay Society)

PO Box 11 PO 21 5PA. Meets alternate Tues in Littlehampton. Lesbian and gay social and support group which offers befriending and counselling.

Brighton & Hove

ACET (AIDS Care Education and Training)

P O Box 200 BN3 3SB. T:01273-733918. F:01273-770878. A branch of the Christian charity which provides practical home based help to people with HIV/AIDS.

Albatross Cafe

27 Middle Street. T:01273-329462. Mon - Sat 11am - 5pm. Cafe with occasional women only and mixed gay evenings.

Alpha Lodge

19 New Steine BN2 1PD. T:01273-609632 F:01273-690264. Lesbian, gay and TV hotel. Open all year. Accepts Access, Visa and Amex.

Aqarium

Steine Street. T:01273-605525. Open usual pub hours. Gay men's pub.

Avalon Hotel

7 Upper Rock Gardens BN2 1QE. T:01273-692344. Lesbian and gay hotel. Accepts Access and Visa.

Ashley Court Hotel

33 Montpelier Road. T:01273-739916. Lesbian and gay hotel.

Bannings

14 Upper Rock Gardens BN2 1QE. T:01273-681403. Lesbian and gay guest house. Women particularly welcome.

Barrington's Private Hotel

76 Grand Parade BN2 2JA. T:01273-604182. Gay hotel.

Black Horse

112 Church Street. T:01273-606864. Open usual pub hours. Lesbian, gay, straight

pub.

Brighton Belle

2 St. George's Road. T:01273-609713. Tues - Sat 10pm - 2am , Sun 4pm - 7pm. Lesbian and gay drinking club. Membership required.

Bulldog Tavern

31 St. James Street. T:01273-684097. Mon - Sat 11am - 11pm, Sun midday - 3pm, 7pm - 10.30pm. Lesbian and gay pub.

Cardome

47a St.James Street. T:01273-692916. Mon - Sat 9.30am - 5.30pm. Shop selling lesbian and gay books, magazines and cards.

Carlton Lodge Hotel

48 Waterloo Street. T:01273-726580. Lesbian, gay, straight hotel. Open all year.

Catnaps

21 Atlingworth Street Hove. T:01273-685193. Lesbian and gay hotel. Open all year.

Chequers Inn

Preston Street. Open usual pub hours. Lesbian, gay, straight pub with drag.

Cine-a-matique

22 Preston Street. T:01273-239154. Shop selling lesbian and gay videos, cards and toys.

Club Revenge

32-34 Old Steine. T:01273-606164. Mon - Sat 10.30pm - 2am. Lesbian and gay club.

Court Craven

2 Atlingworth Street Hove. T:01273-607710. Gay hotel.

Coward's Guest House

12 Upper Rock Gardens BN2 1QE. T:01273-692677. Lesbian and gay guest house.

Do Tongues

T:01273-604480. Weekly on Weds evenings. Literature and arts promoters who arrange weekly events for lesbian gay straight audience.

Floatarium

3 Duke's Court. T:01273-26965. Lesbian and gay hotel.

Food for Friends

32 Prince Albert Street. T:01273-202310. Mon - Sat 9am - 10pm, Sun 10am - 10pm. Lesbian, gay, straight cafe, restaurant and coffee bar.

Franklin's

41 Regency Square. T:01273-327016. Largely lesbian hotel. Gay men welcome. Open all year. All major credit cards accepted.

Freedom Youth UK (Brighton)

c/o PO Box 649 Harrow Middlesex. T:01956-351789. Brighton branch of national lesbian and gay youth network. Contact via this address and telephone number.

Hudson's Guesthouse

22 Devonshire Place. T:01273-683642. F:01273-696088. Lesbian and gay guest house. Open all year. Accepts Visa, Access and AMEX.

Legend's Bar @ New Europe Hotel

31 -32 Marine Parade T:01273-624462. Mon - Sat 11am - 11pm. Lesbian and gay bar.

Lesbian and Gay Switchboard

The Lesbian Avengers

meet at the london women's centre
wesley house, 4, wild court
london wc2 (holborn tube)

at 7.30pm each tuesday evening, accessible venue, signing facilities available

contact us for information about your local group at:
po box 501, london se21 7d5

"We are a non-violent direct-action group committed to raising lesbian visibility and fighting for our survival and our rights"

QUEER AS FUCK - I CAN SEE QUEERLY NOW - DYKE WITH ATTITUDE - THIS FAGGOT'S NOT FOR BURNING - OUTRAGE!

Outrage! T shirts are 100% cotton: £10 (inc. postage)

Available in medium, large, extra large - black or white cotton

5 PETER STREET, LONDON W1 3RR

OutRage! is a broad based group open to all lesbians, gay men and bisexuals committed to radical non-violent direct action and civil disobedience to fight homophobia

P O Box 449 Brighton BN1 1UU. T:01273-690825. Mon - Sat 6pm - 10pm. Sun 8pm - 10pm. Telephone service offering advice, counselling and information.

Lesbian Line

PO Box 449 BN1 1UU. T:01273-603298. Tues and Fri 8pm - 10pm. Telephone service offering advice information and support to lesbians.

Lesbian Walking Group

T:01323-842000. Walks every 3 weeks for 5-8 miles usually starting from Brighton.

Marlborough

Prince's Street. T: 01273-570028. Open usual pub hours. Lesbian and gay pub.

Montpelier Hall

17 Montpelier Terrace BN1 3DF. T:01273-203599. Lesbian and gay hotel. Residents car park.

New Europe Hotel

31-32 Marine Parade BN2 1TR. T:01273-624462. Gay men's hotel with free entry to Club Revenge for guests.

Only Alternative Left

39 Aubyn's. T:01273-324739. Women only non-smoking vegetarian guest house. Open all year. Restaurant and meeting rooms.

Oriental

5 Montpelier Road. T:01273-728808. Open usual pub hours. Lesbian and gay pub.

Open Door

35 Camelford Street BN2 1TQ. T:01273-605706. Mon - Fri 10am - 4pm. A drop-in for people affected by HIV / AIDS.

Our House

P O Box 1317 BN2 4YB. T:01273-693266. F:01273-622006. Self help group for those affected by HIV / AIDS. Offers assistance, care and advice, speakers, resource library. Sunday lunch service.

Out ! Brighton

4 and 7 Dorset Street BN2 1WA. T:01273-623356. Lesbian and gay bookshop. Also stocks magazines, cards, toys, t-shirts, jewellery, rubber, leather and stainless steel.

Pavilion

75 Grand Parade. T:01273-698181. Mon - Sat (except Tues) 8pm - 1am and Sun 2pm -11.30pm. Lesbian and gay restaurant and club. Club open Mon - Sat 10pm - 2am.

Pink Promotions

T:01903-723625. Promotes women's discos twice monthly at private venues.

Portland House Hotel

55-56 Regency Square BN1 2FF. T:01273-820464. F:01273-746036. Lesbian and gay hotel.

Public House Book shop

21 Little Preston Street. T:01273-28357. Mon - Sat 10am-5.30pm. Book shop with lesbian and gay literature and magazines. Mail order available.

Queen's Arms

7 George Street. T:01273-602939. Open usual pub hours. Lesbian and gay pub with disco on Sat.

Queen's Head

10 Steine Street. T:01273-602939. Open usual pub hours. Lesbian and gay pub.

Read All About It

69 East Street. T:01273-204824. Gay run bookshop with lesbian and gay literature and magazines.

Scene 22

129 St. James Street BN1 2HN. T:01273-29884. Shop that sells lesbian and gay books, cards, magazines and leather/rubber items. Cafe.

Shalimar Hotel

23 Broad Street. T:01273-605316. Lesbian and gay hotel. Open all year. Accepts major credit cards.

Secret's

25 Steine Street. T:01273-609672. Mon - Thurs 10pm - 2am, Fri and Sat 9.30pm -2am. Gay bar and disco.

Shameless Hussies

T:01273-731170 or 01273-702506. Monthy lesbian disco.

Sinclair's Guest House

23 Upper Rock Gardens BN2 1QE. T:01273-600006. Mobile:0831-248361. Lesbian and gay guest house. Open all year.

Sussex Beacon

Bevendean Road BN2DE. T:01273-694222. F:01273-682740. A continuing care hospice facility for people with HIV / AIDS.

Sussex Club

5 Regency Square. T:01273-208564. Mon - Sat 6pm -1pm, Sun 7pm - 10.30pm. Private lesbian club for women over 25.

Sussex Safer Sex Supplies Ltd

Graham Wilkinson House 3 Cavendish Street BN2 1RN. T:01273-608511. F:01273-670223. Supplies condoms and associated products to lesbians and gay men.

Sussex University Lesbian Gay and Bisexual Society

c/o Students Union Falmer House University of Sussex BN1 9PH.. T:01273-678152. Meets Room 232 Falmer House Thurs evenings during term. Lesbian, gay and bisexual social and support group for students.

Threshold Women's Counselling

2nd Floor 79 Buckingham Road BN1 3RB. T:01273-749800. Provides free or low cost counselling and therapy (in particular re HIV). Run by women for women. Creche.

Trans-Sister @ The Beachcomber

King's Road Arches. First Thurs each month 9pm - 2am. Lesbian, gay, TV/TS club. Glamour and trash nights with 70s disco.

Victoria House

23 Wilbury Road BN3 9PB. T:01273-326838. Lesbian and gay bed and breakfast.

Whosoever

PO Box 817 BN1 1UU. Organises social and religious interdenominational events. Worship every Sun 7.45pm at Unitarian Chuch, New Road.

Wildcat International

16 Preston Street BN1

2HN. T:01273-323758. Mon - Sat 10am - 6pm. Sells body piercing jewellery, tattoo magazines and steel toys.

Wild Fruit @ The Paradox

78 West Street. T:01273-321628. First Mon each month 10pm - 2am. Lesbian and gay club.

Wiseguys and Outreach Team

Graham Wilkinson House 3 Cavendish Street BN2 1RN. T:01273-625222. F:01273-670223. Health education group aimed at gay men and other men who have sex with men.

Women's Centre

10 St George's Mews off Trafalgar Street. T:01273-600526. Open Mon, Wed & Fri 10.30am - 3pm and 7pm - 9pm. Lesbian and straight women's resource centre.

Zanzibar

129 St. James Street. T:01273-622100. Mon - Sat midday - 2am, Sun 7pm - 10.30pm. Gay club bar and cafe.

Bromley

Lesbian and Gay Group

33 Highland Road BR1 4AA. T:0181-464-1068. Local social group for under 30s.

Camberley

Bucklands

Buckland House 121 Yorktown Road Sandhurst Camberley GU17 8BW. T:01252-874865. F:01252-877422. Mon - Fri 9am - 5pm. Solicitor practice covering conveyancing, probate, wills, matrimonial, criminal and litigation. Accepts legal aid work. Disabled access.

Canterbury

Carpenter's Arms

Black Griffin Lane. Weds and Sat from 7pm. Lesbian, gay, straight pub. GALA disco third Sat monthly (see GALA).

East Kent Friend

P O Box 40 CT1 2YE. T:01843-558762. Tues 7.30pm - 10pm. Telephone service offering advice, support and information to lesbians, gay men and bisexuals.

Four Seasons

77 Strurry Road CT1 1BV. T:01277-787078. Gay run bed and breakfast. Open all year.

GALA (Gay and Lesbian Association)

PO Box 40 CT1 2YE. Contact via East Kent Friend. Lesbian and gay social and support group. Disco at Carpenter's Arms third Sat each month.

Kent and Canterbury Lesbian Line

PO Box 163 CT2 8AX. T:01227-464570. Fri 7.30pm-10pm. Telephone service offering advice, information and counselling for lesbians.

Seymour Place

28 High Street Wingham near Canterbury CT3 1AB. T:01227-720134. Lesbian and gay hotel. 15th century country house. In-house massage and gym.

Chatham

Lesbian and Gay Christian Movement

(Medway Towns)

Richard Frost P O Box 53 Chatham Kent ME5 7ED. T:01634-408869. Lesbian, gay, straight. Exists to bring gay liberation to the churches of Christ.

MAGIC

PO Box 10c NE4 6TX. T:01634-716951. Lesbian and gay social group which runs a weekly disco and organises regular socials. Produces a newsletter and lease manages The Vaults (see Rochester listings) where most of their activities take place.

Positive Contact

P O Box 153 Chatham ME4 5DF. A self-help group for people in the Medway area living with HIV / AIDS. Partners and families welcome. Holds monthly meetings. Monthly newsletter.

Chelmsford

Evangelical Fellowship within the Lesbian and Gay Christian Movement

45 Hillary Close CM1 5RP. T:01245-252214. To support lesbian or gay evangelical Christians in coming to terms with their sexuality. To encourage other evangelical Christians to re-examine their understanding of human sexuality.

LOGIC

PO Box 2210 CN1 3HX. T: 01245-442992 or 01245-257802. Mon and Fri 6pm-8pm. Lesbian and gay social group which meets weekly.

Cheshunt

Terrence McLellan Aids Foundation

Mill House Russell Street EN7 6JH. T:01992-623762. Provides practical help for people living with HIV / AIDS. Also befriending and support.

Chichester

AIDS Network

P O Box 92 PO19 2EJ. T:01243-538484 (helpline). Mon 6pm - 8pm. Tues - Fri 6pm - 7pm. Support for all affected by HIV / AIDS. Resource centre, training and education, hardship fund.

Bush

16 The Hornet. T:01243-779945. Open usual pub hours. Lesbian, gay, straight pub and bed and breakfast.

Coggeshaw

Queen's Head

Colchester Road. Mon - Sat 7pm-11pm, Sun 7pm-10.30pm. Gay pub. Discos and cabaret Fri, Sat and Sun.

Colchester

Lesbian and Gay Switchboard

15 Queen Street Colchester CO1 2PH. T:01206-767043. Mon - Fri 7pm - 10pm. Sat 10.30am - 1pm, drop-in only. Telephone helplines and drop-in. Helplines also operate as HIV/ AIDS helplines and advice, information and counselling services for the lesbian and gay community. Also has a buddy service.

Lesbian Line

T:01206-870051. Sun 8pm-10pm. Telephone service offering advice, information and counselling for lesbians.

Malsters Arms

Haven Road. T:01206-860323. Open usual pub hours. Lesbian and gay pub.

Open Road

78 Maldon Road CO3 3AL. T:01206-766096. HIV counselling, testing, information on safer sex and drug use, therapy programme.

Thelma's

Colchester Arts Centre St Mary at-the-Walls Church Street. T:01206-577301. First Fri monthly 9pm-1.30am. Lesbian and gay disco.

Crawley

Body Positive

P O Box 235 RH10 1FW. T:01293-552111. A self-help group for people affected by HIV / AIDS offering moral support in a relaxed atmosphere. Also complementary therapies, information, advice, closed and open groups.

Lesbian Line

T:01293-520478. Mon 7pm-8pm, Thurs 7pm-8pm. Telephone service offering advice information and support for lesbians.

Women's Social Group

T:01293-531459. Meets alternate Mon at local pub. Lesbian social group.

Dartford

Baily and Goff

53-55 Spital Street Dartford Kent DA1 2EB. T:01322-220235. F:01322-293841. Mon - Fri 9am - 5pm. Solicitor general practice (not crime) covering conveyancing, landlord and tenant, wills and probate, family, accident, enviromental law and planning. Accepts legal aid work.

Duke's

PO Box 163 DA1 5JG. Social group with regular meetings for gay men.

Eastbourne

HARASS (Hastings and Rother AIDS Support Society)

65d Susans Road BN21 3TG. T:01323-643322. Drop-in centre. Mon - Fri 9am - 1pm. Support for people with HIV / AIDS. Services adapted to client's individual needs. Befriending team of volunteers and support groups.

Hartington Hotel

89 Cavendish Place. T:01323-643151. Mon-Sat 11.30am-11pm, Sun usual pub hours. Lesbian and gay pub.

East Grinstead

Fairlight Hotel

41 Silverdale Road. T:01323-721770. Lesbian, gay, straight hotel. Accepts Access and Visa.

The Haven

3 Dexter Drive RH19 4SU. T:01342-300763. A support group for those affected by HIV / AIDS.

Englefield Green

RAFT (Runnymede AIDS Friendship)

P O Box 8 Virginia Water GU25 4YS. Provides a range of services to people who are worried, affected or infected by HIV /

AIDS.

Farnham

Queen's Arms

Farnham Road Ewshots T:01252-850241. Open usual pub hours. Lesbian, gay, straight pub (particularly Sat).

Ralph's Cellar Disco

Shortheath Road. T:01252-715844. Gay disco Sat twice monthly 10pm-1am.

Fleet

Stanburys

140 Fleet Road Fleet Hampshire GU13 8BE. T:01252-617913. F:01252-815236. Opens 9am - 5.30pm. Solicitor practice specialising in crime, matrimonial, landlord and tenant, conveyancing, general. Accepts legal aid work. Emergency service.

Folkestone

Bottom's

Carlton Hotel The Lees. T:01303-53290. Sun 8pm-1am. Gay disco.

East Kent Buddy Groups

c/o Royal Victoria Hospital Radnor Park Avenue CT19 5BN. T:01303-220018. Runs three buddy groups in Ramsgate, Ashford and Folkestone. Emotional and / or practical support for anyone who is HIV+ or who has an AIDS diagnosis.

Funtington

Funtington Hall Nursing Home

Funtington PO18 9LL. T:01243-573183. Lesbian and gay nursing home.

Gravesend

The City of London

27 The Terrace Gravesend Kent DA12 2BA. T:01474-329370. Mon - Sat 11am - 11pm. Sun midday - 3pm, 7pm - 10.30pm. Lesbian, gay, straight pub.

Guildford

Gay Society

T:01483-733045. Meets alternate Wed. Gay social and befriending group.

Greyhound

11 High Street. T:01483-300490. Open usual pub hours. Lesbian, gay, straight pub.

Hart Brown and Co

66 Woodbridge Road Guildford GU11 4RE. T:01483-68267. Emergency: 01483-573783. F:01483-39313. Mon - Fri 9am - 5.30pm. Solicitor practice covering crime, housing, matrimonial, childcare, civil, personal injury, medical negligence, conveyancing, landlord and tenant, probate, wills, financial and investment, immigration, mental health, employment. Accepts legal aid work. Emergency service. Speaks French, German, and Spanish. Disabled access.

Surrey and East Hampshire AIDSLINK Ltd

T:01483-300150. Daily 8pm - 10pm. Telephone service offering advice, information and support to people affected by HIV/AIDS. The organisation runs a buddy group offering practical and emotional support to people with HIV/

AIDS. Also social activities and a family and friends support group.

Harlow

Harlow and District AIDS Support Group

c/o Harlow Advice Centre 2 East Gate CM20 1ND. T:01279-446622. Fundraising and trust fund for people with AIDS. Also provides confidential advice, information, support and education.

Lesbian and Gay Switchboard

T:01279-639637. Sun, Wed, Thur 8pm-11pm, Fri 8pm-midnight, Tues 8pm-11pm (women only). First and third Mon (TV/TS). Telephone service offering advice information and support for lesbians, gay men, bisexuals and TV/TS.

Outcome

North Essex Health Promotion Forth Avenue CM20 1DT. T:01279-450500. F:01279-450728. Mon-Fri 9am-5pm. Health project for gay and bisexual men looking at issues around HIV/AIDS.

Ruby's

2a Wych Elm. T:01279-451677. Mon - Wed 8pm-11pm, Thurs 8pm-midnight, Fri 8pm-2am disco, Sat lunch midday - 3pm, 8pm-2am disco, Sun lunch midday -3pm, quiz 8pm-10.30pm. Last Mon of month is Mellow Mon for the over 30s.Lesbian and gay centre and club.

Harrow

Harrow and Brent Lesbian and Gay Group

P O Box 649 Harrow HA3 0LE. Mon 8pm - 11pm. A social group for lesbians and gay men.

Hastings

Funnell and Herring

192 Queens Road Hastings. T:01424-426287. Emergency :0831-583251. F:01421-434372. Mon - Fri 9am - 1pm, 2.15pm - 5.15pm. Solicitor practice covering criminal, matrimonial, civil litigation, conveyancing, probate, commercial. Accepts legal aid work. Emergency service. Speaks some French. Disabled access.

Hastings Befrienders

PO Box 6 St. Leonard's on Sea. T:01424-721394. Fri 8pm-10pm. Telephone service offering support information and advice for lesbians and gay men.

Hastings and Rother AIDS Support Society

2 Cambridge Gardens TN34 1EN. T:01424-429901. Mon - Fri 9am - 4pm (24hr answerphone). Gives advice, information and support around HIV / AIDS.

Lesbian Line

PO Box 46 St. Leonard's on Sea. T:01424-721394.. Mon 7pm-9pm. Telephone service offering advice information and support to lesbians.

Margaret House

5 Milward Road. T:01424-713698. Lesbian, gay, straight bed and breakfast.

Hemel Hempstead

AIDSline

T:0442-242042. Telephone service offering advice, support and counselling for people affected by HIV/ AIDS.

Henley-on-Thames

Benson's

Remenham Hill Henley on Thames RG9 3EP (Trevor, Mel). T:01491 575430. F:01491-573471. Office Mon - Fri 10am - 3pm. Club Mon - Sat 9pm - 2am. Lesbian, gay, straight nightclub. Sun 9pm-1am women only.

Herne Bay

Roman Galley

Thanet Way. Telephone East Kent Friend for details (see Canterbury). Open usual pub hours. Lesbian, gay, straight pub. East Kent Friend run occasional discos at this venue.

Hertford

Herts Aid

Cedar Cottage Goldings Lane SG14 2PX. T:01992-556616. F:01992-556618. A confidential service offering information, counselling, support, home support, befriending to people with HIV/ AIDS.

High Wycombe

Chilternaids

P O Box 377 HP13 6HV. T:01494-444818. Thurs 8pm - 10pm. Service offering direct support through practical assistance, befriending, transport and a financial support fund for people with HIV / AIDS.

Hillingdon

Hillingdon AIDS Response Trust

Beasleys Yard 126 High Street UB8 1JU. T:01895-813874. Mon - Fri 9am - 5pm. Advice and support for anyone affected by HIV / AIDS.

Horsham

AVERT (AIDS Education and Research Trust)

11 Denne Parade RH12 1JD. T:01403-210202. Produces a number of educational leaflets and pamphlets around HIV funded by donations and funds research projects.

Isleworth

Bennett and Ryan

Grove House 551 London Road Isleworth TW7 4DS. T:0181-568-2800 or 568-0597. F:0181-569-7480. Mon - Fri 9.30am - 5.30pm. Solictor practice covering most areas and specialising in matrimonial, children, property, litigation and crime. Accepts legal aid work. Speaks German. Provision for disabled clients.

Kingston-upon-Thames

Kingston and Richmond Area Gay Society

PO Box 158a Surbiton KT6 6RS. T:0181-397-4903. Lesbian and gay social group which organises pub outings and coffee mornings.

Lewes

Estcourt (Dr), Ashby (Dr), Elliot

(Dr), Hill (Dr)

Health Centre Newick near Lewes BN8 4LR. Ask for Dr Estcourt, Elliot or Hill. T:01825-722272. Phone for opening hours. Male and female medical practice. NHS / private. East Sussex FHSA. Disabled access.

Little Bromley

Fox and Hounds

Harwich Road. T:01206-392797. Open usual pub hours, (midnight on Sat). Disco Wed and Sat. Lesbian and gay pub.

Luton

Shirley Temple

1 Liverpool Road. T: 01582-25491. Open usual pub hours. Gay pub.

Tallulah's

15 Upper George Street LU1 2RD. T:01582-30344. Mon - Sat 7pm - midnight, Sun 9pm - midnight. Lesbian and gay restaurant.

Williams and Co

22 King Street Luton LU1 2DP. T:01582-23322. F: 01582-455885. Mon - Fri 9am - 5.30pm. Solicitor practice covering wills and probate, personal injury, crime, family, civil litigation, conveyancing. Accepts legal aid work. Disabled access.

Maidstone

Burrough's

38 King Street Maidstone Kent ME14 1BS. T:01622-676976. Solicitor practice covering crime, divorce, liquor licensing, public entertainment licencing, conveyancing, wills, probate, juvenile crime, care proceedings, drink & drive. Emergency service.

Margate

Boys and Maughan

India House Hawley Street Margate Kent CT9 1PZ. T:01843-220288. Emergency pager 01426-841279. Mon - Fri 9am - 1pm, 2pm - 5pm. Sat 9.30am - midday. Practice covers debt, housing, family, PI, crime, welfare, consumer, employment, immigration, conveyancing, wills and probate. Accepts legal aid work. Emergency service. Speaks French, Hindi, Punjabi.

Club Freedom

17 Cliff Terrace CT9 1RU. T:01843-231766. Tues - Say 10pm-2am. Gay club.

New Inn

New Street. T:01843-223799. Open usual pub hours. Lesbian and gay pub with disco.

Pillow Talk

13 Marine Drive. T:01843-294069. Gay sex shop that stocks leather, rubber, magazine and cards. Mail order service.

Trinity Bed and Breakfast

1 Trinity Square. T:01843-226249. Lesbian and gay bed and breakfast. Accepts credit cards.

Tudor's

55 Godwin Road Cliftonville. T:01843-299174. Lesbian run lesbian, gay, straight bed and breakfast.

Milton Keynes

Lesbian and Gay Switchboard

Pink Directory

P O Box 153 Milton Keynes MK1 1AA. T:01908-666226. F:01908-282459. Mon 7pm - 10pm (men), Thurs 7pm - 9pm (women). Lesbian, gay, bisexual, straight, TV/TS. Telephone service providing support, advice and information.

MK Beam

Neath Hill Health Centre 1 Tower Crescent Neath Hill MK14 6JY. T:01908-241685. A voluntary organisation offering befriending, education and information and practical and emotional support for people with HIV/AIDS.

Pagham

Millburgh Beach House HIV Respite Centre

T:01798-867646. Respite care for people with HIV/AIDS. A bungalow located on the West Sussex coast within 30 minutes of Millburgh Hall HIV/AIDS Centre. The unit is open all year. 24hour care worker supervision.

Petworth

Millburgh Hall HIV/AIDS Treatment Centre and Hospice

Selham GU28 0PT. T:01798-867646. F:01798-867684. A treatment centre and hospice for people with HIV/AIDS who require respite, convalescence or terminal care.

Ramsgate

Madam Sinnz

13 Turner Street CT11 8NJ. T:01843-587667. Open usual pub hours. Lesbian and gay pub with disco in basement.

Reading

Awareness

Arts Centre 21 South Street Reading. Contact Lesbian and Gay Helpline for details. Lesbian and gay disco on the 1st Friday of each month 9pm - 1am.

Buddies

Voluntary practical and emotional support for people with HIV and AIDS. Contact via Lesbian and Gay Helpline or T:01734-770939 / 770940.

Lesbian Disco

Park Community Hall London Road. T:01734-311939. Second Sat each month at 8pm. Lesbian disco and social.

Lesbian and Gay Helpline

Tues and Fri 8pm - 10pm, Sun 4pm - 6pm. PO Box 75 Reading RG1 7DU. T:01734-597269. Telephone advice, support and information line.

Lesbian Social and Befriending Group

Contact via Women's Centre. T:01734-311939.

Number 5 Youth Counselling

Mon - Fri 10am - 10pm. Counselling service that can arrange face-to-face meetings. Not specifically gay oriented.

Reading Gays and Lesbians

P O Box 75 Reading RG1 7DU. T:01734-507404 (Andy or Len). Befriending and social group. Currently mainly men.

Usually meets weekly.

Reading Survivors

T:01734-560820. Tues 7pm - 10pm. Male rape and abuse counselling and support service.

Reading University Lesbian and Gay Society

c/o Reading University Union PO BOx 230 Whiteknights RG6 2AZ. Wed 8.30pm during term time. Social 8pm Mon at Wynford Arms.

Women's Centre

6 Silver Street. T:01734-311939. Drop-in for women on Monday evenings.

The Wynford Arms

110 Kings Road Reading. T:01734-589814. Mon - Fri midday - 3pm, 7pm - 11pm. Sat midday - 11pm. Sun midday - 3pm, 7pm - 10.30pm. Lesbian and gay pub.

Redhill

Elmshades

26 Pendleton Road. T:01737-766052. Open usual pub hours. Lesbian, gay, straight pub with private loftbar on Thurs - Sun evenings.

Goodhand and Forsyth

2 High Street Redhill Surrey. T:01737-773533. Emergency:01883-743654. F:01737-761222. Mon - Fri 8am - 6pm. Solicitor practice covering criminal, litigation, matrimonial. Accepts Legal Aid work. Emergency service. Facilities can be made available to disabled people.

St Peter's House Project

26 Station Road KT20 7BG. T:01767-241044. Daily 3.30pm - 10pm. Telephone service offering advice, support and information to people with HIV/AIDS. Also runs a respite centre for people with AIDS. Offers gay men's health promotion services and outreach work.

Robertsbridge

Eliot-Pyle (Dr E) & McNeily (Dr R)

Oldswood Surgery Station Road Robertsbridge TN32 5DG. T:01580-880790. By appointment only. Medical practice. NHS / private. East Sussex FHSA. Disabled access.

Rochester

Ship Inn

347 High Street. T:01634-844264. Open usual pub hours. Lesbian and gay pub.

Vaults

168 High Street. T:01634-818433. Tues - Thurs pub hours, Fri and Sat open until 2am with disco. Lesbian and gay pub leased by the MAGIC group. (See Chatham listing for further details).

St Albans

The Crescent

19 Russell Avenue AL3 5ES. T:01727-844230. Mon - Fri 10am - 4pm. Telephone service offering advice, counselling and information for people affected by HIV/ AIDS. Also operates a buddy service, a body positive self-help group, support groups and complementary therapies.

Diva Fever @

Spritzers

T:01582-794053. First and third Thurs of each month. Women only disco.

Spritzers

Redbourn Road. Open usual pub hours. Lesbian and gay pub.

Verulam MSC

PO Box 158 AL2 3UQ. T:01727-868563. Gay men's leather club which meets first Tues of each month at Spritzers.

St Leonards on Sea

Hastings Befrienders

P O Box 6 St Leonards on Sea. T:01424-444777. Mon 7pm - 9pm (men), Fri 8pm - 10pm (women). Helpline. Offers safer sex information, counselling and befriending to lesbians, gay men and bisexuals.

Sherwood Guest House

15 Grosvenor Crescent St Leonards on Sea TN38 0AA. T:01424-433331. Gay and straight guest house. Not open all year (ring for details). Accepts Visa, Access.

Victoria

Battle Road. Open usual pub hours. Lesbian, gay, straight pub.

Slough

Parkside Guest House

1 Upton Court Road. T:01753-22553. Lesbian, gay, straight bed and breakfast.

SWAGG (Slough and Windsor Area Gay Group)

T:01932-761932. Gay social group which holds regular meetings in the area.

TVPS (Thames Valley Postive Support)

P O Box 1433 SL1 6YG. T:01628-603400. Tues Wed Thurs 11am - 4pm. Drop-in centre for people with HIV/ AIDS. Also has a weekly support group and separate monthly support groups for gay men, women and partners, families and friends. Also offers individual counselling and has a buddy scheme.

Southall

Portland Road Video and Photo Centre

R P Ramji Efta House 3-5 Western Road Southall UB2 5HB. T:0181-843-9942. F:0181-843-9942. Mon - Sat 11am - 5pm. Lesbian, gay, straight. Photoprocessors, studio, photo-lab, for developing and printing, video filming and confidential services.

Wilson Houlder and Co

91 South Road Southall UB1 1SH. T:0181-574-2626. Emergency : 0850-818377. F:0181-571-3118. Mon - Fri 9am-12.45pm, 2pm - 5pm. Crime, family, personal injury, housing and propoerty disptes, debt collection, immigration, conveyancing, wills and probate. Accepts Legal Aid work. Emergency service. Disabled access.

Southend-on-Sea

The Cliff

48 Hamlet Road

Southend-on-Sea SS1 1HH. T:01702-344466. Mon - Sat midday - 11pm. Sun 12.30pm - 3.30pm, 7pm - 10.30pm. Lesbian, gay, TV pub.

Essex Women's Social Group

T:01702-344466. Meets at Cliff Hotel every first and third Tues of month. Ask at the bar for Jo.

Garden

Chartwell Square Victoria Circus Precinct. Thursday 9.30pm-2am. Gay club.

SAIDSO (Southend AIDS Organisation)

Southend Hospital Prittlewell Chase Westcliff-on-Sea Southend-on-Sea SSO ORY. T:01702-391750. Mon - Fri 6pm - 10pm. Telephone service offering advice, support and information to people with HIV/AIDS. Also operates a buddy service.

Stevenage

Brignalls

Queensway Chambers Queensway Stevenage Hertfordshire SG1 1BA. T:01438-359311. Emergency : 01438-820339. F:01438-740127. Mon - Fri 9am - 5.30pm. Solicitor practice covering accident claims, crime, family, wills and probate, conveyancing, company and commercial. Accepts legal aid work. Emergency service. Disabled access.

Sutton

Lesbian Support Group

c/o The Women's Centre 3 Palmerston Road Sutton SM1 4QL. T:0181-661-1991. Meets on the first and third Friday of the month 8pm - 10pm.

Women's Centre

Marian Thorn 3 Palmerston Road Sutton SM1 4PL. T:0181-661-1991. Mon - Wed 10am - 2.30pm. Thurs midday - 4.30pm. Fri 10am - 5.30pm. A resource centre for all women and children.

Thatcham

Condomania UK Ltd.

Julie Long or Maria Brown Unit 5 Rivermead Pipers Way Thatcham Berkshire RG13 4EP. T:01635-874393 (24hr ansaphone). F:01635-877622. Condom suppliers and retailers.

Twickenham

Gay Ski Group

37 St Margarets Road Twickenham TW1 2LN. T:0181-892-9735. Provides contacts and information to lesbians and gays on skiing resorts and sympathetic establishments on the slopes.

Wallington

Phoenix

P O Box 103 Wallington Surrey SM6 9SJ. Social and contact group for mature gay men and their admirers.

Waltham Abbey

Lantern Trust

72 Honey Lane EN9 3BS. T:01992-714900. F:01922-712779. A registered charity which provides accredited courses for caregivers in the areas of HIV/AIDS.

Watford

Hertfordshire Gay Community

P O Box 228 Watford WD2 6DX. Social and support group for lesbians and gay men in Hertfordshire and the surrounding districts.

Windsor

Adam and Eve

29 Thames STreet SL4 1PR. T:01753-864359. Open usual pub hours. Lesbian and gay pub.

Behind Closed Doors

Keith Stenning 16 Mountbatten Square Ward Royal Windsor SL4 1SX. T:01753-869004 (24hr answerphone). Gay and straight (men only). Anxiety and phobia relaxation therapy by massage or psychology.

Greyhound

Conebrook Bypass (A4) near Heathrow Airport. T:01753-684920. Mon-Fri 8pm-2am, Sat 8pm-3am, Sun 7pm-midnight. Nearest lesbian and gay pub to Heathrow Airport.

Noah's Ark

Arthur Road. T:01753-866316. Open usual pub hours Mon - Thurs until midnight, Fri and Sat until 1am. Lesbian, gay, TV club. (Sign on the door says "Members and guests only" but this is just to fool the tourists!)

Woking

The Crescent Project

Heathside Crescent Woking Surrey GU22 7AG. T:01483-767005. F:01483-723392. 24 hours. Lesbian, gay, bisexual,straight. Provides accommodation, training, information and counselling for young people (16-25). Performs facilitation work with specific groups.

Sunrise

P O Box 26 GU21 4FB. T:01486-723816. Christian organisation which provides a free confidential service for people who are affected by HIV/ AIDS. Aims to give emotional, spiritual and practical support.

Woodford Green

Beavis (Dr A K)

4 St Barnabas Road Woodford Green IG8 7DA. T:0181-504-0032. Mon - Fri 9am - 12.30pm, 2pm - 6.30pm (Thurs pm closed). Male doctor medical practice. NHS / private. Redbridge and Waltham Forest FHSA.

Hunter Publications

Don Dawson 1a Finchingfield Avenue Woodford Green Essex IG6 7LA. T:0181-502-9644 or 0860-128948. Mon - Fri 7.30am - 12.30pm. Lesbian, gay, straight. Publishers and distributors of contact magazines. Publishes *Gay Galaxy*.

LONDON

Sexual Politics

ORDER FORM

To order titles direct from Cassell see the form at the back of the directory : here we list some 30 innovative and acclaimed new books in our Lesbian and Gay Studies, Women on Women and AIDS Awareness series.

PUB QUIZ

Throughout 1995 Cassell and *The Pink Paper* shall be running a nationwide tournament of pub quizzes. If you run a pub and would be interested in taking part, contact Cassell's Sexual Politics Quiz, Villiers House, 41/47 Strand, London WC2N 5JE.

MAKE CASH! HOLD A BOOK PARTY!

If you are interested in hosting a book party for you and your friends contact Cassell's Sexual Politics Book Party, Villiers House, 41/47 Strand, London WC2N 5JE.

MAILING LIST

For regular information about our forthcoming titles, catalogues and news of special offers and book events in your area, fill in the form below and return to Cassell's Sexual Politics Mailing List, Villiers House, 41/47 Strand, London WC2N 5JE. No charge and no obligation.

Please include my details on the Sexual Politics Mailing List for receipt of details of forthcoming titles, news of special offers and of Cassell book events:

Name ....
Address ....
....
....
....

Send to Cassell Sexual Politics Mailing List, Villiers House, 41/47 Strand, London WC2N 5JE.

LONDON Hotels, Guest Houses and B&Bs

Bromptons

294 Old Brompton Road Earls Court SW5 9JF. T:0171-373-6559. Gay men only. Accepts Visa, Access, AMEX, Diners. Earls Court tube.

Camelot Hotel

45-47 Norfolk Square Paddington W2 1RX. T:0171-723-9118 and 0171-262-1980. F:0171-402-3412. Lesbian, gay, straight, TV/TS. Accepts Visa, Access. Paddington tube.

Gloucester House Hotel

140 Cavendish Road Clapham South SW12 0DD. Clapham South tube. T:0181-675-4167. F:0181-675-4167. Lesbian, gay, straight, TV/TS. Accepts Visa, Access.

Kensington International

4 Templeton Place Earls Court SW5 9LZ. T:0171-370-4333. Lesbian, gay, straight. Accepts Visa, Access, AMEX, Diners. Earls Court tube.

Manor House Hotel

53 Manor Park Lewisham SE13 5RA. T:181-318-5590. F:0181-244-4196. Lesbian, gay, straight. Accepts Visa, Access. Disabled access.

New York Hotel

32 Philbeach Gardens Earls Court SW5 9EB. T:0171-244-6884. F:0171-370-4691. Lesbian, gay, straight. Visa, Access, AMEX. Earls Court tube.

Number 7 Guesthouse

7 Josephine Avenue Brixton SW2 2JU. T:0181-674-1880 (phone and minicom). F:0181-671-6032. Lesbian, gay. No smoking. Accepts Visa, Access. Brixton tube.

Number 16 Hotel

16 Sumner Place South Kensington SW7. T:0171-589-5232. Lesbian, gay, straight. Accepts Visa, Access, AMEX, Diners. South Kensington tube.

Philbeach Hotel

30 Philbeach Gardens Earls Court SW5 9EB. T:0171-373-1244 (bookings) or 0171-373-4544 (visitors). Lesbian, gay, TV/TS. Accepts Visa, Access, AMEX. Earls Court tube.

Redcliffe Hotel

268 Fulham Road SW10 9EW. T:0171-823-3494. F:0171-351-2467. Lesbian, gay, TV/TS. Accepts Visa, Access, AMEX. Earls Court or South Kensington tubes.

Reeves Hotel for Women

48 Shepherds Bush Green W12 8PJ. T:0181-740-1158. Lesbian, straight (women only) hotel. Open all year, residents car park. Accepts Visa, AMEX. No disabled access. Shepherds Bush tube.

Richmond House Hotel

38b Charlewood Street Victoria SW1V 2DX. T:0171-834-4577. F:0171-630-7467. Lesbian, gay, straight hotel. Pimlico or Victoria tube.

Rogers B&B

Clive Rogers 59a Golders Green Road

Golders Green NW11 8EL. T:0181-458-6870. Gay, TV / TS. Bed and breakfast accommodation in a private flat. Golders Green tube.

Wanstead Guest House

39 Woodlands Avenue Wanstead E11 3RA. T:0181-989-3466. Lesbian, gay, straight. Wanstead tube.

Bars, Clubs, Pubs, Cafes, Restaurants

Ace of Clubs

52 Piccadilly W1. T:0171-408-4457. Sat 9.30am - 4am. Lesbian club. Green Park tube.

Amazonas Restaurant

75 Westbourne Grove W2. Mon 7pm - 11.30pm. Tues - Thurs midday - 2.30pm, 7pm - 11.30pm. Fri Sat midday - 2.30pm, 7pm - 1am. Sun 7pm - 10.30pm. Lesbian, gay, straight restaurant.

Angel

65 Graham Street Islington N1. T:0171-608-2656. Mon - Sat midday - midnight. Sun midday - 11.30pm. Lesbian, gay cafe and bar. Angel tube.

Anvil

88 Tooley Street SE1. T:0171-407-0371. Tues - Sun 8.30pm - late. Gay leather bar. London Bridge tube.

Artful Dodger

139 Southgate Road N1. T:0171-226-0841. Mon - Fri 5pm - midnight. Sat midday - 11pm.Sun midday - 3pm, 7pm - 10.30pm. Lesbian, gay pub.

Artful Dodger

Brunner Road Walthamstow E17. T:0181-520-4836. Mon Tues 7pm - 11pm. Wed - Fri midday - 3pm, 7pm - 11pm. Sat midday - 4.30pm, 7pm - 11pm. Sun midday - 3pm, 7pm - 10.30pm. Gay pub.

Attic Bar

The Peacock 13/14 Maiden Lane Covent Garden WC2. T:0171-836-8260. Mon - Sat 5.30pm - 11pm. Gay pub. Covent Garden tube.

Attitude @ The Trafalgar

Trafalgar Avenue SE15. T:0171-701-2175. Mon - Fri 7pm - 11pm. Sat midday - 11pm. Sun midday - 3pm, 7pm - 10.30pm. Gay pub.

Backstreet

Wentworth Mews Burdett Road E3. T:0181-981-5812. Thurs - Sat 10pm - 3am. Sun 9pm - 1am. Gay (leather/rubber) club.

Balans

60 Old Compton Street W1. T:0171-437-5212. Mon - Sat 9am - 1.30am. Sun 9am - midnight. Lesbian, gay straight cafe. Piccadilly Circus tube.

Bam-b's

7 Plough Way Surrey Quays SE16. T:0171-237-7928. Thurs - Sat 7pm - 11pm. Lesbian bar. Surrey Quays tube.

Bell

257-259 Pentonville Road N1. T:0171-837-5617. Mon - Sat 1pm - 2am. Sun 5pm - midnight. Lesbian and gay bar and club. Kings Cross tube.

Benjys

562a Mile End Road E3. T:0181-980-6427. Sun 9pm - 1am. Gay

club. Mile End tube.

Bistro Carapace

30 Winchester Street SW1. T:0171-828-3366. Gay restaurant. Mon - Sat 7pm - 11pm. Sun 12.30pm - 3pm , 7pm - 10.30pm. Victoria tube.

Black Cap

171 Camden High Street NW1. T:0171-485-1742. Mon - Sat 1pm - 2am. Sun midday - 3pm, 7pm - 10.30pm. Gay pub and club. Camden Town tube.

Block

1/5 Parkfield Street Islington N1. T:0171-226-7453. Sun & Mon 11pm - 3am. Fri & Sat 11pm - 5am. Gay club. Angel tube.

Box

Seven Dials 22 Monmouth Street Covent Garden WC2. T:0171-240-5828. Mon - Sat 11am - 11pm. Sun midday - 10.30pm. Lesbian and gay cafe and bar. Lesbian only Sunday evening (Girl Bar). Covent Garden tube.

Bridge

425 New Kings Road SW6. T:0171-736-2324. Mon - Thurs midday - 1am, Fri - Sat midday - 3am. Sun midday - 3pm, 7pm - midnight. Putney Bridge tube.

Brief Encounter

42 St Martins Lane WC2. T:0171-240-2221. Mon - Sat midday - 11.30pm. Sun midday - 3pm, 7pm - 10.30pm. Gay bar. Leicester Square tube.

Brixtonian Backyard

4 Neals Yard. Covent Garden WC2. T:0171-240-2769. Daily 12.30pm - 11pm. Sat evening women only (Wow Bar). Lesbian, gay, straight bar and cafe. Covent Garden tube.

Bromptons

294 Old Brompton Road SW5. T;0171-370-1344. Mon - Wed 8pm - 1am, Thurs - Sat 8pm - 2am Sun 8pm - midnight. Gay bar and club. Earls Court tube.

Bull and Pump

72 Shoreditch High Street E1. T:0171-739-4365. Mon - Sat 5pm - 11pm. Sun 7pm - 10.30pm. Gay pub. Liverpool Street tube.

Carioca @ Ruby's

49 Carnaby Street W1. T:0171-287-3957. Sun 3.15 onwards. Lesbian and gay tea dance. Oxford Circus tube.

Central Station

37 Wharfdale Road N1. T:0171-278-3294. Mon - Wed 5pm - 1am, Thurs 5pm - 3am, Fri 5pm - 5am, Sat midday - 5am, Sun midday - midnight. Gay pub and club. Kings Cross tube.

Champion

1 Wellington Terrace Bayswater Road W2. T:0171-229-5056. Mon - Sat midday - 11pm. Sun midday - 3pm, 7pm - 10.30pm. Gay pub.

Cheekies @ The Frog and Night Gown

148 Old Kent Road SE1. T:0171-701-1689. Sun 7pm - midnight. Mainly lesbian pub.

City of Quebec

12 Old Quebec Street W1. T:0171-629-6159. Mon - Sat 11am - 11pm. Sun midday - 3pm, 7pm - 11pm. Gay pub. Marble Arch tube.

Clockhouse

156 Clapham Park Road SW4. T:0171-622-2597. Mon - Fri 5pm - 11pm, Sat midday - 11pm. Sun midday - 10.30pm. Lesbian, gay, straight bar. Clapham Common tube.

Club 180

180 Earls Court Road SW5. T:0171-835-1826. Mon - Sat 10pm - 2am. Gay club. Earls Court tube.

Coleherne

261 Old Brompton Road SW5. T:0171-373-9859. Daily 11am - 11pm. Earls Court tube.

Comptons

53 Old Compton Street W1. T:0171-437-4445. Mon - Sat midday - 11.30pm. Sun 7pm - 10.30pm. Gay pub. Leicester Square tube.

Creole Garden

85 Battersea Rise SW11. T:0171-924-4454. Daily 6pm - 11pm. Lesbian and gay restaurant.

Crews

14 Upper St Martins Lane WC2. T:0171-379-4880. Mon - Sat midday - 11pm. Sun midday - 3pm, 7pm - 10.30pm. Gay bar. Leicester Square tube.

Cruella's @ WKD

18 Kentish Town Road NW1. T:0171-267-1869. Last Wed of the month 8pm - late. Women only cafe /bar/disco. Camden Town tube.

Detour

261 Old Brompton Road SW5. T:0171-373-9859. Sun 3pm - 11pm. Gay cafe and bar. Earls Court tube.

Diva Dive @ Club Tiempo

64/65 Wilton Road SW1. Fri 9pm - 2am. Lesbian only club. Victoria tube.

Dress Circle @ Silver Screen Cafe

233 Earls Court Road W8. T:0171-370-5700. Thurs evening. Lesbian only cafe/bar upstairs. Earls Court tube.

Drill Hall

16 Chenies Street WC1. T:0171-631-1353. Mon 6pm - 11pm. Women only bar. Theatre and performance venue rest of the week which showcases lesbian and gay performers predominently. Goodge Street tube.

Duke of Clarence

140 Rotherfield Street N1. T:0171-226-6526. Mon - Fri 5.30pm - 11pm. Sat 7pm - 11pm. Sun midday - 3pm, 7pm - 10.30pm. Women's pub with pool room and beer garden. Food available.

Duke of Wellington

119 Balls Pond Road N1. T:071-249-3729. Mon - Fri 6pm - midnight. Sat 1pm - midnight. Sun midday - 3pm, 7pm - 10.30pm. Women only room. Lesbian and gay pub.

Eagle

2 Shepherdess Walk, City Road N1. T:0171-253-4715. Sat midday - 11pm, Sun midday - 3pm, 7pm - 10.30pm. Gay pub. Old Street tube.

Earls

180 Earls Court Road SW5. T:0171-835-1826. Mon - Sat 4pm - midnight, Sun midday - midnight. Gay pub. Earls Court tube.

Edge

11 Soho Square W1. T:0171-379-4880.

T:0171-439-1223. Mon - Thurs 11am - 1am. Fri - Sat 10am - 1am. Sun midday - 10.30pm. Lesbian, gay, straight cafe and bar. Tottenham Court Road tube.

Edward VI

25 Bromfield Street N1. T:0171-704-0745. Mon - Sat midday - midnight. Sun midday - 3pm, 7pm - 11.30pm. Gay pub. Angel tube.

Eliza Doolittle's

3 Ossulston Street NW1. Fri 7.30pm - 11pm. Sat 8pm - late. Women only nights at straight pub. Euston tube.

Empire

Little Turnstile High Holborn WC1. T:0171-405-6791. Mon - Fri midday - midnight. Sat 7pm - 11pm. Gay and straight pub. Holborn tube.

Fannys

305a North End Road W14. T:0171-385-9359. Tues - Sat 7pm - late. Lesbian, gay, bisexual, TV/TS pub.

Father Redcap

319 Camberwell Road SE5. T:0171-708-4474. Mon - Sat midday - 11pm, Sun midday - 3pm, 7pm - 10.30pm. Lesbian and gay pub.

First Out

52 St Giles High Street WC2. T:0171-240-8042. Mon - Sat 10am - 11pm. Sun 1pm - 10.30pm. Women only Sat evening. Lesbian and gay cafe and bar. Tottenham Court Road tube.

Fist @ Club 101

Tinworth Street SE11. Last Friday of the month 10pm - 4am . Lesbian and gay fetish club. Vauxhall tube.

Fountain

36 Deptford Broadway SE8. T:0181-692-1954. Mon - Sat midday - 3pm, 7pm - 11pm, Sun midday - 3pm, 7pm - 10.30pm. Gay pub. New Cross tube.

Freedom

60-66 Wardour Street W1. T:0171-734-0071. Daily 9am - 11pm. Lesbian, gay, straight cafe and bar. Piccadilly Circus tube.

Gate

Above Ryman's 68 Notting Hill Gate W2. Mon - Sat 10pm - 1am. Sun 2.30pm - 7pm, 10pm - midnight. Gay club. Notting Hill tube.

Gillys

Wild Rent Bermondsey SE1. T:0171-403-2729. Mon - Sat midday - midnight. Sun midday - 3pm, 7pm - 10.30pm. Gay bar and club. Borough tube.

Girls on Top @ The Royal Oak

62 Glenthorne Road W6. T:0181-748-2781. Wed 7pm onwards. Mainly lesbian bar. Hammersmith tube.

Gloucester

1 King William Walk Greenwich SE10. T:0181-858-2666. Mon - Sat 11am - 11pm. Sun midday - 3pm,7pm - 10.30pm. Gay pub.

(Le) Gourmet

312 Kings Road SW3 5UH. T:0171-352-4483. Mon - Sat 6.30pm - 11.30pm. Sun 1.30pm - 3.30pm, 7pm - 11pm. Lesbian, gay, straight, TV / TS restaurant.

Grapes

121 Borough High Street SE1. T:0171-407-1856. Mon - Sat 11am - 11pm. Sun

midday - 10.30pm. Gay pub. London Bridge tube.

Green Room

62 Lavender Hill Battersea SW11. T:0171-223-4618. Daily 7pm - late and Sun lunch 1pm - 4.30pm. Lesbian, gay, straight restaurant.

Halfway to Heaven

7 Duncannon Street WC2. T:0171-930-8312. Mon - Fri 3pm - 11pm, Sat 1pm - 11pm. Sun 7pm - 10.30pm. Gay pub. Charing Cross tube.

Heaven

Villiers Street WC2. T:0171-839-5210. Wed (Fruit Machine) 10pm - late, Fri (Garage) 10pm - late, Sat 10pm - late. Lesbian and gay club. Embankment tube.

Hujo's

11 Berwick Street W1. T:0171-734-5144. Mon - Sat 10am - midnight. Piccadilly Circus tube. Lesbian, gay, straight cafe.

ICA (Institute of Contemporary Arts)

The Mall SW1. T:0171-930-0493. Lesbian, gay, straight multi-media arts institute which regularly programmes lesbian and gay events. Membership available. Cafe and bar. Charing Cross tube.

Jonathons

1st Floor 16 Irving Street WC2. T:0171-930-4770. Mon - Sat 3pm - 11pm. Sun 1pm - 3pm, 7pm - 10.30pm. Gay bar. Leicester Square tube.

Kings Arms

Poland Street W1. T:0171-734-5907. Mon - Sat midday - 11pm, Sun midday - 3pm, 7pm - 10.30pm. Lesbian and gay bar. Oxford Circus tube.

King William IV

77 Hampstead High Street NW3. T:0171-435-5747. Mon - Sat 11am - 11pm, Sun midday - 3pm, 7pm - 10.30pm. Gay pub. Hampstead tube.

Kit Kat Cafe

1166 London Road Norbury SW16. T:0181-764-9044. Wed - Fri 7pm - midnight. Sat Sun midday - midnight. Sat women only. Lesbian and gay club and restaurant.

Koko

50 Old Compton Street W1. Open every day 9am -11pm. Lesbian, straight, gay cafe.

Kudos

10 Adelaide Street WC2. T:0171-379-4573. Mon - Fri 11am - 11pm. Sat 10am - 11pm. Sun midday - 10.30pm. Gay cafe and bar.

La Liberte @ The New York Hotel

32 Philbeach Gardens Earls Court SW5. Daily 7pm - 11pm. Gay restaurant. Earls Court tube.

Lantern Bar

255 Gipsy Road West Norwood SE27. T:0181-766-6348. Mon - Thurs 11am - 11pm. Fri Sat 11am - midnight. Sun midday - 3pm, 7pm - 10.30pm. Gay bar.

La Rue's

Manette Street W1. T:0171-437-5002. Mon - Sat midday - 2.30am. Leicester Square tube. Gay cafe and bar.

Le Beau Jest

94 Merton Road SW18. T:0181-870-

5040. Mon - Sat 7pm - midnight. Lesbian, gay, straight bar.

Little Apple

98 Kennington Lane SE11. T:0171-735-2039. Mon - Sat midday - midnight. Sun midday - 11pm. Lesbian, gay, straight pub. Kennington tube.

Locomotion

First Floor Bar 18 Bear Street WC2. T:0171-839-3252. Mon - Sat midday - 11pm. Sun 3pm - 10.30pm. Lesbian, gay cafe bar. Leicester Square tube.

London Apprentice (L.A.)

333 Old Street EC1. T:0171-250-3409. Mon - Thurs 9am - 3am, Fri Sat 9pm - 5am, Sun 9pm -4am. Gay bar and club. Old Street tube.

Lone Sailor

62 Thames Street SE10. T:0181-858-7906. Mon - Sat 11am - 11pm, Sun midday - 3pm, 7pm - 10.30pm. Gay pub.

Lowdown

Falconberg Mews W1. T:0171-437-1660. Mon - Sat 5pm - 3am. Sun 7.30pm - 11.30pm. Gay bar and club.Tottenham Court Road tube.

Maggie Jones

6 Old Court Place Kensington Church Street W8 4PL. T:0171-937-6464. Lesbian, gay, straight restaurant.

Malt and Hops

33 Caledonian Road N1. T:0171-837-9558. Mon - Fri 11am - 11pm. Sat midday - 11pm. Sun midday - 3pm, 7pm - 10.30pm. Lesbian, gay, straight pub. Kings Cross tube.

Manhattans

268 Fulham Road SW10. T:0171-823-3494. Mon - Sat 7pm - 1am. Gay bar and club.

Manleys

8-9 Manley Court Stoke Newington N16 0PB. T:0171-249-4566. Lesbian, gay, TV / TS. Tues - Sat midday - 6pm. Tea room with monthly art exhibitions.

Market Tavern

Market Towers 1 Nine Elms Lane SW8. T:0171-622-5655. Mon Wed Thur 9pm - 4am. Fri Sat 9pm - 5am. Sun 1pm - 7.30pm, 9pm - 2am. Vauxhall tube. Gay bar and club.

New Cotton Inn

2 St Pauls Way Bow E3. Mon - Sat 11am - midnight. Sun midday - 3pm, 7pm - 10.30pm. Gay pub.

Old Compton Cafe

34 Old Compton Street W1. 24-hours. Lesbian and gay cafe. T:0171-439-3309.

Oval House Theatre

52 Kennington Oval. T:0171-735-2786.Lesbian, gay straight theatre and cafe.

Partners

305 Kennington Road SE11. T:0171-582-9900. Mon - Sat 5pm - midnight. Sun 1pm - 10.30pm. Gay bar and cafe. Kennington tube.

Patisserie Valerie

44 Old Compton Street. T:0171-437-3466. Mon - Fri 8am - 8pm. Sat 8am - 7pm. Sun 10am - 5.30pm. Lesbian, gay, straight cafe. Leicester Square tube. Also at 215 Brompton Road SW3. T:0171-823-9971. Earls Court tube.

Peasant

240 St John Street EC1. Mon - Sat midday - 11pm. Lesbian, gay straight restaurant. Angel tube.

Penny Farthing

135 King Street Hammersmith W6. T:0181-748-7045. Mon - Sat midday - 11pm. Sun midday - 3pm, 7pm - 10.30pm. Gay pub. Hammersmith tube.

Pride

269 Stepney Way E1. T:0171-265-9375. Mon - Thurs 8pm - midnight. Fri and Sat 8pm - 2am. Gay pub.

Queen's Arms

63 Court Hill Lewisham SE13. T:0181-852-8041. Mon - Sat 11am - 11pm. Sun midday -3pm, 7pm - 10.30pm. Gay pub.

Queens Arms

223 Hanworth Road Hounslow. T:0181-570-9724. Mon - Sat 11am - 11pm. Sun midday - 3pm, 7pm - 10.30pm. Gay pub. Hounslow tube.

Queen of England

320 Goldhawk Road Hammersmith W6. T:0181-741-0457. Mon -Sat 11am - 11pm. Sun midday - 10.30pm. Gay pub. Stamford Brook tube.

Queens Head

27 Tryon Street Chelsea SW3. Mon - Sat 11am - 11pm. Sun midday - 3pm, 7pm - 10.30pm. Gay pub. Sloane Square tube.

Rage @ Caspers

2 St Annes Court W1. T:0171-494-4941. Mon 6pm - 1am. Gay bar and restaurant with telephones on the tables. Tottenham Court Road tube.

Red

8 Egerton Garden Mews Knightsbridge SW3 2EH. T:0171-584-7007 or 0171-584-0972. Lesbian, gay, straight, TV / TS restaurant.

Reflections

8 Bridge Road E15. T0181-519-5115. Mon - Thurs 9am - 2am, Fri - Sat 9pm - 5am. Sun midday - 1am. Lesbian and gay bar and club.

Rose and Crown

13 Mare Street Hackney E8. T:0181-986-7497. Mon - Sat midday - midnight. Sun midday - 3pm, 7pm - 10.30pm. Lesbian, gay, straight pub. Bethnal Green tube.

Rossana's

17 Strutton Ground Westminster SW1P 2HY. T:0171-233-1701. Mon - Fri 7pm onwards. Mon - Wed lesbian and gay restaurant. Thurs and Fri lesbian only.

Roundhouse

Woolwich Manor Way Woolwich. T:0171-476-1320. Mon - Sat 11am - 11pm. Sun midday - 3pm, 7pm - 10.30pm. Lesbian and gay pub.

Royal George

7 Selby Street Vallance Road E1. T:0171-377-8828. Mon - Sat 11am - 11pm. Sun midday - 3pm, 7pm - 10.30pm. Gay pub.

Royal Oak

73 Columbia Road E2. T:0171-739-8204. Mon - Sat 11am - late. Sun 8am - 5pm, 7pm - 11pm. Gay pub.

Royal Oak

62 Glenthorne Road Hammersmith W6. T:0181-748-2781.Hammersmith tube. T:0181-748-2781. Mon - Sat

midday - 2am. Sun midday - midnight. Gay pub.

Royal Oak

79 Green Lanes N16. T:0171-354-2791. Mon - Sat 11am - 11pm. Sun midday - 3pm, 7pm - 10.30pm. Lesbian, gay, straight pub.

Roys West End

11 Upper St Martins Lane WC2. T:0171-836-5121. Mon - Fri midday - midnight. Sat 6pm - midnight. Gay restaurant. Leicester Square tube.

Salmon and Compasses

58 Penton Street Islington N1. T;0171-837-3891. Mon - Sat midday - 2am. Sun midday - 5pm, 7pm - 10.30pm. Gay pub. Angel tube.

Septembers

Hackney Road E2. T:0171-739-9854. T:0171-739-9851. Daily 8pm - late. Gay pub.

79CXR

79 Charing Cross Road W1. Mon - Thurs midday - 1am.. Fri - Sat midday - 1am. Sun midday - 11.30pm. Leicester Square tube.

Ship and Whale

2 Gulliver Street SE16. T:0171-237-3305. Mon - Sat 8pm - 2am. Sun midday - 3pm, 8pm - midnight. Lesbian and gay bar. Surrey Quays tube.

Silver Screen Cafe

233 Earls Court Road SW5. T:0171-370-5700. Mon - Sat midday - 11pm. Sun 1pm - 10.30pm. Lesbian, gay, straight bar and cafe. Earls Court tube.

Stella's

68 Brigstock Road Thornton Heath. T:0181-689-7887. Mon - Fri 5pm - 11pm. Sat 11am - 11pm. Sun 7pm - 10.30pm. Lesbian and gay bar.

Steph's Restaurant

39 Dean Street W1V 5AP. T:0171-734-5976. Mon - Thurs midday - 3pm, 5.30pm - 11.30pm. Fri Sat 5.30pm - midnight. Lesbian, gay, straight, restaurant.

Substation

Falconberg Court W1. Mon - Fri 5pm - 3am. Sat 10.30pm - 6am (men only). Sundays 7pm - 1am (women only). Lesbian and gay bar and club. Tottenham Court Road tube.

Thats Grand!

98 Kennington Road SE11. T:0171-735-2039. Mon - Thurs 7pm - midnight. Fri 6pm - midnight. Sat 7pm - midnight. Sun 1pm - 11.30pm. Gay bar.

13's Piano Bar

13 Gerrard Street W1. Mon - Sat 10pm - 3am. Gay bar. Piccadilly Circus tube.

Truly Western Experience @ Powerhaus

1 Liverpool Road N1. 2nd Tues of the month. 8pm - late. Lesbian country and western dance night. Angel tube.

Two Brewers

114 Clapham High Street Clapham SW4. T:0171-622-3621. Mon - Thurs 6pm - 1am. Fri Sat 6pm - 2am. Sun midday - 3pm, 7pm - midnight. Gay pub and club.

Vauxhall Tavern

372 Kennington Lane SE11. T:0171-582-

0833. Mon & Thurs 8pm - 1am. Tues & Wed 8pm - midnight. Fri & Sat 8pm - 2am. Sun midday - 3pm, 7pm - 10.30pm. Lesbian and gay pub. Fri 9pm - 2am Vixens at The Vauxhall, women only cabaret and bar.

Vibrating Passions @ Carpenters Arms

70 Whitfield Street W1. T:0171-636-1250. Sun midday - 3pm, 7pm - 10.30pm. Women only bar. Warren Street tube.

Victoria

451 Queensbridge Road E8. T:0171-249-7393. Mon - Wed midday - 5pm, 7pm - midnight. Thurs - Sat noon - 5pm, 7pm - 2am. Sun 1pm - 8pm. Thurs evening women only. Fri evening men only. Lesbian and gay pub.

Village Soho

81 Wardour Street W1. T:0171-436-2468. Mon - Sat 11.30am - 11pm. Sun midday - 10.30pm. Gay cafe and bar. Piccadilly Circus tube.

Wagamama

4 Streatham Street WC1. T:0171-323-9223. Mon - Fri midday - 2.30pm, 6pm - 11pm. Sat 1pm - 3pm, 6pm - 11pm. Lesbian, gay, straight restaurant. Tottenham Court Road tube.

White Swan

556 Commercial Road E14. T:0171-791-0747. Sun - Thurs 8.30pm - midnight. Fri and Sat 8.30pm - 2am. Gay pub and club.

Wilde about Oscar

30-31 Philbeach Gardens SW6. Daily 7pm - midnight. Sun 12.30pm - 4.30pm. Gay restaurant. Earls Court tube.

Woodman

119 Stratford High Road E15. T:0181-519-8765. Mon - Sat 11am - 11pm. Sun midday - 3pm, 7pm - 10.30pm. Gay pub.

Yard

57 Rupert Street W1. T:0171-437-2652. Mon - Sat midday - 11pm. Gay bar. Piccadilly Circus tube.

Ye Old Rose and Crown

1 Crooms Hill SE10. T:0181-858-0154. Mon - Sat 11am - 11pm. Sun midday - 3pm, 7pm - 10.30pm. Gay pub.

Businesses

Accomodation Address Service

66 Castle Road NW1 8SN. T:0171-267-7887. Mon - Sat 9.30am - 7pm. Sun 10am - 1pm. Confidential service for lesbians and gay men who choose not to receive some or all of their mail at their home.

Alexandra Surgery

125 Alexandra Park Road N22 4UN. T:0181-888-2518. Mon - Fri 9am - midday, 4.30pm - 6.30pm (not Wed). NHS and private patients. Offers acupuncture. Enfield and Harringay FHSA. Disabled access.

Alfalfa Productions

225a Brecknock Road N19. T:0171-284-0551. Television production company which produced part of Channel Four's lesbian and gay *Out* programme.

All Out

Productions

49 Wellington Street Covent Garden WC2E 7BN. T:0171-240-2070. F:0171-240-2071. Contact David Cook and David Prosser. Independent lesbian and gay radio production company. Produces *Out This Week* for Radio 5 (909MW and 693MW at 9.35pm each Sat).

Amplett Lissimore

29 Westlow Street Crystal Palace SE19 3RW and 103 Sydenham Road Sydenham SE26 5UA. T:0181-771-5254, F:0181-771-9276 (Crystal Palace). T:0181-778-2738, F:0181-676-9685 (Sydenham). Mon - Fri 9.15am - 5.30pm. Solicitor practice covering crime, conveyancing, personal injury, family, housing, general contract, wills and probate. Accepts legal aid work. Emergency service for existing clients. Disabled access.

Angelo

26 Glennie Road SE27 OLY. T:0181-761-5597 or 0850-767283. 24-hour answering service. Lesbian, gay, straight electrician and plumber.

Ashdown Building and Decorative Specialists

7 - 11 Kensington High Street W8 5NP. T:0181-3491 / 0850-741699. F:0181-547-1190. Daily 7am - 10pm. Lesbian, gay straight. Various building and decoration services.

Aston (Frannie)

28 Morrish Road Brixton SW2 4EH. T:0181-671-0581. Lesbian, gay, straight. Acupuncturist.

Attitude

Northern and Shell Tower City Harbour E14 9GL. T:0171-987-5090. Monthly gay men's style magazine. Editor: Tim Nicholson.

Avis Cycling and Leisure

70 Clerkenwell Road EC1M 5QA. T:0171-250-1534. Mon - Fri 9am - 5.30pm. Cycle shop specialising in accessories and clothing. Offers repair service.

Bhatt (Dr G B)

38 Bushey Hill Road Camberwell SE5 8QS. T:0171-703-5874. Medical practice. Male doctor. Private patients only by appointment. Lambeth Lewisham Southwark FHSA. No disabled access.

Bishop (Dr C)

79 Harley Street W1N 1AE. T:0171-486-1104. Doctor practice. Mon - Wed Fri 10am - 5pm. Private patients only. Offers plastic surgery service. Disabled access.

Boldface Typesetting and Design

17a Clerkenwell Road EC1M 5RD. T:0171-253-2014. F:0171-251-3443. Mon - Fri 9am - 6pm. Design and typesetting (Compugraphic and Applemac) with facilities for scanning, disk conversion, OCR etc.

Book Works

P O Box 3821 N5 1UY. T:0171-609-3427. Lesbian and gay. Mail order book service specialising in fiction and photographic titles.

Boyz

Pink Directory

13 Hercules Street N7 6AT. T:0171-281-2404. F:0171-263-2572 (editorial). 77 City Garden Row N1 8EZ . T:0171-608-3051 (advertising and administration) and T:0171-608-3053 , F:0171-608-2544 (accounts). Weekly gay magazine. Editor: Simon Gage.

Brentfield Medical Centre

10 Kingfisher Way Brentfield Road NW10 8TF. T:0181-459-8833. Phone for opening hours. Male and female medical practice. NHS and private. Physiotherapy. Brent and Harrow FHSA. Disabled access.

Brompton's Opticians

306 Old Brompton Road SW5. T:0171-373-5753. F:0171-370-3932. Lesbian and gay friendly opticians.

Brixton Cycles

435-437 Coldharbour Lane SW2 . T:0171-733-6055. Lesbian and gay friendly cycle and accessory shop. Repair service.

Burgess Richard

44 Chesilton Road SW6 5AB. T:0171-736-4949. Mon - Fri 9am - 6pm. Lesbian, gay, straight. Chartered Accountant offers financial advice and assistance.

Burton Judith & Co

Museum House 25 Museum Street WC1A 1JT. T:0171-491-0048. F:0171-493-9241. All lesbian solicitor practice. Covers commercial and residential conveyancing, wills and probate, company and partnership matters, family, civil actions, employment, landlord and tenant, debt personal injury. Accepts Legal Aid work. Speaks Cantonese, Italian, French and Spanish.

Capital Gay

1 Tavistock Chambers Bloomsbury Way WC1A 2SE. T:0171-242-2750. Weekly London based newspaper for lesbians and gay men. Editor: Gillian Rodgerson.

Cassell plc

Villiers House, 41-47 Strand WC2E 5JN. T:0171-839-4900. F:0171-839-1804. Mainstream publishers of sexual politics and lesbian and gay studies books (non-fiction). Contact Steve Cook, Roz Hopkins or Liz Gibbs.

Central London Law Centre

47-49 Charing Cross Road WC2H 0AN. T:0171-437-5854 (day and emergency). F:0171-734-3563. Mon - Fri 10am - 5.30pm. Employment advice Tue 3pm - 7pm. Immigration 3pm - 7pm.Law centre covering immigration, housing, employment and other areas. Accepts Legal Aid work. Speaks Bengali, Mandarin, Spanish, French, Urdu, Hindi, German and Cantonese. Home visits for disabled clients.

Chain Reaction

3 Montgomery Court St Thomas Road W4 3LE. T:0181-995-8140 or 0181-773-2909. Night club promoters for lesbian and gay venues.

Challenge Training, Advice and Consultancy

c/o Femi Otitoju, 37 Rectory Gardens N8

7PJ. T:0181-340-4167. F:0181-342-8433. Mon - Fri 10am - 5.30pm. Training and consultancy in equal opportunities and related areas.

Chelsea Funeral Directors

260b Fulham Road SW10 9EL. T:0171-352-0008.

Clone Zone

64 Old Compton Street W1 & 266 Old Brompton Road Earls Court. T:0171-287-3530. Gay run shop selling cards, magazines and sex toys.

CMA Ltd

Brain McLaughlin PO Box 48 Henley-on-Thames RG9 3NS. T:01491-572550. F:01491-411737. Office hours. Organises the Gay Lifestyles. Annual two day exhibition in London.

Cinenova

113 Roman Road E2 0HU. T:0181-981-6828. F:0181-983-4441. Lesbian and women only. Distributor of independent films and videos made by women. Publishes a catalogue.

Crip Strip Productions

Val Stein. T:0171-485-3537. Mon - Fri 10am - 6pm. Produces cartoons and illustrations to highlight lesbian and disability issues using subversive humour. Aims to further disability rights.

Cohen and Co

338 Regents Park Road Finchley N3 2LN. T:0181-346-2550. F:0181-349-2851. Mon - Fri 9.30am - 5.30pm (other times by arrangement). Solicitor practice specialising in conveyancing, debt collection, licensing, probate, wills, trusts, landlord and tenant.

Colleys

6 Bowden Street Cleaver Square SE11 4DS. T:0171-587-0880. F:0171-820-0805. Mon - Fri 9am - 5.30pm. General solicitor practice specialising in housing, family, welfare benefits, landlord and tenant.

Coote & Associates

10-14 Macklin Street Covent Garden WC2B 5NF. T:0171-430-1921, mobile 0836-637898. F:0171-430-1942. Office hours. Marketing, PR and advertising consultancy plus writing and publishing company newsletters and brochures.

Covent Garden Cycles

275 West End Lane NW6 1QS. T:0171 - 435-3725. F:0171-794-4484 and 53-55 Pimlico Road SW1W 8NE T:0171-730-6668 F:0171-730-3783 and 2 Nottingham Court WC2 9AY T:0171-836-1752. Mon-Fri 8am-7pm, Sat 10am-6pm. Lesbian and gay friendly cycle and accessory shops.

Coxon (Dr A)

78 Harley Street W1. T:0171-486-2534. Mon - Fri 9am - 6pm. Sat 9am - 12.30pm. Medical practice. Female doctor. NHS only. Partial disabled access.

Dangerous to Know

PO Box 1701 SW9 OXD. Video distribution company which specialises in international lesbian and gay films.

Daniel and Harris

338 Kilburn High Road NW6 2QN. T:0171-625-0202. F:0171-372-5029. Mon - Fri 9.30am - 5.30pm. Solicitor practice. Housing (tenant work), family, domestic violence, injunctions, personal injury, medical negligence, conveyancing, wills and probate. Accepts Legal Aid work.

Darlington & Parkinson

259 Horn Lane Acton W3 9EH. T:0181-992-5054/5055/4271/0887. Emergency:0181-812-1694. F:0181-992-8296. Mon - Fri 9.30am - 5.30pm. Solicitor practice covering crime, family, housing, immigration, mental health, probate. Accepts Legal Aid work.

Davies (Titus)

6 Lambert Street N1 1JE. T:0171-609-7200, 24-hour ansaphone. Mon - Fri 9am - 5pm. Lesbian, gay, straight. Maker of furniture tailored to customer requirements.

Davis (Dr J A)

105 Malvern Road NW6 5PU. T;0171-328-3625. Phone for surgery hours. Medical practice. Female doctor. NHS only. Brent and Harrow FHSA. Disabled access.

Daw C A & Son

27 Palace Gate W8 5LS. T:0171-584-1234. Lesbian and gay friendly. Property agency.

Dawson (Peter)

53 Cliff Point Columbia Road E2 7PP. T:0171-739-7226. Illustrator providing finished illustrations, logos, letterheads for businesses, book publishers, bars/clubs. Also trompe l'oeil finishes on walls.

Daykin Carr

416 Mare Street Hackney E8 1HP. T;0181-986-5438. F:0181-986-0216. Mon - Fri 9.30am - 1pm, 2pm - 5pm. Solicitor practice covering housing and family law. Accepts legal aid work. Speaks French.

Denovo

Syracusae Studio 4 134 Liverpool Road N1 1LA. T:0171-609-9797. F:0171-609-9798. Mon - Fri 8am - 6pm. Graphic designers. Produces brochures, corporate IDs, packaging, retail graphics, exhibitions, corporate stationery, CDi etc.

Desmond Banks and Co

25 Powis Terrace W11 1JJ. T:0171-221-1455. F:0171-229-2414. Mon - Fri 9.30am - 5.30pm. Solicitor practice covering crime, conveyancing, business law, leases and general law (not family). Accepts Legal Aid work.

Detonator

24 Offley Road SW9 OLS. T:0171-430-1921 and 0836-637968. F:0171-430-1942. Opens office hours. Publishers of *Gay to Z* Directory and *Trade Press* (GBA newsletter).

Diffley (Dr), Hodges (Dr), Brew-Graves (Dr)

1 Richmond House East Street SE17 2DU. T:0171-703-7393. Mon - Fri 10pm - midday, 4.30pm - 6.30pm (7pm Mon and Wed). NHS only.

Offers a counselling service. Lambeth, Southwark and Lewisham FHSA. Disabled access and facilities.

Diva

Millivres Ltd, Ground Floor Worldwide House 116-134 Bayham Street NW1. T:0171 482 2576. Lesbian bi-monthly lifestyle magazine. Editor: Frances Williams.

Donmall (Dr), Otty (Dr), Coyle(Dr)

Albion Street Health Centre 87 Albion Street SE16 1JX. T:0171-237-2092. Mon - Fri 9am - 6.30pm. Medical practice. Male and female doctors. NHS only. Lambeth, Lewisham and Southwark FHSA. Disabled access.

Don't Panic!

52 Dean Street Soho W1. T:0171-976-5585. F:0171-976-5587. Mail order T:0800-393-183. Lesbian and gay retail and mail order outlet selling clothing and gay paraphenalia.

Duthie Hart and Duthie

517-519 Barking Road Greengate Plaistow E13 8PT. T:0181-472-0138. Emergency 0181-471-8115. F:0181-470-7628. Mon - Fri 9am - 5.30pm. Solicitor practice covering criminal litigation, civil litigation, personal injury, matrimonial, housing, family, mental health, commercial and residential conveyancing, wills and probate. Accepts legal aid work. Emergency service. Speaks Cantonese, Greek, Bengali. Disabled access.

Earth

Glen Donovan 49 Frith Street Soho W1V 5TE. T:0171-734-3426. F:0171-734-3427. Mon - Fri 9.30am - 6pm. Lesbian, gay, straight. Travel and entertainment agent.

Ellison Communications

Unit B11 Lanterns Court E14 9TU. T:0171-712-9141 or 9151. Advertising, marketing, PR company.

Eurocom Cleaning Service

29 Hertslet Road N7 6PH. T:0171-700-0632, F:0171-700-0632. Mon - Fri 9am - 4pm. Cleaning company for lesbians and gays servicing homes, bars and offices. Also provides a cooking and care service for people with HIV and AIDS.

Eurocom Languages

29 Hertslet Road N7 6PH. T:0171-700-0632, F:0171-700-0632. Mon - Fri 9am - 4pm. Lesbian and gay language service offering tuition in your own home and office. Also translations and interpreting.

Everywoman magazine

34 Islington Green N1 8DU. T:0171-359-5496. Monthy magazine for lesbians and straight women which covers current affairs, arts, politics and health.

Expectations

75 Great Eastern Street EC2A 3HU. T:0171-739-0292. F:0171-256-0910. Mon - Thurs 11am - 7pm. Fri 11am - 8pm. Sat 11am - 9pm. Sun midday - 5pm.

Lesbian, gay, straight. Leather, rubber, fetish shop.

Fawcett Library

University of East London Calcutta House Old Castle Street E17. T:0171-283-1030 ext 570. Tues - Fri 10am - 5pm. Women's archive.

Feather (Stuart)

5e Hedgegate Court W11 1JP. T:0171-221-8399. Lesbian, gay and straight commissions accepted by artist.

Fetters

40 Fitzwilliam Road SW4 0DN. T:0171-622-1356. F:0171-622-1356. Mon - Fri 10am - 5.30pm. Lesbian, gay, straight. Suppliers of all forms of restraint equipment (mail order).

Fine (Dr J H)

68 Harley Street W1N 1AE. T:0171-636-7661 or 0171-935-3980.. Male doctor. Mon - Fri 8am - 4pm. Sat 8am - 11am. Private patients only. Offers a psychotherapy and psychiatry service.

Fitzrovia Medical Centre

31 Fitzroy Square W1P 5HH. T:0171-387-5798. Mon - Fri 9pm - 6.30pm. Medical practice. Male and female doctors. NHS and private (by appointment). Also offers acupuncture, dietician, homeopathy, counselling and psychology, physiotherapy. Kensington, Chelsea and Westminster / Camden and Islington FHSA's. Disabled access.

Fizzical Guys (Model Agency)

Frank Wallace. T:0181-675-5858 or 0956-234660. Gay, bisexual, straight modelling agency.

Fizzical Photography

Frank Wallace. T:0181-675-5858 or 0956-234660. Mon - Fri 10am - 6pm. Provides a discreet service for the processing of gay photographic material. Also provides a full photographic service.

Freedom Cars

Old Compton Street Soho W1. T:0171-734-1313. Lesbian and gay taxi service.

Garden Care and Design (Rob Knapp)

Flat 2 41a Cromwell Avenue Highgate N6 5HN. T;0181-341-3808. Gay landscape gardening service and garden maintenance.

GAY radio programme

Broadcasts Mon - Fri at 1am-3am on Spectrum 558AM. Lesbian and gay radio programme presented by Jeremy Joseph.

Gay Community Distribution Services

P O Box 3686 E9 7DQ. T:0171-594-7700. Runs a subscription service for back issues of Capital Gay. All profits are donated to lesbian and gay groups.

Gay Times

Ground Floor Worldwide House 116-134 Bayham Street Camden Town NW1. T:0171-482-2576 (editorial and advertising), T:0171-267-0021 (subscription and mail order). F:0171-284-0329. Monthly colour national lesbian and gay magazine edited

by David Smith. Published by Millivres Limited.

Gay's The Word

66 Marchmont Street WC1. T:0171-278-7654. Open Mon - Wed, Fri, Sat 10am - 6pm, Thurs 10am - 7pm, Sun 2pm - 6pm. Bookshop which stocks lesbian, gay, bisexual literature and magazines.

GBA (Gay Business Association)

Mike McCann (Chair) 225 Valley Road Streatham SW16 2AF. T:0181-677-0020. F:0181-769-1487. Office hours. A trade association for businesses serving the lesbian and gay community. Over 150 members agree to abide by the GBA's code of practice. Offers a regular newsletter, organises seminars on a variety of business topics, campaigns for equal rights and an end to discrimination and holds regular networking and social meetings.

Get Wet

BCM Box 3564 WC1N 3XX. T:0171-627-0290. Mail order business selling leather, rubber and PVC clothes, books, equipment, safer sex items, toys etc.

Gill and Co

22a Theobalds Road WC1X 8PF. T:0171-242-0404. F:0171-831-8537. Mon - Fri 10am - 6pm. Solictor practice covering immigration, criminal, personal injury, civil and commercial litigation, libel and copyright. Accepts Legal Aid work. Speaks French, Spanish and Urdu.

Glazer Delmar

223-229 Rye Lane SE15 4TZ. T:0171-639-8801. Emergency 0171-732-6911. F:0171-358-0581. Solicitor practice covering personal injury, probate wills, family, crime, immigration, conveyancing, housing, medical, negligence. Accepts Legal Aid work. Emergency service (immigration and crime only). Speaks Spanish.

GLR Gay and Lesbian London

Sat 9pm - 10pm. (94.9 FM). Lesbian and gay radio programme presented by Rebecca Sandells and Matthew Linfoot.

Gold, Lerman & Muirhead

43 Streatham Hill SW2 4TP and The Hop Exchange 24 Southwark Street SE1 1TY. T:0181-671-6611, F:0181-674-8004 (Streatham Hill) and T:0171-378-8005, F:0171-378-8025 (Southwark). Mon - Fri 9am - 5.30pm. Solicitor practice covering divorce and family, domestic violence, crime, housing, personal injury, company and commercial, wills and probate and conveyancing. Accepts Legal Aid work. Speaks German. Partial disabled access.

Greenwich Community Law Centre

187 Trafalgar Road SE10 9EQ. T:0181-853-2550. Mon - Fri 10am - 4pm (telephone). Law centre opens Mon Tues 1pm - 3pm. Thurs 6.30pm - 8pm. Law centre covering immigration, employment, housing and welfare rights. Accepts Legal Aid

work. Speaks Punjabi, Urdu, Hindi, Swahili. Disabled access.

Hackney Law Centre

236-238 Mare Street E8 1HE. T:0181-985-8364, 0181-986-9891 (emergency). F:0181-533-2018. Mon - Fri 10am - 1pm. Law centre covering immigration / asylum, employment, housing, actions against the police, education, community groups. Accepts legal aid work. Emergency service. Interpreters arranged where necessary.

Hamptons Survey and Professional

Alistair Beard Hampton House High Street Wimbledon Common SW19 5BA. T:0181-946-8717. F:0181-879-0159. Mon - Fri 9am - 6pm. Lesbian, gay, straight. Residential surveyors with a residential sales and lettings department in South West London.

Hanne and Co

251 Lavender Hill SW11 5TH. T:0171-228-0017 (also emergency number). F:0171-223-4431. Mon - Fri 9.30am - 5.30pm. Solicitor practice covering crime, family, housing, personal injury, consumer, welfare benefits, debt, conveyancing, wills and probate. Accepts Legal Aid work. Emergency paging service. Speaks French, German, Russian, Spanish, Polish, Gujerati, Hindi, Urdu.

Hanwell Health Centre

Dr Naish 20 Church Road Hanwell W7 1DR. T:0181-567-5738. Mon - Fri 8.30am - 6.30pm. Medical practice. Male doctor. NHS and private. Acupuncture, aromatherapy, yoga, aerobics, chiropractor, hypnotherapy (non-NHS), physiotherapy and gym (NHS). Ealing, Hammersmith, Hounslow FHSA. Disabled access.

Hayfield (Anne)

Flat G 219 Underhill Road SE22 0PB. T:0181-693-1618. Independent trainer on issues relating to race, sexuality, Equal Opportunites Policies, employment and women's development.

Hickman and Rose

144 Liverpool Road N1 0RE. T:0171-700-2211. Emergency 0459-138106. F:0171-609-6044. Mon - Fri 9.30am - 5.30pm. Solicitor practice covering criminal law, claims against the police. Accepts Legal Aid work. Emergency service. Speaks Hebrew.

Hodge Jones and Allen

163 Camden High Street NW1 7JY. T:0171-267-9447 (day), 0459-111192 (emergency). F:0171-267-5219. Mon - Fri 9am - 6pm. Solicitor practice covering crime, housing, personal injury, employment and discrimination. Accepts Legal Aid work. Speaks French, German, Italian, Greek, Spanish and Hindi.

Holborn Medical Centre.

64 Lambs Conduit Street WC1N 3LW. T:0171-405-3541. Mon - Fri 9am - 7pm. Medical practice.

Male and female doctors. Camden and Islington FHSA. NHS and private patients. Acupuncture, homeopathy (non NHS). Partial disabled access.

Home Zone

31 Spring Street Paddington W2 1JA. T:0171-402-3188, F:0171-402-1726. Mon - Fri 9.30am - 6pm. Lesbian, gay, straight. Residential letting agents specialising in the renting of self-contained properties.

Hoxton Health Collective

T:0171-729-4704. Mon - Wed Fri 9am - 11am, 4pm - 6pm. Thurs 4pm - 6pm. NHS only. Has a women's health worker, a practice nurse and a counsellor / psychotherapist. City and East FHSA. Disabled accessible.

Islington Green Centre of Alternative Medicine

33 Gaskin Street N1 2RY. T:0171-704-6783. Mon - Sat 10am - 7pm. Lesbian, gay, straight. Shop which sells natural health and homeopathic products.

Iveagh House Surgery

Iveagh House Loughborough Road SW9 7SE. T:0171-274-8850. F:0171-733-2102. Mon - Fri 8.30am - 11am, 3pm - 6pm. Medical practice. Male and female doctors . Lambeth, Southwark and Lewisham FHSA. NHS only. Also offers clinical psychology and a chest specialist. Disabled access.

Jackson (Dr G)

17 Pembridge Road W11 3HG. T:0171-221-0174. Mon - Fri 9.30am - midday, 3.30pm - 6pm. Medical practice. Female doctor. NHS and private. Kensington, Chelsea and Westminster FHSA.

Khaley (Shirley)

41 Penwood House Danebury Avenue SW15 4PJ. T:0181-392-2341. Mon - Fri 9am - 6pm. Lesbian, gay, straight mobile hairdressing and beauty treatment.

Kivity (Oran) (MIROM)

Neals Yard Therapy Rooms Neals Yard Covent Garden WC2H 9DP. T:0171-379-7662. Mon - Fri 9.30am - 9.30pm. Lesbian, gay, straight. Provides acupuncture and massage, advice on lifestyle and diet. Free 15 mins consultations.

KL Associates

140 Grays Inn Road WC1X 8AZ. T:0171-833-8225 or 0171-833-8225. F:0171-278-2679. Mon - Fri 10am - 10pm. Lesbian, gay, straight. Chartered Accountants offering accountancy, taxation and auditing services.

Lake (Moira)

BCM Pleiades WC1N 3XX. T:0181-943-5507. Mon - Fri. Lesbian, gay, straight. Astrology, counselling and psychotherapy.

Ladycabs

Islington (0171-833-4496), Hackney (0181-985-3254), Archway (0171-272-3019). Women's taxi service which will perform school-run.

Lavender Hill Homeopathic Centre

33 Ilminster Gardens

Battersea SW11 1PJ. T:0171-978-4519. Mon - Sat 9am - 7pm. Lesbian, gay, straight. Provides alternative health care including homeopathy, osteopathy, shiatsu and Chinese massage.

Lesbian Link

The G L I Agency BCM GLI 27 Old Gloucester Street WC1N 3XX. T:0181-687-0003. F:0181-687-0004. Mon - Sat 9.30pm - 6pm. Lesbian and gay introduction agency for one-to-one friendships only.

Lesbus Removals

92a Leswin Road N16 7ND. T:0171-254-9766 (24-hour answerphone). Mon - Sat. Lesbian and gay. Small and large removals, short and long distance.

Lewisham Lesbian Mothers Group

c/o 308 Brownhill Road Catford E8. Meets on the 1st Sun of each month. Discussion and support group. Free creche and activities.

Leyton Green Neighbourhood Health Service

180 Essex Road E10 6BT. T:0181-539-0756. Mon Tues Fri 9am - 1pm, 4.30pm - 6.30pm. Wed 9am - 12.15pm, 4.30pm - 6.30pm. Thurs 9am - 1pm. Health service for a designated area (ring for details). All doctors are female. NHS only. Offers osteopathy, psychotherapy and well-women clinics. Redbridge and Waltham Forest FHSA. Disabled access.

London Film Makers Co-op

42 Gloucester Avenue Camden Town NW1 8JD. T:0171-586-4806. F:0171-483-0068. Mon - Sat 10am - 6pm. Lesbian, gay straight. Film-making courses, facilities and distribution. Also has a cinema.

London Spectacle Company

6 Duke Street W1M 5AA. T:0171-486-2483/4. Lesbian and gay friendly opticians and retailers.

Lush

Unit 310 31 Clerkenwell Close EC1R 0AT. T:0171-253-2975. F:0171-490-0063 Mon- Fri 9am - 5pm. Lesbian, gay, straight. Design, manufacture and wholesale mens, ladies underwear and ladies fashion garments.

McDonnell Michael

343a St John Street EC1V 4LB. T:0171-837-5329. Lesbian, gay, straight. Provides massage and reflexology for the treatment of backache, joint and muscular problems and to reduce stress.

Malnick JP & Co

292 Upper Street Islington N1 2TU. T:0171-226-8235. Emergency 0956-326890. F:0171-609-3951. Mon - Fri 9am - 6pm. Solicitor practice covering crime, civil actions, complaints against the police, housing, wills and probate, domestic and commercial conveyancing, data protection complaints. Emergency service. Speaks Spanish.

Malexpress

27 Old Gloucester Street WC1N 3XX. T:0181-340-8644. F:0181-347-7667. Mon - Fri 10am - 6pm. Gay publications mail order service.

Market Street Health Group

52 Market Street East Ham E6 2RA. T:0181-472-0202. Mon - Fri 8am - 6pm. Medical practice. Male doctor. NHS only. City and East London FHSA. Disabled access.

Ivan Massow Associates

195 Wardour Street W1V 3FA. T:0171-494-1848. Gay financial consultants.

Millers (Solicitors)

30 Princethorpe Road SE26 4PF. T:0181-473-3924. F:0181-473-3922. Mon - Fri 9.30am - 5.30pm. Solicitor practice covering property, wills and probate, partnership and company. Speaks Spanish. Disabled access.

Millivres Ltd

283 Camden High Street NW1 7BX. Publishers of *Gay Times, Diva, Zipper, Vulcan, Overload* and Millivres Books.

Morris Sultman

108 High Road East Finchley N2 9EB. T:0181-444-1818. F:0181-444-1663. Mon - Fri 9am - 5pm. Sat 9am - midday. Lesbian, gay, straight. Independent financial advisors specialising in pensions, life assurance and lump sum investments.

Morrow Reis Designs

36 Leysfield Road W12 9JF. T:0181-749-5898. Interior designers.

New Cross Natural Therapy Centre Ltd

Sarah Leigh 394 New Cross Road SE14 6TY. T:0181-469-0858. Mon - Sat 9am - 9pm. Lesbian, gay, straight. Offers a range of alternative therapies practiced by qualified practioners.

New Surgery

31 Linom Road London SW4 7PB. T:0171-274-4220. Mon - Fri 8.30am - 6.30pm. Sat 9.30am - 11.30am. Medical practice. Male and female doctors. NHS only. Acupuncture, clinical psychology, chiropody, minor surgery. Lambeth, Southwark and Lewisham Health Commission. Disabled access.

Newtec

Caroline Grant 22 Deanery Street Stratford E15 4LP. T:0181-519-5843. F:0181-519-9704. Mon - Fri 9am - 5pm. Training of women in manual skills and new technology (women only).

No Fuss Feasts

Andrew Crisp 5 De Beauvoir Court Northchurch Road Islington N1 3NX. T:0171-226-7087. F:0171-226-7087. Mon - Fri 9am - 6pm. Sat 10am - 6pm. Lesbian, gay, straight outside catering.

North Islington Law Centre

161 Hornsey Road Hornsey N7 6DU. T:0171-607-2461. F:0171-700-0072. Mon 10.30am - 2.30pm. Wed 10.30pm - 2.30pm. Thurs 1.30pm - 5.30pm. Fri 9.30am - 1.30pm. Covers

immigration, housing, employment. Accepts Legal Aid work. Speaks Punjabi, Hindi and Gujerati. Disabled access and toilet.

North Kensington Law Centre

74 Golborne Road W10 5PS. T:0181-969-7473 (also emergency number). F:0181-968-0934. Mon, Tues, Thurs, Fri 10am - 1pm, 2pm - 6pm. Wed 2pm - 6pm. Covers community care, employment, education, housing, crime, human rights and immigration. Accepts Legal Aid work. Emergency service for people detained by the police. Disabled access.

North Lambeth LAw Centre

14 Bowden Street SE11 4DS. T:0171-582-4425 or 0171-582-4373. F:0171-582-2148. Mon and Fri 10am - 1.30pm, Wed and Thurs 2pm - 5.30pm. Covers housing, employment, immigration, welfare benefits for people who live in SE1 and SE11. Accepts Legal Aid work. Speaks French and Spanish.

Onlywomen Press

71 Great Russell Street W1. Lesbian feminist independent publishing house which published fiction and non-fiction books.

OPM Development Consultants

Kamil Kellner 59 Kentish Town Road London NW1X 8NX. T:0171-284-1694. Gay business and managment consultancy for small businesses, local government and the voluntary sector. Also offers training courses.

Osmond Bard and Co

413 Hoe Street E17 9AR. T:0181-520-2182. Emergency numbers 0860-343562, 0860-870931. F:0181-509-3170. Mon - Fri 9am - 5.30pm. Solicitor practice covering criminal, matrimonial, conveyancing, corporate affairs, debts, employment, housing, consumer, bankruptcy, off-shore trusts, Spanish properties, landlord / tenant. Accepts legal aid work. Emergency service. Speaks Afrikaana, Dutch, German and French.

Out on a Limb Limited

c/o Val Martin Battersea Studios Television Centre Thackeray Road SW8 3TW. T:0171-498-9643, F:0171-498-1494. Mon - Fri 10am - 6pm. Film and video distributors of material made by or of interest to lesbians and gays.

Ova Women's Music Resource Centre

Highgate Newtown Community Centre 25 Bertram Street N19. T:0171-281-2528. Recording studio and tuition open to women and girls.

Parfett (Michael)

Unit 407 Clerkenwell Workshops 31 Clerkenwell Close EC1R 0AT. T:0171-490-8768. F:0171-490-0063. Mon - Fri 9am - 6pm. Lesbian, gay, straight. Antique restoration and conservation specialising in musical instruments, gilding and fine antiques.

Park House Medical Centre

T:0181-969-7711. Mon - Fri 8am - 6pm. NHS and private. Brent and Harrow, Camden and Islington, Westminster, Chelsea, Barnet, Hammersmith and Hounslow FHSA's. Offers manipulation. Disabled access.

Phintons

Phillippe Hinton 41 Chester Court Lomond Grove Camberwell SE5 7HS. Lesbian, gay, straight. T:0171-703-5347. Mon - Fri 9am - 6pm. Painter, decorator and interior floor and wall tiler, paper hanging, plastering and carpentry.

Pink Paper

13 Hercules Street N7 6AT. T:0171-272-2155. F:0171-263-2572. Lesbian and gay weekly free newspaper. Editor: Alison Gregory.

Pink Property Services

3rd Floor 60-62 Old Compton Street Soho W1. T:0171-734-3118. 24-hour answerphone. Lesbian and gay residential letting agency.

Piranha Productions

United House North Road N7 9DP. T:0171-607-3355. Lesbian, gay, straight television production company. Produced part of Channel Four *Out* series.

Pitshanger Family Practice

Dr Simon Valentine 209 Pitshanger Lane W5 1RQ. T:0181-997-4747. Phone for surgery times. Ealing Hammersmith and Hounslow FHSA. NHS and private. Disabled access.

Plumstead Community

105 Plumstead High Street Plumstead SE18 1SB. T:0181-855-9817. F:0181-316-7903. Law centre covering employment, housing, immigration, welfare rights plus advice in other areas for people who live in SE2, SE9, SE18 and SE28. Accepts Legal Aid work. Speaks Punjabi, Gugerati, Hindi, Urdu, French and Spanish. Disabled access.

Pollecoff Rangeley

123/125 City Road EC1V 1JB. T:0171-608-2568. F:0171-808-2751. Office hours. Solicitor practice with a large gay clientele. Covers all aspects of legal work.

Powell Spencer and Partners

290 Kilburn High Road NW6 2DB. T:0171-624-8888. Emergency:01459-118181. F:0171-328-1221. Mon - Fri 8.30am - 6.30pm. Solicitor practice covering criminal defence, child care, personal injury. Accepts Legal Aid work. Emergency service. Speaks Spanish. Disabled access and facilities.

Practice (The)

Matthew Kalitowski 17 Mansell Road N4 2EF. T:0171-354-9879. 24-hr answerphone. Mon - Sat office hours and evenings. Lesbian, gay, straight hypnotherapy and psychotherapy service.

Prowler Press Ltd

33 Highgate High

Street N6 5JT. T:0181-348-9963. F:0181-348-0023. Mon - Fri 10am - 6pm. Gay picture magazine publishers and distributors, mail order, video makers and book distributors.

Queensbridge Road Surgery

206 Queensbridge Road Hackney E8 3NB. T:0171-254-1101. Mon Wed Thurs 9am - 7pm, Tues 9am - 8pm, Fri 9am - 6pm. Medical practice. Male and female doctors. City and East London FHSA. No disabled access.

Queer Steps

Spike T:0181-802-0492. Queer Ballroom and Latin American dance group. Will instruct and perform for charities, groups, at fundraisers, celebrations and political events.

QX (Queer Xtra)

Unit 14 132 Charing Cross Road WC2H OLA. T:0171-379-7525. F:0171-379-7525. Weekly free lesbian and gay London listings magazine.Available from most West End lesbian and gay venues and elsewhere. Editors : Tony Claffey and Jacqui Gibbons.

Rabbs (Dr C) Chathrath (Dr V) Hassan (Dr A K R) Pillay (Dr G)

42 Station Road NW4 3SU. T:0181-202-3733. Phone for surgery hours. Medical practice. Male and female doctors. NHS only. Barnet FHSA.

Radford and Co

459 Harrow Road W10 4RG. T:0181-969-7268. Mon - Fri 9.30am - 5.30pm. Female solicitor practice specialising in relationship breakdown, child law, domestic violence and housing.

Radford Smith and Partners

46 Chiswick High Road W4 1SZ and 51 Wallingford Avenue W10 6PZ. T:0181-995-8351 (Chiswick) and T:0181-969-8070 (Wallingford Av-enue). Financial consultants

Rainbow Decorators

85 Steeds Road N10 1JB. T:0181-883-5518. Lesbian, gay, straight. Decorating and building trade service.

Regulation Ltd / The Art of Control

17a St Albans Place Islington N1 0NX. T:0171-226-0665. F:0171-226-0658. Mon - Sat 10.30am - 6.30pm. Lesbian, gay straight shop which sells fetish, military, rubber, leather clothing and toys.

River Place Health Centre

River Place Essex Road N1 2DE. T:0171-226-1473 (also emergency number). Mon - Fri 9am - 6.30pm. Sat 9.30am - midday. Medical practice. Male and female doctors. NHS only. Camden and Islington FHSA. Operates an asthma clinic, a blood pressure clinic, an antenatal clinic, a family planning and well woman clinic and has practice nurses and health visitors. Disabled access.

Rouge

BM Rouge WC1N 3XX. T:0171-377-

9426. Lesbian and gay quarterly magazine. Editor: Roger Evans.

Rox

49 Old Compton Street Soho W1V 5PN. T:0171-287-0666. Lesbian and gay hairdressing salon. Also has sunbed facilities.

Russell, Cooke, Potter and Chapman

2 Putney Hill, Putney SW15 6AB. T:0181-789-9111. F:0181-780-1194. Mon - Fri 9am - 6pm. Solicitor practice specialising in crime, matrimonial, employment, personal injury, conveyancing, commercial, care work and probate. Speaks French and Spanish. Disabled access.

Russell (Julia)

Sequinpark Women's Health Club 17 Crouch Hill N4 and 134 Stoke Newington Chruch Street Stoke Newington N16. T:0171-272-6857 (Crouch Hill), T:0171-241-1449 (Stoke Newington). Massage and reflexology for women (men by referral only).

Rylett Road Surgery

45 Rylet Road W12 9ST. T:0181-749-7863 (24hrs). Phone for surgery times. medical practice. Male and female doctors. Ealing Hammersmith and Hounslow FHSA. NHS only. Disabled access.

Salsa-Fusion

11 Woburn Court Bernard Street WC1N 1LA. T:0171-837-3752. F:0171-837-3752. Organises lesbian and gay salsa dance classes and courses.

Sanders (Dr Stuart)

22 Harmont House 20 Harley Street W1N 1AL. T:0171-935-5687. Mon - Fri 9am - 5pm. Private patients only. Has X-Ray, Cardiography, ECG and Patholgy facilities. Disabled access.

Scarlet Press

5 Montague Road E8 5HN. T:0171-241-3702. Independent feminist publishing house which produces feminist and lesbian non-fiction books.

Securitron

140 Grays Inn Road WC1X 8AZ. T:0171-833-8225. F:0171-278-2679. Mon - Fri 10am - 10pm. Lesbian, gay, straight. Security services for pubs, clubs, offices, and outdoor events and festivals.

Sh!

22 Coronet Street N1 6HD. T:0171-613-5458. Mon, Wed - Sat 11.30am - 6.30pm. Lesbian, straight women's sex shop. Relaxed, friendly and unscary men are welcome as guests of women only.

Shebang!

13 Hercules Street N7 6AT. T:0171-272-2155. F:0171-263-2572. Bi-monthly free lesbian magazine. Editor: Alison Gregory.

Silver Moon Women's Bookshop

64-68 Charing Cross Road WC2H 0BB. T:0171-836-7906. F:0171-379-1018. Largest women's book store in Europe (only women's bookshop in UK). Sizeable lesbian stock. Also operates a worldwide mail order service and a quarterly newsletter.

Slome (Dr J)

146 Walm Lane NW2 4RU. T:0181-452-3003. Mon - Fri 9am - 5pm by appointment. Medical practice. Male doctor. NHS and private patients. Offers acupuncture and counselling. Brent and Harrow FHSA. Disabled access.

Smoothies

Fiona Bloomfield 28 Foulden Road Stoke Newington N16 7UR. Lesbian, gay, straight. Plastering service.

Somerset How Independent Financial Advisors

52 Ockenden Road Islington N1 3NW. T:0171-226-5584. F:0171-226-4513. Mon - Fri 9am - 6pm. Lesbian, gay, straight financial advisory service to companies and individuals.

South Islington Law Practice

131-132 Upper Street N1 1QP. T:0171-354-1033. F:0171-354-8155. Mon - Fri 10am - 1pm, 2pm - 6pm also Wed evenings 6pm - 8.30pm by appointment. Housing, employment and immigration specialists attend at certain times - phone for details. Covers general law, housing, employment, immigration and education. Accepts Legal Aid work. Speaks Italian, Bengali and Tamil. Disabled access and facilities (will arrange home visits).

South Lambeth Road Practice

272 South Lambeth Road SW8 1UL. T:0171-622-1923. Mon - Fri 9am - 6.30pm. Medical practice. Male and female doctors. NHS only. Lambeth, Southwark and Lewisham FHSA. Disabled access.

Staverton Surgery

51 Staverton Road NW2 5HA. T:0181-459-1359. Opens Mon - Sat ring for details. Medical practice. Male and female doctors. NHS only. Also offers yoga. Brent and Harrow FHSA. Disabled access.

Stevens Consulting

56 Pennethorne Road SE15 5TQ. T:0171-732-9713. Mon - Fri 8am - 10pm. Lesbian, gay, straight. General builder specialising in kitchen and bathroom installation. Experienced in plumbing, electrical, carpentry, and decorating work.

Stockwell Group Practice

107 Stockwell Road SW9 9TJ. T:0171-224-3225. Medical practice. Ring for surgery hours. Ask for Dr Jenkins (male). NHS only. Lambeth, Southwark and Lewisham FHSA. Disabled access.

Stopes (Marie) International

Marie Stopes House 108 Whitfield Street W1P 6BE. T:0171-388-2585 or 0171-388-0662. Lesbian, gay, straight. Family planning, male and female health screening, abortion advice male and female sterilisation. Private patients only.

Supershape Aromena

55 Goldborne Road W10 5NR. T:0181-960-1888. F:0181-

968-4587. Mon and Thurs 10am - 9pm. Fri and Sat 10am - 6pm. Lesbian, gay, straight, TV/TS. Beauty salon offering permanent facial and body hair removal, waxing, facials, massage, steam room, nail extensions, aromatherapy and reflexology.

Taylor Nichol

3a Station Place N4. T:0171-272-8336 (also emergency). F:0171-281-9148. Mon - Fri 9.30am - 5.30am. Solicitor practice covering crime and court martials. Accepts Legal Aid work. Emergency service for people detained in police stations. Speaks German, French, Spanish. Disabled access.

Taylor (Robert)

T:0171-792-9787. Photographer who accepts commissions for lesbians, gay men and straights.

Thomas (Dr H W) Chung (Dr C Y C)

27-29 Brandon Street SE17 1JR. T:0171-703-6050. Ask for Dr Thomas. Mon,Tues,Wed,Fri 10am - midday, 5pm - 7pm. Thurs and Sat 10am - midday. Medical practice. Male doctors. NHS and private patients. Lambeth, Southwark and Lewisham FHSA. Disabled access.

Time Out

Universal House 251 Tottenham Court Road W1P OAB. Weekly London listings magazine. Lesbian and gay section lists clubs, pub, venues and one-off special events and runs reviews. Section Editor: Paul Burston.

Tottenham Neighbourhood Law Centre

15 West Green Road N15. T:0181-802-0911. Emergency: 0181-802-0911 and 0181-802-9497. F:0181-809-7078. Mon - Fri 10am - 6pm. Ring for appointment. Law centre covering employment, housing, welfare rights, nationality and immigration, family and child rights. Accepts Legal Aid work. Speaks French, Ibo, Bengali, Gujerati, Swahili, Italian. Disabled access.

Transformation

52 Eversholt Street NW1 1DA. T:0171-388-0627. Mon - Sat 9am - 8pm. Business and shop that specialises in turning men into beautiful women. The company sells a full range of clothing and services to TV's/TS's.

Upstream

1 Warwick Court Choumert Road SE15. T:0171-358-1344. Workers co-operative. Design, typesetting, printing, leaflet production, publicity, brochures, annual reports, stickers, catalogues and raffle tickets.

Victorian Fireplaces Company

Unit 53 West Yard Camden Lock NW1 8AF. T:0171-482-2543. F:0191-417-9946. Lesbian and gay friendly antique cast iron fireplace manufacturer.

Waldron Health Centre

Stanley Street SE8 4BG. T:0181-692-2314. Mon - Fri 9am - 11am, 4pm - 5.30pm, Sat 9am - 11am. Medical practice.

Male and female doctors. NHS only. Offers counselling service. Lambeth Southwark and Lewisham FHSA. Disabled access.

Ward (Mary) Legal Advice Centre

42 Queen Square London WC1N 3AQ. T:0171-831-7079. F:0171-831-5431. Opens 9.30am - 5.30pm. Covers housing, employment, personal injury, family, debt, welfare benefits, tax. Accepts Legal Aid work. Speaks Urdu, Hindi, Punjabi, Bengali and others by arrangement. Disabled access.

Waterloo Health Centre

5 Lower Marsh SE1 7RJ. Mon - Fri 9am - 12.45pm. 2pm - 6pm. Medical practice. Male and female doctors. NHS only. Acupuncture and counselling. Lambeth, Southwark and Lewisham FHSA. Disabled access.

Watson (Dr J), Hockney (Dr E), Flood (Dr E)

Essex House Station Road Barnes SW13 0LW. T:0181-876-1033. Medical practice. Male and female doctors. Mon - Fri 8.30pm - 6.45pm (emergencies on Sat morning). NHS only. Physiotherapy and clinical psychology. Kingston and Richmond FHSA. Disabled access.

Wells Park Road Practice

1 Wells Park Road Sydenham SE26 6JE. T:0181-699-2840 (day), 0181-676-8893 (night). Medical practice. Male and female doctors. NHS and private. Phone for surgery hours. Acupuncture, osteopathy, minor surgery, chiropody, dietician. Disabled access.

Whitehead Associates Independent Financial Advisors

Sovereign House 91-93 Buckingham Palace Road SW1V 0RS. T:0171-828-5565. F:0171-630-9000. Mon - Fri 9am - 5pm. Provides independent financial advice to lesbians and gay men. Specialises in health and life insurance, mortgages, pensions and investments.

Wilson and Co

697 High Road Tottenham N17 8AD. T:0181-808-7535 (also is an emergency number). F:0181-880-3393. Mon - Fri 9am - 5.30pm. Out-of-hours appointments available. Solicitor practice covering immigration, crime, housing, family and children, actions against the police, mental health, conveyancing and wills. Accepts Legal Aid work. Emergency service. Speaks Turkish, French and Somali and interpreters are provided for other languages when this service is requested. Disabled access.

Winstanley Burgess

378 City Road EC1V 2QA. T:0171-278-7911. Emergency 0860-337895. F:0171-831-2135. Mon - Fri 9.30am - 5.30pm. Solicitor practice covering crime, family, actions against the police, immigration, landlord and tenant, conveyancing, personal injury, trusts,

wills and probate. Accepts Legal Aid work. Emergency service. Speaks French and Turkish. Disabled access.

Winter Stewart

78 Lots Road SW10 0RN. T:0171-376-5552. Accountants.

Women's Book Club

45-46 Poland Street W1V 4AU. T:0171-437-1019. F:0171-437-4117. Mon - Sat 9.30am - 6.30pm, late night Thurs until 7.30pm. International book club for women which produces quarterly catalogue offering broad span of fiction and non-fiction books at discounted prices. Accepts telephone credit card orders.

Women's Computer Centre Ltd

Rose Maxwell Wesley House 4 Wild Court Holborn WC2B 5AU. T:0171-430-0112. Lesbian and straight (women only). Computer training and practice facilities for women in London.

Women's Press

34 Great Sutton Street EC1V ODX. T:0171-251-3007. Feminist publishing house with broad range of lesbian and feminist fiction and non-fiction.

Wonderfaux

Stuart Feather 5e Hedgegate Court W11 1JP. T:0171-221-8399. Lesbian, gay, straight. Decoration and painting of special effects on furniture and interiors.

Words into Action

Sarah Roelofs 22b Pemberton Terrace N19 5RY. T:0171-281-4834 or 0171-833-7098. F:0171-833-4371. Phone or fax for operating hours. Equal Opportunities Policy consultancy which provides organisations with supportive advice and educative information either by briefing managers or facilitating staff discussion groups.

Workshop

81 Lenthall Road Hackney E8 2JN. T:0171-241-6584. Mon - Fri 10am - 6pm. Gay run business which prints t-shirts, offers darkroom hire and operates a photographic printing service.

Wright Morris & Co

Chancery House 1 Lochaline Street W6 9JJ. T:0181-748-4122. F:0181-748-3267. Mon - Fri 8am - 6.30pm. Solicitor practice covering corporate / commercial, litigation, conveyancing, wills and probate, insolvency, criminal and family. Accepts legal aid work. Speaks French. Disabled access.

X-On Software

21 Great Tower Street EC3R 5AQ. T:0171-522-0088. F:0171-522-0090. Lesbian, gay, straight computcr software company.

Zeki Gonul

T:0831-694786. Gay photography service.

Organisations

ACE Project

ACE Centre Queen's Hospital Queen's Road CR9 2PS. T:0181-665-5000. A support and education centre for people affected by HIV / AIDS. Free and confidential services include a drop-in, complementary therapies, counselling, buddy service, support groups.

ACT-UP London (AIDS Coalition to Unleash Power)

BM 2995 WC1N 3XX. Meets each Wed at 7.30pm at Jan Rebane Centre, 12-14 Thornton Street SW9. A diverse and non-partisan group committed to direct action to end the AIDS crisis.

African Communities HIV Project

c/o London Borough of Croydon Social Services Rees House 2-4 Morland Road CR0 6NA. T:0181-654-8100 x220. F:0181-655-1875. Works with African community groups who provide personal care and support to people affected by HIV / AIDS. Has a development worker who facilitates meetings, advises on fund raising, resources, premises etc.

AGLOW (Association of Greater London Older Women - 50+)

Louie Hart Manor Gardens Centre 9 Manor Gardens N7 6LA. T:0171-281-3485. Mon - Fri 10am - 5pm. Lesbian and straight (women only). Membership organisation open to all women aged 50 or over. Runs conferences, seminars and events, produces reports and leaflets on issues of concern to older women and produces a quarterly newsletter. Offers speakers, runs a small library and will lend a photographic exhibition. Steering group of older lesbians meets monthly and organises lesbian only events.

AHRTAG (Appropriate Health Resources & Technologies Action Group)

Farringdon Point 29-35 Farringdon Road EC1M 3JB. T:0171-242-0041. International development agency which provides information and resources about HIV/AIDS. Publishes quarterly newsletter, *AIDS Action* and produces AIDS Information and Enquiry Service Database.

AIDS AHEAD (AIDS Health Education and Advice for the Deaf)

FACTS Centre 23-25 Weston Park N8 SY. T:0181-340-5864. Department of British Deaf Association providing information to all deaf people about HIV/AIDS. Provides interpreters, gives grants to deaf people with AIDS, provides training in use of explicit sexual signing, lends minicoms to deaf people with AIDS.

AIDS Crisis Trust

38 Ebury Street SW1 OLU. T:0171-730-0130. Grant making trust to HIV/AIDS organisations.

AIDS & Housing Project

Livingstone House 11 Carteret Street SW1H 9DL. T:0171-222-6933. Aims to advise housing organisations on the provision of quality housing for people with HIV/AIDS.

Alcohol Advisory Service (Camden and Islington)

Jane Pullin 32 Drayton Park N5 1PB. T:0171-607-7363. F: 0171-609-5109. Mon - Fri 9am - 8pm. Tues - Thurs 9am - 5pm. Fri 9am - 2pm. Lesbian, gay, straight. Confidential advice, assessment and counselling service for people with alcohol problems residing in Camden and Islington and North East Westminster.

Alcohol Recovery Project

Linda Ginesi or Delores Young 318 New Cross Road SE14 6AF. T:0181-691-2886 or 0181-691-5975. Mon - Fri 9.30am - 12.30pm (drop-in, Wed women only) afternoons by appointment only. Counselling for all young people with alcohol problems.

All Party Parliamentary Group on AIDS

1 The Abbey Garden Great College Street SW1P 3SE. T:0171-219-5761. Aims to raise awareness of HIV/AIDS in parliament. Holds major parliamentary meetings annually and circulates occasional briefing papers.

Angel Drug Project

Karen Mawson 38-44 Liverpool Road N1 0PU. T:0171-226-3113 (helpline), 0171-354-4777 (office). F:0171-359-4644. Mon, Wed, Fri 2pm - 5pm. Tues, Thurs 2pm - 7pm. Lesbian, gay and straight. Free and confidential service to drug users, partners and families. Advice, counselling, assessment, basic health care, needle exchange, condoms, dental dams. Also has a drop-in open to the public.

April Housing Co-op

Unit C1 Metropoltian Workshops Enfield Road N1 5AZ. T:0171-254-8129. Lesbian and gay housing co-operative affiliated to Hackney Short Life User Group. Any lesbian or gay man wanting to go on to the waiting list must attend 3 meetings. Disabled access.

Association of Lesbian, Gay and Bisexual Psychologies - UK

Andy McKeown 90 Coniston Road N10 2BN. Lesbian, gay, straight. Campaigning group challenging heterosexist and homophobic theories, assumptions and practices within the field of psychology.

At Ease

28 Commercial Street E1 6LS. T:0171-247-5164. Sun 5pm - 7pm. Lesbian, gay, straight. Independent advisory service for members past and present of the armed forces. Offers confidential advice including applications for discharge, complaints procedure, court martials, conscientious objection and being lesbian and gay in the military.

Audre Lorde Clinic

Royal London Hospital Turner Street E1 1BB. T:0171-377-7307. Fri 9am-midday by appointment. STD clinic for lesbians offering free advice and information on sexual health for lesbians, safer sex advice, free dental dams, cervical smear tests and breast cancer screening.

Badminton

Sports Centre, Ladbroke Grove W11. T:0181-891-6748. Meets each Tues 8pm -10pm. Lesbian and gay badminton club which welcomes new members.

Barnet College Gay, Lesbian and Bisexual Befriending Group

Graham 8 The Beeches Simmons Way Whetstone N20 0TQ. T:0181-361-4182. Group associated with Barnet College. Meets first Thurs of the month at Barnet College.

Barnet General Hospital

Clare Simpson House 3-5 Wellhouse Lane EN5 3DL. T:0181-732-4110. Mon and Thurs open clinic 9am-11.30am, HIV clinic Tues 2pm - 5pm. Offers HIV testing and counselling, free condoms and information and advice on sexual health.

Barnet Health Agency

HIV Testing Service Colindale Hospital Colindale Avenue NW9 5GH. T:0181-905-9779. Mon and Weds offers same day testing and results for HIV.

Basement Project

Peter Argyll 4 Hogarth Road SW5 0PT. T:0171-373-2335. F:0171-259-2085. Mon Wed Thurs Fri 11am - 4pm. Lesbian, gay, straight. Advice and counselling on a broad range of issues but more specifically around homelessness, health, substance use and benefits.

Bear Hug

The Secretary PO Box 3147 E5 9RX. Wed and Sat 9.30pm onwards. Gay social group which meets at The Empire (pub), Little Turnstile, High Holborn WC2. Group is for bearded, hairy men and their admirers. Regular monthly social events organised.

Beaumont Society

BM 3084 WC1N 3XX. T:01582-412220 (24hr ansaphone). Self-help group for TV / TS's.

Beckenham Hospital

Department of Genito-Urinary Medicine 379 Croydon Road Beckenham BR3 3QL. T:0181-663-6832. Mon, Weds 9am - midday, Thurs 12.30-6.30pm, Fri 9.30am - midday. Offers pre-HIV test counselling, HIV testing, advice and support on sexual health and HIV-related matters.

Beit Klal Yisrael

PO Box 1828 W10 5RT (Rabbi Shelia Shulman). Reform synagogue that welcomes lesbians and gay men.

Bexley and Greenwich Health Promotion Service

32 Passey Place Eltham SE9 5DQ. T:0181-859-6372. Develops projects with gay and bisexual men. Offers advice and information for gay and bisexual men and sex workers. HIV tests and counselling.

BHAN (Black HIV/ AIDS Network)

St. Stephen's House 41 Uxbridge Road W12 8LH. T:0181-749-2828. Offers support counselling and advice for black people affected by HIV/AIDS. A full range of multilingual counselling is available; specifically in Swahili, Luganda, Yoruba, Hindi and Urdu.

BHAN Drop-in and Resource Centre

111 Devonport Road W12 8PB. T:0181-749-2828. Mon - Fri 9.30am - 5.30pm. Offers health surgery, welfare advice and counselling for black people affected by HIV/AIDS.

Bisexual Group

PO Box 3325 N1 9EQ. Meets Fri 8pm at London Friend. Social and befriending group for bisexual men and women.

Bisexual Helpline

BM BI WC1N 3XX. T:0181-569-7500. Tues and Weds 7.30pm - 9.30pm. Telephone service offering counselling information and support for all bisexual people.

Black Experience

Unit 63b Eurolink Business Centre Brixton SW2 1BZ. T:0171-738-7025. Lesbian, gay, bisexual. An organisation for people of African descent organising social and other events including AIDS / HIV awareness.

Black Lesbian and Gay Centre

Arch 196 Bellenden Road SE15 4RF. T:0171-732-3885. Lesbian and gay. Operates a phoneline, Tues and Thurs 2pm - 4.30pm. Provides social information, support, advice and other information to black lesbians and gay men. Activities and specialist groups.

Blackliners

Unit 46 Eurolink Centre 49 Effra Road SW2 1BZ. T:0171-738-7468 (administration) or 0171-738-5274 (helpline). Helpline operates Mon - Fri 10am - 8.30pm and Sat 1pm - 6pm. Counselling, care and support service for people affected by HIV/AIDS who are of African, Asian or Caribbean descent. Buddying and outreach work and produces promotional information on safer sex.

Blenheim Project

Rachel Fox 7 Thorpe Close W10 5XL. T:0181-960-5599. F:0181-968-6950. Mon - Fri 10am - 5pm. Lesbian, gay straight. Drop-in centre for drug users offering telephone counselling, one-to-one counselling, needle exchange, acupuncture and detox herbal teas.

Bloomsbury Swimming Club

Bloomsbury Swimming Pool W1. Telephone Pete for details on 0181-349-1844. Sat 9am-3pm, Sun 9.15am-12.15pm. Lesbian and gay swimming tuition for aquaphobic adult lesbians and gay men on one-to-one basis.

Body Positive

51b Philbeach Gardens SW5 9EB. T:0171-835-1045 (office) and 0171-373-

9124 (helpline). Helpline operates Mon - Fri 7pm -10pm Sat and Sun 4pm - 10pm. Telephone service offering support information and advice for people affected by HIV/ AIDS.

Body Positive Drop-in Centre

51b Philbeach Gardens SW5 9EB. T:0171-244-7495. Mon and Fri 11am - 9pm, Tues, Weds, Thurs and Sun 11am - 5pm. Offers information, social space, laundry facilities, health and legal advice. Positive Youth meets Fri 6pm -9pm, Women's group Tues 6pm -9pm, Prisoner's Support group, Sunday support group for newly diagnosed people, their families, friends and carers Sun 2pm - 3.30pm.

Bromley Citizen's Advice Bureau

83 Tweedy Road BR1 1RG. T:0181-313-1244. Mon - Fri 9.30am - 5pm. Advice and assistance on benefits, HIV/AIDS issues, housing, debt and legal issues.

Bromley Health Home Care and Respite Care

c/o St. Christopher's Hospice 51-53 Lawrie Park Road SE26 6DZ. T:0181-778-9252 (24-hour emergency cover). Home care, respite care and day care for people affected by HIV/ AIDS.

Bromley Positive

c/o Beckenham Hospital 379 Croydon Road BR3 3QL. T:0181-663-0884. Self-help voluntary organisation for people affected by HIV/AIDS.

Brothers and Sisters

BM B&S London WC1N 3XX. Meets Fri evenings at the Black Cap. Lesbian and gay social group for people who are deaf or are hard of hearing.

BTCV

80 York Way N1 9AG. T:0171-278-4293. Conservation group with a lesbian, gay and bisexual section.

CAGS (Croydon Area Gay Society)

P O Box 464 SE25 4AT. Long running gay social and support group. Produces a newsletter.

Camberwell Circle Project

T:0171-703-6545. Mon - Fri 10am - 5pm. Housing for single homeless people (25-55). Target policy of 35-65% of bed spaces for lesbians and gay men. Also has a small hostel for gay men.

Camden Citizen's Advice Bureau

94 Avenue Road NW3 3EX. T:0171-483-4283. Mon, Wed and Fri 11am - 1pm, Tues and Thurs 2pm - 4pm. Advice and information for people affected by HIV/ AIDS.

Camden Community Law Centre

2 Prince of Wales Road NW5 3LG. T:0171-485-6672. F:0171-267-6218. Covers housing, family, immigration, education, employment, council tax. Accepts Legal Aid work. Speaks Bengali and Spanish. Disabled access and facilities.

Camden Lesbian Centre and Black Lesbian Group

54-56 Phoenix Road NW1 1ES. T:0171-383-5405. Community centre for lesbians and their children. Offers counselling, housing advice and referral, meetings space, helps to set up other groups.

Campaign for Homosexual Equality

The Secretary P O Box 342 WC1X 0DU. T:0171-833-3912 (answerphone) or 0181-743-6252 (Griffith). Mon, Wed, Fri afternoons (usually). Organisation devoted entirely to campaigning, disseminating information and educating the general public on homosexuality. Open to lesbians, gay men and bisexuals. Produces a newsletter.

Capital Housing Project

2-4 Bian Gardens South Kensington. T:0171-373-6635. Accommodation for young homeless people. The project accepts referrals only through other agencies. A quota of places are allocated to lesbians and gay men.

CARA (Care and Resources for People Affected by HIV/AIDS)

178 Lancaster Road W11 1QU. T:0171-792-8299. Organisation which aims to enable churches to set up creative responses to HIV/AIDS. Offers non-judgmental spiritual, emotional and practical support to those affected by HIV/AIDS. Drop-in lunch Tues 12.30-2.30pm. Monthly Sun lunch. Complementary therapies, counselling and 24-hour emergency support.

Cara Housing Project

T:0181-800-2744. Mon - Fri 9am - 5pm. Accommodation for single homeless Irish people. Welcomes lesbians and gay men and has lesbian and gay staff.

Centrepiece

3 Gloucester Avenue NW1 7AS. T:0171-267-8316. Tues 11am-4pm (women's drop-in). Place where people affected by HIV/AIDS can meet, find support, share experiences and relax.

Central Swimming Club

Palace Pool Palace Road W6. T:0171-359-1570. Sun 2pm - 6pm. Swimming lessons for adult lesbians and gay men.

Centrepoint Soho

Haberdashers House 306 Queens Road SE14 5TY. T:0171-277-5137/8. Mon - Fri 9am - 5pm. Short stay hostel accommodation for 9 -16 year olds. Lesbians and gay men welcome.

Centrepoint Vauxhall

11/13 Bondway Vauxhall SW8 1SII. T:0171-735-7999. Homeless hostel space for 60. Maximum stay 6 months. Lesbian and gay quota.

Chalk Farm Oasis AIDS Support Centre

The Salvation Army Hall Haverstock Hill NW3 2BL. T:0171-485-2466. Mon 4pm onwards (drop-in). Also has busy social programme, newsletter, supplies safer sex information and operates a Names Project workshop.

CGOT (Capital Gay On Tape)

c/o 66 Marchmont Street WC1N 1AB. T: 0171-328-3660 (Martin). CGOT is a voluntary organisation which provides a recorded version of Capital Gay each week, free of charge to subscribers anywhere in the UK. Contact the above address for subscriptions, donations or volunteers.

Changes @ London Friend

86 Caledonian Road N1 9DN. T:0171-837-2782. Meets fortnightly on Mon 6.30pm - 8.30pm. Discussion group for women exploring their sexuality and coming out. Disabled access.

CLASH (Central London Action on Street Health)

15 Bateman Buildings Soho Square W1V 5TW. T:0171-734-1794. F:0171-287-1368. HIV prevention project, drop-in with STD clinic (Fri), provides condoms, dental dams, emergency needle exchange, crisis counselling and referral to other services. Works particularly with women and men in the sex industry.

Communication Club

1 Walcott Street SW1P 2NG. T:0171-834-7566 or 0171-437-1819 or 0171-233-666 (info). Lesbian and gay. Meets first Thurs of the month at 6.30pm L'Equipe Anglais 21-23 Duke Street W1. Social and professional network for people working in the media, advertising, journalism, PR, print and communications.

Continuum

PO Box 2754 NW10 8UF. T:0181-961-1170. F:0181-961-2330. Mon - Fri 9am - 5pm. Organisation for long term survivors of HIV/AIDS. Offers personal and telephone advice, information support, alternative therapy suggestions, research information, nutritional and lifestyle information. Bimonthly publication called *Continuum.*

Corduroy Group

Charles Stevens 118 Coleman Court Burr Road Southfields SW18 4PB. T:0181-870-7335. Phone 7pm - 10pm weekdays and at weekends. For gay and straight men who partucularly enjoy corduroy clothing articles. Publishes a newsletter three times a year.

Countdown on Spanner

c/o Central Station 37 Wharfdale Road N1. Meets Sun 7.30pm at Central Station. Campaign group set up as a result of the Operation Spanner court case.

Croydon Area Gay Youth

Roy Nixon P O Box 464 SE25 4AT. T:0181-773-2909 (24hr helpline). Lesbian, gay. Provides support and social events (under 30).

Croydon Friend

P O Box 464 SE25 4AT. T:0181-683-4239. Mon Fri 7.30pm - 9.30pm. Lesbian, gay, bisexual and straight group. Information, befriending, advice, counselling services for lesbians and gays and those with sexual identity problems.

CRUSAID

1 Walcott Street SW1P 2NG. T:0171-834-7566. F:0171-834-7565. Charity for raising and distributing funds for the support and care for people with HIV/AIDS. Manages a fund for individuals in financial hardship, administers Positively Women's Children Fund.

DAWN (Drugs and Alcohol Services for Women)

30-31 Great Sutton Street EC1V ODX. T:0171-253-6221. Mon - Fri 9am-5pm. Network organisation for nationwide services for drug and alcohol advice for women.

Deaf MESMAC

c/o Facts Centre 23-25 Western Park N8 9SY. T:0181-341-4848 (minicom). F:0181-340-5864. Meets first week of each month. Outreach project for gay men who are deaf or hard of hearing.

DELGA (Liberal Democrats for Lesbian and Gay Action)

105 Larch Close Balham London. T;0181-673-3157. Represents the views of lesbians, gay men and bisexuals within the Liberal Democrats and campaigns on legal and social equality issues in the party. Promotes the principles of liberal democracy within the lesbian and gay community.

Deptford Centre

Speedwell Street Deptford SE8 4AT. T:0181-692-5251. Day centre which provides amenities and services to single homeless people (under 25) without children. Has lesbian and gay staff.

Desert Winds

Suite 20 Mary Ward House 5 Tavistock Place WC1H 9SN. T:0171-387-9681 ext 206. F:0171-387-8968. Organisation for the facilitation of emotional, physical, and spiritual well-being of people living with and affected by HIV and AIDS. Follows a Native American Philosophy offering retreats, counselling and support.

Dining Club

97 Adelaide Grove Shepherds' Bush W12 0JX. T:0181-743-3222. Gay dining club which organises fortnightly events. Issues a newsletter.

Diversity

New Actors Centre 1a Tower Street WC2. T:0171-377-1926. Meets weekly on Tues evenings. Lesbian and gay choir rehearse weekly. Welcome new singers and pianists. Repertoire covers everything from classical to pop.

Domestic Violence Intervention Women's Support Service

Aii Ling DVIP Womens Support Service P O Box 2838 W6 9ZE. T:0181-748-6512 (24-hour answerphone). Lesbian and straight women only. Provides help and support for any woman dealing with the effects of physical, sexual or emotional abuse from a partner or ex-partner.

Drink Crisis Centre Women's Services

Bernie Cahill P O Box 719 SE5 8QB. T:0171-252-6900. F:0171-701-8253. Mon - Fri 9.30am - 5pm. Provides women only services for women with alcohol and drug problems. Can offer temporary women only accomodation for those in housing need.

Dynamo Dykes

T:0171 281-7838. Meets weekly each Tues. Lesbian volley-ball team. Welcomes new members.

ECC (Edward Carpenter Community)

37 Ritherdon Road SW17 8QE. T:0181-672-8857. Gay. A non-profit making organisation commit-ted to caring, trusting, personal growth, sharing, creativity, and other principles and intentions aimed at nurturing commu-nity. Run by gay men. Organises residential weeks to further the above objectives at secluded and rural locations.

Elton John AIDS Foundation

32 Galena Road W6 OLT. T:0181-741-9933. F:0181-741-3938. Provides funds for direct care services and prevention education projects on a national basis for HIV/AIDS. Hardship funds are adminis-tered by CRUSAID and Body Positive London.

English Collective of Prostitutes

PO Box 287 NW6 5QU. T:0171-837-7509 (minicom). F:0171-833-4817. Network of women working within the sex industry. Cam-paigns for the aboli-tion of prostitution laws and against women's poverty. Gives advice and support to prostitutes about health, legal matters, police illegality and racism, child custody and benefits. Publishes *Prostitute Women and AIDS, Resisting The Virus Of Repression.*

Evergreens @ London Friend

86 Caledonian Road N1 9DN. T:0171-837-3337. Tues 7.30pm - 10pm. Social group for gay men aged 40+ and their friends. Disabled access.

FACTS (Foundation for AIDS Counselling Treatment and Support)

23-25 Western Park N8 9SY. T:0181-348-9195. F:0181-340-5864. Mon - Fri. Out patients clinic (GP referral is not always necessary). Offers specialised GP-type care for people affected by HIV/ AIDS. Gym, support groups, cafe and offers a range of non-medical services.

Fat Women's Group

c/o Wesley House 4 Wild Court WC2B 5AU. Lesbian, bisexual, straight. Support meetings at Wesley House on the 1st Wed of each month. Also produces a newsletter called *Fat News.*

Feminist Audio Books

52-54 Featherstone Street EC1Y 8RT. T:0171-251-2908. 24-hour answerphone. Lesbian and straight women only. Voluntary organisation providing a tape library of books by, for and about women for the visually impaired and print disabled.

Feminist Library

Juliet Eve 5a Westminster Bridge Road SE1 7XW. T:0171-928-7789. Tues 11am - 8pm. Sat and Sun 2pm - 5pm. Lesbian, bisexual, straight women. Lending and research housing fiction and non-fiction and a large selection of journals. Also information on women's studies courses.

First Step

BM Box 1992 WC1N 3XX. T:0181-461-4112. Meets Mon 7pm - 10pm. Lesbian and gay support group for young people in South London. Also provides advice and information.

Fizzical

Frank Wallace 33 Rowfant Road Balham SW17 7AP. T:0181-675-5858 or 0956-234660. 10am - 11pm. Membership group for gay men who have an interest in body building and weight training.

Food Chain

52 Deptford Broadway SE8 4PH. T:0181-692-1222. F:0181-694-9900. Prepares and delivers free three course meals tailored to the specific needs of house-bound people affected by HIV-related illnesses in Greater London. Produces bi-monthly newsletter called *Link.*

Freedom Youth UK

P O Box 649 Harrow HA3 0LE (send SAE). Lesbian, gay, bisexual. A national organisation for young (under 26) lesbians, gay men, bisexuals and those exploring their sexuality. Operates a European exchange project, a penpal scheme, newsletter, youth groups, a phone line, befriending scheme and competitions.

Fusion

c/o London Friend 86 Caledonian Road N1 9DN. T:0181-889-5162 (9am - midday). Meets Sat 8pm - 11pm at London Friend. A multi-racial gay social group which holds discussions, has guest speakers and provides videos.

Gap House

76 Oakley Square NW1 1NH. T:0171-383-4103. Long-stay hostel for young women aged 16 - 18 1/2 year olds. 50% target lesbian bed space.

Gay Authors Workshop

GAW BM Box 5700 WC1N 3XX. Send SAE. Nationwide group of lesbians, gay men and bisexuals who meet regularly to read and discuss work in progress and foster serious gay writing.

Gay Classic Cars Group

BM Box 5901 WC1N 3XX. National lesbian and gay social group with a mutual interest in classic cars. Meets regularly at The Queens Arms, Chelsea.

Gay East London Social Group

Oxford House Derbyshire Street Bethnal Green E2. T:0181-471-6066 (Derek) or

0181-980-0766 (Darren). Meets 1st and 3rd Fri of each month at Oxford House, 8.30pm - 11pm plus various social events throughout the month. Social group for gay men who are predominantly from East London.

Gay Football Supporters Network

C Andrews c/o The Central Station 37 Wharfdale Road N1 9SE. T:0171-278-3294, (please write in the first instance). Lesbian and gay group meets on the last Fri of the month. Socials, trips, contact directory for lesbian and gay football fans across the UK.

Gay Islington

The Old Fire Station 84 Maton Street off Seven Sisters Road N7. Meets Tues 7pm - 10pm. Youth social group for gay men.

Gay London Professionals

Club Circa 59 Berkeley Square W1 Fri at 6pm - 11pm. Social and networking group for gay professional men.

Gay London Swimmers

BM GLS WC1N 3XX. T:0181-800-8880. Swimming group for gay and bisexual men. Call for details.

Gay Meditation Group

Asian Community Centre 57-59 Trinity Road SW17. Sun 3pm -5pm. Lesbian and gay meditation group which welcomes people of any/no faiths.

Gay Nudist Group

BM 372 WC1N 3XX. Gay social group for men interested in nudism.

Gay Sweatshop

Holborn Centre for Arts 3 Caps Yard Sandland Street WC1. T:0171-242-1168/3143. Professional lesbian and gay touring theatre company.

Gay Young Brent

P O Box 649 Harrow HA3 0LE (send SAE). T:0181-903-9893 or 0956-351789. Mon 8pm - 10pm. Lesbian, gay, bisexual. West London youth group (under 26) affiliated to Freedom Youth UK. Offers support workshops, socials, counselling, day trips, befriending scheme, penpal scheme, visits to Europe and a safe and friendly environment.

Gay Young Harrow

P O Box 649 Harrow HA3 0LE (send SAE). T:0181-903-9893 or 0956-351789. Lesbian, gay, bisexual. West London youth group affiliated to Freedom Youth UK. Offers support workshops, socials, counselling, day trips, befriending scheme, penpal scheme, visits to Europe and a safe and friendly environment.

Gay Young Hillingdon

P O Box 649 Harrow HA3 0LE (send SAE). T:0956-351789. Sun 5pm - 10pm. Lesbian, gay, bisexual. Harrow youth group (under 26) affiliated to Freedom Youth UK. Offers support workshops, socials, counselling, day trips, befriending scheme, penpal scheme, visits to Europe and a safe and friendly environment.

Gay Young London

c/o Kings Cross Neighbourhood Centre 51 Argyle Street WC1. Meets Mon 7.30pm - 9pm. Gay youth group.

Gays the Word Discussion Group

66 Marchmont Street WC1. T:0171-278-7654. Wed 7.45pm - 9pm. Discussion group for lesbians who are making their first entry on to the scene.

GEMMA

Elsa Beckett BM Box 5700 WC1N 3XX. T:0171-485-4024. Mon - Fri 3pm - 8pm. Lesbian and bisexual women. Exists to lessen the isolation of lesbian and bisexual women via a national friendship of pen, tape and phone friends.

GLAAS (Greater London Association of Alcohol Services)

30-31 Great Sutton Street EC1V ODX. T:0171-253-6221. Mon - Fri 9am-5pm. Networking organisation for alcohol services throughout London.

Globe Centre

159 Mile End Road E1 5AQ. T:0171-791-2855. F:0171-780-9551. Day centre for people affected by HIV/AIDS offering a wide range of services including gym, hydrotherapy pool, cafe, meeting hall, day care and drop-in, advice. Has a closed support group for gay men with HIV/AIDS (Weds evening).

GMFA (Gay Men Fighting AIDS)

Unit 42 Eurolink Centre 49 Effra Road SW2 1BZ. T:0171-738-6872. F:0171-738-7140. Volunteer led organisation of gay men which aims to link research to health education campaigns. Promotes safer sex amongst gay men. Organises safer sex education activities for gay men on the commercial scene in London. Monthly newsletter called *F***Sheet.*

Hammersmith and Fulham Young Lesbian Group

T:0181-748-4910. Group for all young women aged 16-25 who think they are lesbian. Allows for meetings in a safe place.

Harrow and Brent Lesbian and Gay Group

Contact via Switchboard. Meets 8.30pm Mon. North London lesbian and gay social group. Organises sports, games and social evenings. Has a women's sub-group.

Healing Circle

c/o Helios Centre 61 Collier Street N1. T:0171-713-7120. Mon - Sat 10am - 8pm, visitor times by appointment. Group for gay men wishing to remain HIV healthy. Manages well-person project which aims to counsel, support and advise people with diminishing T4 cells. Has a comprehensive natural remedies advice service.

Heal Trust

41c Ramsden Road SW12 8QX. T:0181-265-3989. F:0181-265-3989. Aims to promote nutritional holistic and non-toxic therapies as first line treatment for AIDS-related illnesses.

Hiking Dykes

HD Walking Group PO Box 3670 N17 8NH. Group for lesbians who enjoy walking and camping. Organises mainly one day walks within travelling distance of London. Also long distance walks, company trips and youth hostelling. Quarterly meetings and newsletter.

Hineinu

Contact via Jewish Helpline. Youth support and social group for young Jewish lesbians, gays and bisexuals.

HIV Counselling Project

c/o Newham Independent Counselling Service 365 High Street North E12 6PG. T:0181-552-9799. Short, medium and long term counselling to individuals and couples who live in Newham and are affected by HIV/AIDS. Employs principal HIV/AIDS counsellor with specific brief for gay men.

HIV Project

82-86 Seymour Place W1H 5DB. T:0171-724-7443. F:0171-723-7688. Mon - Fri 9.30am - 5pm. Works to reduce the incidence of HIV transmission and to promote sexual health by raising skills and professional standards and by providing support for staff working in HIV prevention and sexual health promotion. Offers training, research and strategic co-ordination to staff within the field.

Hungerford Drug Project

32a Wardour Street W1V 3HJ. T;0171-287-8743. F:0171-287-1274. Lesbian, gay, straight. Drop-in and telephone line operate Mon - Fri 2pm - 5pm. Tues, Wed, Thurs, Fri 10am - 1am, Wed 6pm - 9pm by appointment only. Advice, information and counselling for people who use drugs and their partners, families and friends. Education on HIV and drugs for young people. Training around drug and HIV-related issues for other organisations.

Ian Charleson Day Centre

Pond Street NW3 2QJ. T:0171-830-2062. T:0171-794-0500 ext. 3082 (helpline). Mon-Fri 8.30am-6pm. Six bed ward and suite of rooms offering a full range of treatment and care for people living with HIV/AIDS.

Immunity Legal Centre

1st Floor 32-38 Osnaburgh Street NW1 3ND. T:0171-388-6776. F:0171-388-6371. Mon - Fri 10am - 1pm and 2pm - 5pm. Free legal advice and information for anyone affected by HIV / AIDS.

Institute for the Study of Christianity and Sexuality

c/o ISCS Oxford House Derbyshire Street E2 6HG. T:0171-613-1095. Mon - Fri 9am - 5pm. Provides a forum for discussion of sexuality from a theological perspective.

Ishigaki Jujitsu Club

University of London Union Malet Street WC1. T:0171-232-2895. Meets each Thurs 7.30pm - 9pm. Lesbian and gay martial arts club.

Islington Lesbian and Gay Committee

Committee Clerk Islington Council Town Hall N1 2UD. T:0171-477-3260. Promotes equality and non-discrimination against lesbians and gay men and monitors council policy to ensure the needs of lesbians and gay men are being met. Open meetings.

Islington Young Lesbians

The Old Fire Station 84 Maton Street off Seven Sisters Road N7. Lesbian youth and social group. Wed 7pm - 10pm.

Jewish Lesbian and Gay Group

BM Box JGLG WC1N 3XX. Meets once a month. Jewish lesbian and gay social group.

Jewish Lesbian and Gay Helpline

BM Jewish Helpline WC1N 3XX. T:0171-706-3123. Mon Thurs 7pm - 10pm. Telephone service offering advice, counselling and support to Jewish lesbian and gay people.

Junction @ London Friend

86 Caledonian Road N1 9DN. T:0171-837-3337. Thurs 7.30pm - 10.30pm. Social group for gay men disaffected by the commercial scene.

Kenric

BM Kenric London WC1N 3XX. National lesbian social group which has been existence for over 25 years. Initial contact by letter only. Publishes monthly newsletter containing a diary of events, contact ads etc. Has regional representatives organising numerous local social events.

Labour Campaign for Lesbian and Gay Rights

PO Box 306 N5 2JY. T:0171-582-8401. Lesbian and gay. Works within the labour movement for the rights of lesbians and gay men.

LAFS (Lesbians at Friend on Sundays)

T:0171-837-3337. Social group for lesbians disaffected with the commercial scene.

LAGER (Lesbian and Gay Employment Rights)

Anne Hayfield LAGER Unit 1g Leroy House 436 Essex Road N1 3QP. T:0171-704-8066 (lesbian), 0171-704-6066 (gay). F:0171-704-6067. Mon - Fri 11am - 5pm. Advice to lesbians and gays with employment problems.

LAGPA (Lesbian and Gay Police Association)

BM LAGPA WC1N 3XX. T:01426-943011 (24-hour answerphone). Lesbian, gay, straight. Offers advice, support and socials to all police officers, special constables and civilians employed by police forces in the UK.

Landmark

47a Tulse Hill SW2 2TN. T:0181-678-6686. F:0181-678-6825. Centre for all people living with HIV/AIDS, their partners and carers. Drop-in centre, supplies meals and offers broad range of advice, counselling and other services including housing, legal, money and benefits, nursing,dental and dietary advice, holistic therapies, social work support, counselling and reach out home support service.

LEAN (London East AIDS Network)

44 Romford Road E15 4BZ. T:0181-522-0066. F:0181-519-9947. Offers advice and support services for people affected by HIV/AIDS. Staff also provide welfare and housing advice, hardship fund for registered clients, legal advice, advocacy service, training on welfare benefits, housing, HIV awareness, prevention and care issues.

Lesbian Archive and Information Centre

Jackie Forster London Womens Centre Wild Court Holborn WC2B 4AU. Lesbian and straight women. T:0171-405-6475. Sat 2pm - 6pm although out of London visitors may arrange an appointment. Multi-media collection (books, magazines, videos, cassettes, photos, postcards, film) about lesbians in the UK and world-wide from many cultures.

Lesbian Avengers

National Groups Coordinator P O Box 501 SE21 7DS. Meets weekly on Tues at 7pm at London Women's Centre. Lesbian non-violent direct action group which aims to increase lesbian visibility. All lesbians welcome.

Lesbian Custody Project

Rights of Women 52 Featherstone Street EC1Y 8RT. T:0171-251-6576. Mon - Fri 10am - 5pm or later by appointment. Advice and support to lesbians involved in mothering or wanting to mother in relation to the law.

Lesbian Drop-In

Jean Cross c/o West Hampstead Women's Centre 55 Hemstal Road NW6 2AD. T:0171-328-7389. Tues 6pm - 8pm. Provides the opportunity to relax in a friendly enviroment, socialise and meet new women.

Lesbian and Gay Bereavement Project

Vaughan Williams Centre Colindale Hospital Colindale Avenue NW9 5HG. T:0181-455-8894 (helpline), T:0181-200-0511 (admin office). F:0181-905-9250. Helpline operates daily 7pm - midnight. Admin office Mon - Fri 3pm - 6pm. Telephone counselling for lesbians and gay men bereaved by the loss of a same sex partner or otherwise affected by bereavement. Project publishes a will form and is often able to find suitable clergy or secular officiants for funerals. The project also offers speakers and discussion leaders for any group concerned with death or dying.

Lesbian and Gay Christian Movement

LGCM Oxford House Derbyshire Street E2 6HG. T:0171-739-1249. Mon - Fri 10am - 6pm. Religious group which promotes advocacy, caring and education.

Lesbian and Gay Fostering and Adoptive Parents Network

c/o London Friend 86 Caledonian Road N1 9DN. Meets 1st Sun of the month at 3pm at London Friend. Support group for lesbians and gay men interested in fostering or adoption of children and young people. The group supplies information and co-ordinates campaigning on this issue.

Lesbian and Gay Freedom Movement

Club Room Conway Hall Red Lion Square. Sun 2pm - 6pm. Discussion group for lesbians and gay men on sexual politics and anarchism.

Lesbian and Gay Teenage Group

Manor Gardens Centre 6-9 Manor Gardens N7 6LA. Meets Wed 7pm - 10pm and Sun 3pm - 7pm. Social and support group for lesbian and gay people aged 19 or under.

Lesbian Survivors of Lesbian Abuse

Jean Cross c/o West Hampstead Women's Centre 55 Hemstal Road NW6 2AD. T:0171-328-7389. Phoneline operates Thurs 7pm - 9pm.. Self-help support group for lesbians who have been physically, emotionally or sexually abused in a lesbian relationship.

Lesbian Umbrella Group

Jean Cross c/o West Hampstead Women's Centre 55 Hemstal Road NW6 2AD. T:0171-328-7389. 2nd and 4th Sunday of the month 3pm - 6pm. Social group for lesbians. Videos, outings, parties, discussions.

Lewisham Gay Alliance

c/o Voluntary Action Lewisham 120 Rushey Green SE6 4HQ. A social and campaigning group for gay men in Lewisham. Undertakes local projects with council and other groups.

Libertines (Lewisham 50+ Gay Group)

c/o Age Concern Box 55 20 Brownhill Road Catford SE6 2EN. T:0181-859-8644 (Kingsley), 01689-859806 (Dave), 0181-695-6000 x 3348 (Ralph). Meets Fri fortnightly in the cafe at the above address at 7.30pm - 9.30pm. Open to lesbians but currently solely gay men. Social, befriending, support group for over 50's.

Liberty

21 Tabard Street SE1 4LA. T:0171-403-3888. F:0171-407-5354. Mon - Fri 10am - 1pm, 2pm - 5.30pm. Lesbian, gay, straight campaigning group for international civil liberties.

Link

7 Church Studios North Villas off

Camden Park Road NW1 9AY. T:0171-267-1100. F:0171-267-0400. Lesbian, gay, straight. A resource centre for men, women and children affected by HIV / AIDS. Offers housing advice, advocacy, welfare rights, access to social workers, clinical nurse, specialist advice, clinical psychology, dieticians, physiotherapy, counselling services, legal advice, social support, massage, holistic therapies, support and self-help groups, a cafe and a drop-in. Disabled access.

London Black Women's Health Action Project

Cornwall Avenue Community Centre 1 Cornwall Avenue E2 OHW. T:0181-980-3503. F:0181-980-6314. Tues - Thurs 9am-5pm, Fri 10am - 12.30pm. Promotes general health and well-being of black women in London. Produces educational material for black women, offers counselling, health classes, conferences, workshops and discussion groups, translation services and newsletter.

London Blues

BM London Blues WC1N 3XX. T:0171-635-9764. F:0171-720-1413. Wed 9pm - 11.30pm at Central Station. Gay uniform, denim and western gear club.

London Borough of Richmond

Yorh House Richmond Road Twickenham TW1 3AA. T:0181-891-7830. Runs an HIV/ AIDS prevention project for gay and bisexual men.

London Connection

12 Adelaide Street WC2N 4HW. T:0171-930-3440. Thurs 6pm - 9pm. Lesbian, gay and bisexual social and support group for young people (16-25) which offers advice on housing, unemployment.

London Friend

86 Caledonian Road N1 9DN. T:0171-837-3337 (men and women). T:0171-837-2782 (women only). Phone helplines operate as follows. Men and women, daily 7.30pm -10pm, women only Sun - Tues 7.30pm -10pm. Also minicom available on these numbers. Lesbian, gay, bisexual. A registered charity and voluntary organisation offering a range of counselling and support services. Aims to welcome people from groups that are traditionally discriminated against on the grounds of gender, race, disability, nationality and religion. Disabled access.

London Irish Women's Centre

Maggie O'Keefe 59 Stoke Newington Church Street N16 0AR. T:0171-249-7318. Tues Wed Thurs 10am - 1pm, 2pm - 5pm. Lesbian and straight Irish women. Caters for needs of Irish women living in London especially those discriminated against (travellers, lesbians, single parents, disabled). Offers housing and welfare advice and information, counselling service, Irish classes for children, information sessions on domestic violence, racial harassment and homelessness.

London Lesbian and Gay Switchboard

PO Box 7324 N1 1QS. T:0171-837-7324. 24-hour telephone service offering confidential advice information and support to lesbians, gay men and bisexuals. Takes national calls. Has produced a range of resources on HIV/AIDS including a booklet called *Rough Sex Safer Sex*, posters, and a leaflet offering advice for lesbians on HIV.

London Lesbian and Gay Theatre Group

Deborah or Tony 6-9 Manor Gardens N7 6LA. T:0171-263-5932. Wed 7pm - 10pm. Sun 3am - 7pm. Lesbian, gay, bisexual. A voluntary project for young people (15-25). Offers a safe place, away from the scene to meet other lesbians, gays or bisexuals for support, advice and fun.

London Lesbians in Healthcare

c/o The Women's Centre 4 Wild Court Kingsway WC2B 5AU. Meets 3rd Thurs of the month 8pm - 10pm. For lesbian healthcare workers. Social, discussion, campaigning, support group.

London Lesbian Line

BM 1514 WC1 3XX. T:0171-253-0924. Mon, Fri 2pm -10pm, Tues to Thurs 7pm - 10pm. Telephone service offering advice information and support for lesbians. National calls taken.

London Lighthouse

111-117 Lancaster Road W11 1QT. T:0171-792-1200 or 0171-792-2979 (minicom). F:0171-964-2543. Purpose built residential and support centre for people affected by HIV/AIDS which provides a comprehensive range of services including a drop-in area, cafe and garden, support and information service, legal advice, welfare advice, pastoral care, camouflage make-up sessions for people with KS, exercise classes, hair cutting service, safer sex resources, social activities, women's sessions, play groups and child care, counselling services, support groups, therapy and activities, day care, training, home support service. Lighthouse has a residential unit with 23 beds providing clinical care in a safe supportive and non-institutionalised environment.

London Women's Centre

Wesley House 4 Wild Court WC2B 5AU. Mon - Sat 8am - 10pm. Women's resource centre which houses many women's organisations and provides various other services including information archives, computer training, sport information, counselling etc. Disabled access.

Long Yang Club

BCM Wisdom WC1N 3XX. T:0181-397-2737 (24-hour). F:0181-391-9117. International organisation for lesbian and gay orientals and friends of any nationality.

Magnet

97 Sandstone Road Grove Park SE12 0UT. T:0181-857-3271. Mon - Fri before 10pm. Sat, Sun after midday. Lesbian and gay group which provides social and recreational activities in South East London and North West Kent.

Mainliners

205 Stockwell Road SW9 9SL. T:0171-737-3141 (helpline). F:0171-737-3361. Helpline operates Mon - Fri 10am - 5pm. Telephone service offering support advice and information for people affected by HIV/AIDS and drug use. Also operates a drop-in, needle exchange, produces *Mainliners* newsletter monthly, organises open days and social events, produces posters and has an outreach team.

Metro Centre

Sakthi Suriyapprakasam 2nd Floor 17 Bowater Road Woolwich SE18 5TF. T:0181-316-5954. F:0181-316-5528. Phoneline operates Mon - Thurs 2pm - 7pm. Lesbian, gay, bisexual. Provides services, groups, counselling, phoneline, cafe/bar, alternative therapies and sexual health information for lesbians and gay men.

Metropolitan Church of East London

BM Handshake WC1N 3XX. T:0171-538-8376. Phone anytime. Services Sun at 327a Mile End Road E1. A church of the lesbian and gay community open to all.

Mildmay Mission Hospital

Hackney Road E2 7NA. T:0171-739-2331. F:0171-729-5361. Provides a comprehensive palliative care service for people affected by HIV/AIDS. Residential AIDS unit comprising of 28 individual rooms with leisure and relaxation areas including a conservatory and roof gardens. Family care centre, coordinates residential care and communnity liaison response, nursery and runs educational and training programmes.

Monday Group for Homosexual Equality

LMG c/o R Cook 105 Portland Road W11 4LN. T:0171-229-8272 (Bob), 0181-803-3728 (Ron). Meets every Mon (not bank hols) at The Central Station, Kings Cross. Campaigning and social gay men's group.

MSC

Salmon and Compasses pub 58 Penton Street N1. Fri 9pm - late. Weekly meetings of leather, denim and motorcycle club. Angel tube.

Murrays

94-96 Walworth Road SE1 6SW. T:0171-701-8653. F:0171-708-1469. Emergency 24 hr pager 0459-122895. Solictor practice covering crime, childcare, conveyancing. Accepts Legal Aid work. Emergency service. Speaks French and Hebrew. Disabled access.

NACRO

Jackie Lowthian 1 Thorpe Close Ladbroke Grove W10

5XL. T:0181-968-3121. Mon - Fri 9.30am - 5.30pm. Lesbian, bisexual, straight women only. Provides advice, information and support to women in custody.

NAM (National AIDS Manual)

Unit 52 Eurolink Centre 49 Effra Road SW2 1BZ. T:0171-737-1846. F:0171-737-6190. Provides information on HIV/AIDS in UK. Publishes the *National AIDS Manual, The Topics Volume, The AIDS Directory, The HIV/AIDS Treatment Directory, The AIDS Trainers Directory, The AIDS Treatment Update* (newsletter), seven language editions of *The European Union Directory of AIDS Service Organisations, The Directory of Alternative and Complementary Therapies.* Also undertakes research projects for a range of organisations.

NATFHE - Lesbian and Gay Network.

27 Britannia Street WC1X 9JP. T:0171-837-3636. F:0171-837-4403. Mon - Fri 9.15am - 5.45pm. National and local network for lesbian and gay members of National Association of Teachers in Further and Higher Education..

National AIDS Helpline

PO Box LB400 WC2B 6JG. T:0800-567123 or 0800-521361 (minicom, daily 10am-10pm). Telephone service runs 24-hours a day. Telephone service offering advice support and information on any aspect of HIV/AIDS. Operates Language services at the following times : Weds 6pm-10pm 0800-2824455 for Bengali, Gujerati, Hindi, Punjabi, Urdu and English. Tues 6pm-10pm 0800-282446 Cantonese and English. Wed 6pm-10pm 0800-282447 for Arabic and English.

National Aids Trust

6th Floor Eileen House 80 Newington Causeway SE1 6EF. T:0171-972-2845. F:0171-972-2885. Promotes a wider understanding of AIDS and initiates, develops and supports efforts designed to prevent the spread of HIV and AIDS throughout the UK. Promotes collaboration between the voluntary and statutory sector, the human rights of people with HIV, monitors discrimination, encourages employers to adopt the Companies Act charter and provides management support, grants and advice for projects around the UK on how HIV affects women, prisoners, drug users, young gay men, black and ethnic minorities and mothers and their children.

National Union of Students Lesbian, Gay, Bisexual Campaign

Nelson Mandela House 461 Holloway Road N7 6LJ. T:0171-272-8900. Mon-Fri 9am-6pm. Supports student union lesbian, gay and bisexual groups, runs national campaigns, provides material and resources and supports individual students.

NAZ Project

Pallingwick House 241 King Street W6 9LP. T:0181-563-0205. Mon Turkish 6.30pm -10.30pm, Tues Punjabi 6.30pm-10.30pm, Wed Urdu 6.30pm-10.30pm, Thurs Bengali 6.30pm-10.30pm. T:0181-563-0208, Mon Farsi 6.30pm-10.30pm, Tues Hindi 6.30pm-10.30pm, Wed Gujerati 6.30pm-10.30pm, Thurs Arabic 6.30pm-10.30pm. Telephone service offering advice, information, support and education on HIV/AIDS issues for South Asian, Turkish, Arab and Irani communities. Also runs a support group called DOST which organises for gay men affected by HIV/AIDS.

NCROPA (National Campaign for the Reform of the Obscene Publication Acts)

15 Sloane Court West SW3 4TB. T:0171-730-9537. Mon - Fri 9am -5.30pm. Campaign and lobbying group which aims to change censorship laws.

New Beginnings

c/o Central Station 37 Wharfdale Road N1 9SE. T:0181-981-3621. Lesbian, gay, bisexual. Sat 8pm at The Central Station. A discussion group for people coming to terms with their sexuality. Also holds club, theatre and cinema trips and picnics.

Newham Alcohol Advisory Service

Maeve Malley 7 Sebert Road Forest Gate E7 0NG. T:0181-519-3354. F:0181-522-0734. Mon - Fri 9am - 4pm. Operates a free, confidential alcohol advisory service for lesbians and gays. Staffed by lesbian and gay counsellors.

North London Gay Bridge Group

NLGBG c/o Central Station 37 Wharfdale Road N1. T:0171-700-1108 (Paul). Plays duplicate bridge every Tues at Central Station 7.25pm.

North London Healthy Living Group

407 Carole House Regents Park Road NW1 8UE. T:0171-483-1418. Meets Sun 8pm. Support and information group which welcomes people affected by HIV/AIDS. Promotes healthy food and no drugs.

North London Line

Barnsbury Complex Offord Road N1 1OG. T:0171-607-8346. Open all day. Youth centre for lesbian, gay and bisexual people. Funded by Camden Council. Offers a phone helpline, one-to-one counselling, social activities and provides space for various organisations in the evenings.

Octopus

T:0181-594-0708. Mon - Fri 8pm - 10pm. Social and befriending organisation covering East London and the Essex borders. Meets Fri 8.30pm.

Odinshof

BCM Tercel WC1N 3XX. Lesbian, gay, straight, heathen, religious charity. Produces newsletter called *Odalstone*.

Older Lesbian Network

OLN c/o The Wheel 4 Wild Court off Kingsway WC2B 4AU. T:0171-831-6946. Older lesbian (40+) social group for women of all backgrounds, religions or cultures. Meets every third Sat at Millman Street Community Centre Millman Street (Russell Square tube). Accessible to women using wheelchairs.

Orientations

Sumay Hwang c/o London Friend 86 Caledonian Road N1. 3rd Sun of the month 2pm - 5pm. Lesbian, gay, bisexual. Social and support group for South East Asian / East Asians.

Out on Thursday

c/o Hammersmith Counselling Centre 182 Hammersmith Road W6. T:0181-741-8818 (Robert or Hans). Phone for details. Group for young gay men under 25 based in Hammersmith. Meets Thurs 6pm - 10pm.

OutRage!

5 Peter Street WC1V 3RR. T:0171-439-2381. Open meeting Thurs 7.30pm at The Central Club 16 Great Russell Street WC1. Broad-based group for lesbians, gay men and bisexuals committed to radical non-violent direct action and civil disobedience.

OUTSET

Drake House 18 Creekside SE8 3DZ. T:0181-692-7141. F:0181-469-2532 (various London offices). Operates a job placement scheme helping people with HIV/AIDS who wish to return or to enter into employment. Offers training.

Outsider

P O Box 4ZB London W1A 4ZB. T:0171-739-3195. Lesbian, gay, straight. A self-help social network for people with physical or social disabilites and others who might have become emotionally isolated. All events are wheelchair accessible and all information is also available on tape.

Outtake

S E Locality Mental Health Team 26 Shore Road Hackney E9 7TA. T:0181-533-6116. F:0181-985-9815. Lesbian, gay, bisexual or those unsure of their sexuality or gender. Meets at a central Hackney location. Mental health support and social group. Referral via GP, social workers or other agencies. Disabled access.

Out to Swim

Marshall Street Baths off Carnaby Street W1. Every Mon 9pm - 10pm. Lesbian and gay swimming club which meets for coaching and intensive training.

PACE (Project for Advice, Counselling and Education).

34 Hartham Road N7 9JL. Mon - Fri 10am - 6pm. A counselling, education and advice project aimed at providing an accessible and professional counselling service for and by lesbians and gay men. Provides counselling on HIV related issues and anxieties. Programme of HIV prevention initiatives aimed at gay men; includes

men with learning difficulties who have sex with other men. Also provides training to voluntary organisations and to health and local authorities on HIV / AIDS issues and runs in-house courses.

Pain and Strength

c/o The London Women's Centre 4 Wild Court WC1. Self-help and campaigning group for lesbians who have survived abusive (physical, emotional, sexual and / or spiritual) lesbian relationships. Works to raise awareness of the needs of survivors of abusive lesbian relationships within the lesbian and gay community and elsewhere. Organises workshops and training sessions. Disabled access.

Pan - London HIV/AIDS Providers Consortium

111-117 Lancaster Road W11 1QT. T:0171-221-7973. F:0171-229-1258. Consortium of 48 London independent and voluntary sector providers of HIV/ AIDS specific services to statutory purchasers. Aims to minimise bureaucracy and maximise services.

PANOS Institute

9 White Lion Street N1 1PD. T:0171-278-1111. F:0171-278-0345. Provides global perspective on impact of HIV/AIDS. Publications and activities include bi-monthly newsletter called *WorldAIDS*, a series of books and other resources.

Pink Singers

P O Box 3680 N1 8NB. T:0181-555-9997 (Philip). Meets Sun 1.30pm in central London. Established in 1983. New singers always welcome - no audition.

Porters

1a Station Buildings Bruce Grove Tottenham N17 6QY. T:0181-808-4895 or 0181-340-4407 (emergency). F:0181-801-6312. Mon - Fri 9.30am - 5.30pm. Solictor practice specialising in criminal defence, matrimonial and children law. Accepts legal aid work. Emergency service.

POS+NET HIV/ AIDS BBS

52 Deptford Broadway SE8 4PH. T:0181-695-6655. Bulletin board information on HIV/ AIDS, includes general advice on HIV/AIDS, helplines, newsletters, drug trials, body positive computer network, medical treatments and international updates. Linked to international networks.

Positive Discounts

PO Box 2920 W11 1XT. T:0171-388-5500. A non-profit making scheme designed to benefit anyone who is HIV+ and living on benefits. Provides a discount card for a wide variety of goods and services, including food, clothing and entertainment. Write for application details.

Positive Partners and Positively Children

The Annexe Jan Rebane Centre 12-14 Thornton Street SW9 0BL. T:0171-738-7333. Self-help and support group for all people directly affected by HIV/AIDS including people with HIV/AIDS. Positively Children is for under 18s with HIV/AIDS or who have a parent, guardian or adopted parent with HIV/AIDS, and for the parents of children with HIV/AIDS.

Positive Place

52 Deptford Broadway SE8 4PH. T:0181-694-9988 or 0181-694-2230. F:0181-694-9900. A centre for the care and support of people affected by HIV/AIDS in South East London. Mon, Tues,Weds evening and Fri drop-in. Also offers information service, complementary therapies, counselling, support groups, social work surgeries, benefits advice, women only space (Thurs), tea parties and games afternoons.

Positive Transport Scheme

52 Deptford Broadway SE8 4PH. T:0181-694-9988. F:0181-694-9900. Offer individuals and families affected by HIV/AIDS up to 40 miles free travel per month and uses local cab companies whose staff have received awareness training and have signed confidentiality agreements.

Positively Healthy

PO Box 71 Richmond TW9 3DJ. T:0181-878-6443. F:0181-878-6443. A holistic AIDS charity working exclusively with gay men. Researches and publishes magazines indicating the multifactorial nature of AIDS. Examines the impact in AIDS of malnutrition, malabsorption, recreational and prescribed drug abuse, psychosocial counselling and media programming. Promotes global medical systems, produces a quarterly treatment resource called *PHactPHile*. Fortnightly weekend course for gay men on staying well and healthy. Respite care weeks, Staying Alive conferences and conferences on HIV/AIDS therapeutics.

Positively Irish Action on AIDS

St Margarets House 21 Old Ford Road E2 9PL. T:0181-983-4293. F:0181-983-4142. Mon - Fri 11am-1pm and 2pm-4pm. Telephone service offering advice, support and information to Irish people affected by HIV/AIDS in UK.

Positively Women

5 Sebastian Street EC1V OHE. T:0171-490-2327. F:0171-490-1690. Mon-Fri midday - 2pm telephone service offering advice, support and information for women affected by HIV/AIDS. Also support groups, counselling, open days, consultancy, leaflets, training and education for women.

Post Adoption Centre

Eileen Lanigan 5 Torriano Mews Torriano Avenue NW5 2RZ. T:0171-284-0555. Office Mon - Fri 9am - 5pm, Helpline 10.30am - 1pm. Lesbian, gay, bisexual, straight. Counselling on post-adoption issues.

Publishing Triangle

c/o Steve Cook and Liz Gibbs at Cassell Publishers plc Villiers House 41-47 Strand WC2E 5JN. T:0171-839-4900. Meets second Wed each month at a central London location. Lesbian and gay social group for people working in all aspects of publishing. Arranges speakers, debates and Lesbian and Gay Book Week 1995 with the Pride Trust. Open to members and non-members.

Pride Trust

Adam Jeanes (Chair) Teddy Witherington (Secretary and Festival Director) Suite 28 The Eurolink Centre 49 Effra Road SW2 1BZ. T;0171-738-7644 or 0171-737-6903. F:0171-924-0325. Lesbian, gay and bisexual. Organisers of the annual Lesbian and Gay Pride March and Festival as well as other associated events including the inaugural Lesbian and Gay Arts Festival for Pride 1995.

Rainbow Clinic

King's College Hospital 15-22 Caldecot Road SE5 9RS. T:0171-346-3453. F:0171-346-3486. Wed 4pm -6pm. Gay men's sexual health clinic.

Rainbow Support and Social Group

Globe Centre 159 Mile End Road E1. T:0171-585-1239. Meets third Mon each month. Group for bereaved gay men. New members welcome to drop-in.

Rank Outsiders

Mike Sansom / Chris Doherty c/o Stonewall 2 Greycoat Place Westminster SW1P 1SB. T:0171-222-9007. F:0171-222-025. Mon - Fri 10am - 6pm. Lesbian and gay. Provides help, support and advice to lesbians and gay men who are in the armed forces or who have served in the armed forces.

Red Admiral Project

51a Philbeach Gardens SW5 9EB. T:0171-835-1495. F:0171-373-1935. Mon-Fri 10am-6pm. Provides free specialist counselling for all affected by HIV/AIDS weekdays, weekends and most evenings.

Red Hot AIDS Charitable Trust

Unit 32 Eurolink Centre 49 Effra Road SW2 1BZ. T:0171-924-0385. F:0171-738-6354. Fundraises mainly from the music industry, for national and international HIV/AIDS prevention work. Sponsors fundraising concerts and provides HIV/AIDS education in the field of popular culture.

Red Ribbon International

23 Barrett Street W1M 5HP. T:0171-483-3686. F:0171-493-3689. Promotes the international symbol of HIV/AIDS awareness to advance understanding, overcome prejudice and show solidarity with those affected by HIV/AIDS. Provides fundraising materials for organisations.

Regard

BM Regard W1N 3XX. National support and campaigning organisation for disabled people within the lesbian and gay community.

River House

Furnival Gardens W6 9DJ. T:0181-741-4772. F:0181-846-9745. Tues Weds Fri 10am-5pm Drop-in centre for people affected by HIV/AIDS. Also provides lunch and translation services from Spanish, Portuguese and Italian to English. Social work advice sessions, black people's support service.

Route 15

Mansfield Centre 310 Barking Road E13 8HL. T:0171-476-1505. Mon, Wed, Thurs, Fri 9am-5pm drop-in. Provides support groups for people living with HIV/AIDS in East London and befriending, complementary therapies and a carers service.

Rubberstuffers

Chris Markham 333 Gray's Inn Road W1X 8PX. T:0171-278-0508. F:0171-713-1733. Mon-Fri 10am-6pm. Provides a London-wide service supplying affordable appropriate condoms and lubricant to London's gay venues. Also distributes packs nationally.

Safe n Sound

c/o Deptford and Lewisham Womens Centre 74 Deptford High Street SE8 4RT. T:0181-692-1851. Lesbian action group on safety which aims to provide a forum through which lesbians can make their views known.

St. Bartholomew's House

33 Buckhurst Street E1 5QT. T:0171-377-5984. A shared house for 8 people with 5 places reserved for people with HIV/AIDS.

Saint Lazarus Voluntary Ambulance Corps

Gay Outreach Officer 624a Lordship Lane N22 5JH. T:0181-889-5602 (24-hr answerphone). F:0181-808-8930. Teaches first-aid and how to carry it out at public events.

Sappho Rising

June Hood 2 Horsford House 48-52 Devonshire Road Forest Hill SE23 3SU. T:0181-699-3176 (evenings). Lesbian social and discussion group which meets fortnightly. Also quizzes and speakers.

Schools Out!

BM Schools Out London WC1N 3XX. T:0181-685-9429 (John), T:0181-575-2154 (Claire). Lesbian and gay campaign group working for lesbian and gay equality in education.

SHAKTI - South Asian Lesbian Gay and Bisexual Helpline

Fazal Mahmood SHAKTI c/o London Friend 86 Caledonian Road N1. T:0171-278-7806 or 0850-120274. Support group for targetted communities. Meetings on the 2nd Sun and disco on the last Fri of the month. Phone for details.

SHE (Sisters Health Education)

PO Box 3424 NW10 4JS. T:0956-219878. Tues 6pm-9pm. Confidential information and advice and education project run by and for lesbians who are concerned in any way with HIV/ AIDS drug use and sexual health.

Shepherd House Project

Paulette Wallace, Rosealind Regis, Tracey Chandler. Unit 3 25 Downham Road N1 5AA. T:0171-275-7611. F:0171-254-8910. Mon - Fri 10am - 5pm. Lesbian, gay, straight. Provides temporary shared accommodation for single, homeless ex-offenders and to assist access to permanent housing.

Shortstop Housing Project

The Lady Helen Seymour House Florence Road E13 0DW. T:0181-472-9613. Offers emergency housing for up to 20 young residents at a time. Aims to resettle young people in 8 weeks. Lesbian and gay staff. Accepts referrals from nominated agencies.

SIGMA Research

Unit 64 Eurolink Business Centre 49 Effra Road SW2 1BZ. T:0171-737-6223. F:0171-737-7898. Researches and publishes on social and behavioural aspects of HIV/AIDS care, including a UK study of male homosexual behaviour, evaluation of health promotion material, testing facilities, needle exchanges, health needs assessments, male sex work, prevention work audits, palliative care and hospice facilities.

Sisterhood of Karn

George Shuttleworth / Ian Dixon Potter c/o The Kings Arms 23 Poland Street W1V 3DD. T:0171-734-5907. Lesbian and gay Doctor Who fan club. Meets in the upstairs bar at the Kings Arms at 8.30pm on the 2nd and 4th Wed of the month.

Sisters of Perpetual Indulgence

T:0181-653-1794. Gay social and campaigning group with a penchant for outrageous street theatre to promote safer sex and gay visibility.

SK Group

BM SK Group WC1N 3XX. East London lesbian and gay social group. Meets Sat 7.30pm - 11pm. Parties once a month.

Slip of the Tongue Theatre Company

c/o Deptford Womens Centre 74 Deptford High Street SE8. Lesbian. Meets Thurs evenings. Offers all lesbians to get involved in productions and theatre workshops. The group is non-professional (unfunded). Rehearses evenings and weekends.

SM Gays

BM SM Gays WC1N 3XX. Meets third Wed of the month 8pm - midnight. Non-profit making social and educational group for gay men interested in consensual sexual sadomasochism.

Spectrum

c/o Kingsley Hall Powis Road Bow E3. T:0181-981-5017. East London lesbian and gay youth social and support group. Meets Tues 6.30pm - 9.30pm.

SPLASH

c/o 21 -23 Beethoven Street W10 4LG.

T:0181-964-1771. Meets weekly Sat at 4.45pm at ULU Malet Street WC1 during term times. London-wide group for people with HIV/AIDS and their friends who are interested in swimming.

Stonewall Football Club

c/o Central Station 37 Wharfdale Road Kings Cross N1. Social group for gay men interested in playing Sunday soccer. Has a team in a London soccer league.

Stonewall Housing Association

Unit W58 TEC 560 High Road Tottenham N17 9TA. T:0171-359-5767. Mon - Fri 10am - 5pm. Houses young lesbians and gay men who are homeless as a result of their sexuality. Accepts applications through referral agencies. Meets at London Friend once a month.

Stonewall Lobbying Group

2 Greycoat Place SW1P 1SB. T:0171-222-9007. Mon - Fri 10am - 5pm. A campaigning and lobbying group which provides information on lesbian and gay issues. Covers the whole of the UK. Provides an all-party parliamentary working group on lesbian and gay rights and has a range of publications and briefing papers. Quarterly newsletter.

Stopover Lewisham

Farnborough House 152 Kirkdale SE26 4BB. T:0181-699-1574. Short-stay mixed hostel for homeless young people (16-21) with a housing connection with Southwark, Lewisham or Greenwich. Will accept self-referrals. 3 spaces targetted at lesbians and gay men.

Strutton Housing Association

73 Collier Street N1 9JU. T:0171-837-0010. F:0171-278-9067. Provides self-contained housing for people with HIV/AIDS. No waiting list and no direct referrals. Up to 50% of vacancies are split between referral from Blackliners, Positively Women, Turning Point, Terrence Higgins Trust, Threshold Housing Advice Centres, Landmark and LEAN.

Spare Tyre

Liz Hannah 140 Greenwich High Road SE10 T:0181-305-2800. Mon - Fri 10am - 5pm. Lesbian, gay, straight. Creates theatre based on personal experience with disadvantaged groups (i.e. unemployed young people).

Staying Out Project

Address from London Lesbian Line. T:0181-533-2174. Mon - Fri 1pm - 10pm. Lesbian, gay, bisexual youth project based in Hackney. Provides safe and welcoming social advice, support space for young people aged 11-25.

Stepping Out

Nick or Phil c/o The Central Station 37 Wharfdale Road N1. T:0171-278-3294. Lesbian and gay youth (under 26) social group. Meets every Fri evening 8pm - 10pm. Organises games, quizzes, discussions, visiting speakers, social outings, visits to clubs and pubs.

Stonewall Immigration Group

c/o Stonewall 2 Greycoat Place SW1P 1SB. T:0171-222-9007. Mon - Fri 9am - 5pm. Lesbian and gay support group and telephone support for lesbians and gay men suffering under the current UK immigration system.

Sutton Gay Youth

Roy Nixon PO Box 464 SE25 4AT. T:0181-773-2909 (24hour helpline). Lesbian and gay under 30s social and support group.

Survivors

PO Box 2470 W2 1NW. T:0171-833-3737. F:0171-986-2721. Operates a helpline Tues, Wed, Thurs 7pm - 10pm. Support and counselling for men and their partners, regardless of sexuality, who have been the victims of sexual abuse.

Teenage Information Network

102 Harper Road SE1 6AQ. T:0171-403-2444. Mon - Fri 10am - 6pm. Counselling, information, advice and resource centre for young people under 25. Runs a Lesbian, Gay and Bisexual Youth Group.

Terrence Higgins Trust

52-54 Grays Inn Road WC1X 8JU. T:0171-831-0330 or F:0171-242-0121. Lesbian, gay, straight. One of the world's largest HIV/ AIDS service organisations. Exists to inform, advise and help people who are affected by HIV / AIDS. Communications section, advice centre, legal line (0171-405-2381 Mon, Wed 7pm-9pm), community services including extensive buddying service, health promotion, fundraising, training and consultancy.

3F Group

1 Erskine Road NW3 3AJ. T:0171-722-9953. Meets 7.30pm at Central Station on the third Friday of each month. Lesbian and gay group which explores faith and sexuality.

Threshold Housing Advice Centre

101a Tooting High Street SW17 OSU. T:0181-682-0321. Provides range of training courses and information on HIV, housing and related issues, development work with other agencies, training, housing advisors and providers to improve access and provision for people living with HIV/AIDS.

TORCHE (Tory Campaign for Homosexual Equality)

BM TORCHE WC1N 3XX. Social and campaigning group for homosexual supporters of the Conservative Party. Pressurises Conservative MPs to further equality in the law.

Turning Point

c/o London Friend 86 Caledonian Road N1. T:0171-837-3337. Daily 7pm - 9.30pm. A social and support group for gay men who are coming out or coming to terms with being gay.

TV / TS Centre and Support Group

T:0171-729-1466 (also a helpline). National organisation for TV / TS. Premises in East London with a drop-in centre.

UK Coalition of People Living with HIV/AIDS Ltd.

BCM Coalition WC1 3XX. T:0171-262-2648. 24-hours. Daily 11am-7pm. Run by people who are HIV+. Promotes advocacy, activism, support and information for people living with HIV/ AIDS.

UK Forum for HIV and Human Rights

c/o Immunity 32-38 Osnaburgh Street NW1 3ND. T:0171-388-6776. F:0171-388-6371. A forum of several key voluntary organisations working on HIV and/or human rights issues. Aims to facilitate publication and debate and highlight and challenge HIV-related discrimination.

Vicarage Lane Community Centre

Vicarage Lane Centre Govier Close Stratford E15. T:0181-519-0235. Gives priority to community groups serving lesbians and gay men.

Vocal Minority

Holborn Centre for Performing Arts W1. T:0181-677-7999. Meets each Tues 7.30pm - 9.30pm. Gay men's choir which welcomes new members.

Wages Due Lesbians

Kings Cross Women's Centre 71 Tonbridge Street WC1H 9DZ. T:0171-837-7509. F:0171-833-4817. Mon - Fri 11am - 5pm. Campaigning organisation which aims to eradicate economic, social and legal discrimination against lesbians.

WAGS (Wimbledon Area Gay Society)

P O Box 243 SW19 8SN. T:0171-736-2120. Meets 8.30pm - 10.30pm William Mary Hall 267 The Broadway SW19. Lesbian and gay social group. Organises various social activities.

WAMP (Women and Medical Practice)

40 Turnpike Lane N8 OPS. T:0181-365-8285 (HIV line). Mon, Tues, Weds, Fri 10am-5pm and Thurs 10am-8pm. Health information, advice and counselling service for women in North London managed by women from a variety of backgrounds, cultures and experiences. Befriending service which is multicultural. Disabled access.

WASH (Women Against Sexual Harassment)

Paulette Keating 305 The Chandley 50 Westminster Bridge Road SE1 7QY. T:0171-721-7592, F:0171-721-7594. 10am - 5pm. Lesbian, gay, straight. Provides legal advice and counselling for people who are sexually harassed at work. Contact for speakers, training and advice on strategies to tackle sexual harassment.

West Hampstead Women's Centre

55 Hemstal Road NW6. T:0171-328-7389. Lesbian, bisexual, straight women. Venue for social, support and political groups. Disabled access.

West London Lesbian and Gay Bridge Club

Meets at The Champion Bayswater Road W2. T:0181-903-9893. Meets every Mon at 7.30pm. Lesbian and gay bridge club.

WinVisible

The Co-ordinator Kings Cross Womens Centre 71 Tonbridge Street WC1H 9DZ. T:0171-837-7509 (voice and mincom). F:0171-833-4817. Lesbian and straight women. Mon - Fri 11am - 5pm plus answerphone. Provides support, advice and information for women with disabilites.

Women's Counselling and Support Group

Friend's Meeting House Church Crescent Muswell Hill N10. T:0181-524-4723. Weekly meetings on Wed 7.30pm - 9.30pm. Lesbian and straight women welcome for support and counselling.

Women and Health

Sherlee Mitchell 4 Carol Street NW1 0HU and 52 Featherstone Street EC1Y 8RT. T:0171-482-2786 (Carol Street) and 0171-251-6580 (Featherstone Street). F:0171-608-0928 (Featherstone Street). Lesbian and straight women. Health clinic and centre, health groups, workshops and classes. Counsellors speak Spanish, Punjabi, Urdu, Serbo-Croat. Practitioners speak Mandarin, Chinese, Cantonese, French, Spanish and Italian. A sessional doctor speaks Bengali, Hindi, Arabic and Urdu.

Women's Football

South London Studs meet every Sun morning for games. Call 0171-737-6867 for further details.

Women's Therapy Link

Helen Carroll or Mary Sarjeant Women's Therapy Link PO Box 2704 NW1 0EP. T:0171-916-0123. 24-hour confidential answering service. Lesbian and straight women. Provides short term counselling and long term therapy to individuals and couples throughout London and the Home Counties. Qualified practicioners.

X-Rayz Lesbian and Gay Association

c/o 8 Woodcocks Tollgate Road Beckton E16. A housing co-operative for lesbians and gays in Newham. Short life and permanent properties.

IRELAND

Sexual Politics

ORDER FORM

To order titles direct from Cassell see the form at the back of the directory : here we list some 30 innovative and acclaimed new books in our Lesbian and Gay Studies, Women on Women and AIDS Awareness series.

PUB QUIZ

Throughout 1995 Cassell and *The Pink Paper* shall be running a nationwide tournament of pub quizzes. If you run a pub and would be interested in taking part, contact Cassell's Sexual Politics Quiz, Villiers House, 41/47 Strand, London WC2N 5JE.

MAKE CASH! HOLD A BOOK PARTY!

If you are interested in hosting a book party for you and your friends contact Cassell's Sexual Politics Book Party, Villiers House, 41/47 Strand, London WC2N 5JE.

MAILING LIST

For regular information about our forthcoming titles, catalogues and news of special offers and book events in your area, fill in the form below and return to Cassell's Sexual Politics Mailing List, Villiers House, 41/47 Strand, London WC2N 5JE. No charge and no obligation.

Please include my details on the Sexual Politics Mailing List for receipt of details of forthcoming titles, news of special offers and of Cassell book events:

Name ....
Address ....
....
....
....

Send to Cassell Sexual Politics Mailing List, Villiers House, 41/47 Strand, London WC2N 5JE.

DUBLIN Hotels, Guest Houses and B&Bs

Frankies

8 Camden Place Dublin 2. T:(01)-478-3087 / 475-2182. Lesbian and gay guesthouse. Open all year round. Accepts Visa, Access, AMEX.

Horse and Carriage Hotel

15 Aungier Street Dublin 2. T:(01)-478-4010. Lesbian and gay hotel. Open all year round. Accepts Visa, Access, AMEX.

Bars, Clubs, Pubs, Cafes, Restaurants

Block

Above The George Bar (see George). Wed - Sun until 2.30am. Gay club.

Desert Hearts @ Groucho's

rear Powerscourt South William Street Dublin. Lesbian club. Thurs 10pm - 2am.

George

89 South Great St. George's Street Dublin 2. Open usual pub hours. Lesbian and gay pub.

HOT (Boogie an Domhain - Horny Organ Tribe)

POD Old Harcourt Street Railway Station Dublin. Thurs 11pm - 2.30am. Lesbian and gay club.

Playground @ The Shaft

Ormond Hotel Ormond Quay Dublin. Sun 10.30pm - late. Lesbian and gay club.

Salon @ The Gallery

Fownes Street Dublin 2. Sat 11am - 3am. Lesbian club.

Shaft

22 Ely Place Dublin 2. T(01)-711638. Lesbian and gay cafe and bar. Open nightly.

Shelter @ The Temple of Sound

Ormond Hotel Ormond Quay Dublin. Wed 10.30pm - late. Lesbian and gay club.

Businesses

Books Upstairs

36 College Green Dublin 2. T:(01)-676-2050 / (01)-679-6687. Book shop stocking lesbian and gay books.

Cibo's

17a Lower Baggot Street Dublin. T:(01)-676-2050 / (01)-661-4790. Lesbian, gay, straight Italian restaurant.

Condompower

The Basement 57 Dame Street Dublin 2. Lesbian and gay sex shop. Mail order service.

Gay Community News

10 Fownes Street Dublin 2. T:(01)-679-5128. National lesbian, gay newspaper which also covers Northern Ireland. Monthly.

Gym

14/15 Dame Lane Dublin 2. T:(01)-679-5128. Opens Mon-Thurs 1pm - 3am, Fri Sat 1pm - 9am. Sun 2pm - 5am. Gay sauna.

Marks Bros

7 South George's Street Dublin 2. Lesbian, gay, straight cafe.

Sinners

12 Parliament Street Dublin. Lesbian, gay, straight restaurant.

Utopia

Pink Directory

165 Capel Street Dublin 2 & 1 South Richmond Street Dublin 2. T:(01)-872-9045 (Capel Street) or (01)-478-1095 (South Richmond Street). Lesbian and gay bookshop and cafe.

Organisations

AIDS Alliance

53 Parnell Square Dublin 1. (01)-873-3799. Voluntary support and services organisation.

AIDS Helpline

T:(01)-872-4277. Telephone advice and information line for people affected by HIV.

Body Positive

Dame House 24-26 Dame Street Dublin 2. T:(01)-671-2363/4. Self-help group for people affected by HIV/ AIDS.

Caidre

25 St. Mary's Abbey Dublin 7. T:(01)-873-0006 daily. Support group for people who are HIV+, asympto-matic or who have an AIDS diagnosis.

First Out

Contact Dublin Lesbian Line or Switchboard for details. Lesbian support group. Meets 1st Wed and 3rd Sat of the month at 7.30pm.

Gaeilgeori Aerach Aontaithe (Irish Speaking Gay Group)

Contact Roy O'Gealbhain Ionad Hirschfeld 10 Sraid Fobhnais BAC 2. Lesbian and gay social group which is Irish speaking.

Gay Mens Health Project

T:(01)-660-2149. Drop-in centre. Tues, Wed 8pm - 9.30pm.

GLEN (Gay and Lesbian Equality Network)

Hirschfeld Centre 10 Fownes Street Dublin 2. T:(01)-671-0939. Lesbian and gay law reform and equality group.

Hirschfeld Outdoors Group

Lesbian and gay outdoor group. Meets at The Hirschfeld Centre on the last Sunday of the month at 1pm.

Holistic Health Project

Contact via AIDS Alliance. T:(01)-873-2149. Supplies holistic massage, Shiatsu and relaxation sessions for people affected by HIV and AIDS.

Icebreakers

Contact Switchboard for details. Lesbian and gay social group where members can meet each other without the pressures of the commercial scene. Meets 7.30pm, Sat in a Dublin hotel.

Irish Names Quilt Project

53 Parnell Square Dublin 1. T:(01)-873-3799. AIDS memorial quilt project.

Julian Fellowship

PO Box 1871 Churchtown Dublin 14. T(01)-492-2843. Lesbian Christian support and self-help group. Meets first and last Thursdays of the month, 7.30pm - 9pm.

Lesbian and Gay Switchboard

Carmichael House North Brunswick Street Dublin 2. T:(01)-872-1055. Sun - Fri 8pm - 10pm. Sat 3.30pm - 6pm. Telephone service offering advice, support and counselling to lesbians and gay men

Lesbian Line

T:(01)-661-3777. Thurs 7pm - 9pm. Telephone service offering advice, support and information to lesbians.

Muted Cupid Theatre Group

Gay theatre group. Meets Tues 7.30pm at Rumpoles Bar Parliament Street.

NGLF (National Lesbian and Gay Federation)

The Hirschfeld Centre 10 Fownes Street Dublin 2. T:(01)-671-0939. Publishes the Gay Community News and provides information and archive material.

Reach

PO Box 1790 Dublin 6. Gay Christian support and self-help group. Meets monthly on Saturdays.

Thursday Club

T:(01)-832-1240. Gay dining club which meets on the second and fourth Thurs of the month.

Transvestite Line

T:(01)-671-0939. Telephone service offering advice, counselling and information to TVs.

Youth Group Dublin

Contact via NLGF and Dublin Switchboard. Lesbian, gay youth group for under 25s. Meets first and third Sun of the month.

Belfast

AIDS Helpline (Northern Ireland)

The Hope Centre 24 Mount Charles BT7 1NZ.T:01232-326117 (helpline). F:01232-329845. Mon Wed 7.30pm - 10pm. Tues Thu 10am - 1pm Sat 2pm - 5pm. Telephone advice and information line for people affected by HIV.Also offers complementary therapies, support groups, outreach support work, counselling, safer sex promotions. Administers the McKellan Fund for personal hardship as a result of HIV / AIDS.

BC AIDS Homelink Service

Level 5 Outpatient Centre Royal Victoria Hospital Grosvenor Road BT12 6BA. T:01232-439888. Tues 1.30pm - 3.30pm, Thurs 10.30am -12.30am. Helpline for people from Northern Ireland with HIV / AIDS diagnosis who may want to consider moving home.

Body Positive N.I.

308 Bryson House Bedford Street BT2 7FE. T:01232-235515 (helpline). Tues - Fri 2pm - 4pm. Self-help group. Drop-in, hospital visiting, counselling, home visits, therapy advice and information for people affected by HIV/AIDS..

Butterfly Club

PO Box 210 BT1 1BG. Support and social group for TV / TSs. Meets first and third Tues of the month. Produces a magazine.

Cara Friend

P O Box 44 BT 1SH. T:01232-322023. Mon - Wed 7.30pm - 10pm. Telephone service offering advice, counselling and information. .

Crows Friend

Skipper Street off High Street. T:01232-225491. Lesbian, gay, straight pub and disco. Lesbian bar on Friday evenings. Late disco Thurs Fri Sat.

Drop-In Centre

Cathedral Buildings Lower Donegal Street, next to Spice of Life Cafe (ring bell marked CF). Sat 1.30pm - 5pm.

Just Books

7 Winetavern Street. T:01232-325426. Lesbian, gay, straight book shop which sells a large range of lesbian and gay material.

Lavender Lynx

Contact via Lesbian Line. Twice monthly social gathering for lesbians.

Lesbian Line

P O Box 44 BT1 1SH. T:01232-238668. Thurs 7.30pm - 10pm. Telephone service offering advice, information and counselling.

Limelight

Ormeau Avenue. Lesbian, gay straight club. Mon 9pm - 1am.

Mothers Support Group

Contact via Lesbian Line. Support group for mothers of lesbians.

Northern Ireland Gay Christian Fellowship

PO Box 44 BT1 1SH. Gay Christian social group. Meets second and fourth Sun of the month, 3pm at Cathedral Buildings 64 Lower Donegal Street.

NIGRA (Northern Ireland Gay Rights Association)

Cathedral Buildings 64 Lower Donegal Street. T:01232-664111. Thurs 8pm. Gay campaigning group. Also operates a lending library.

Northern Ireland Women's Rights Movement

Contact via Women's Centre. Lesbian, straight campaign group for the improvement of women's everyday lives. Acts as a referral agency.

Older Lesbian Group

Contact via Lesbian Line. Social group for older lesbians.

Parliament Bar

Dunbar Street. Gay straight pub. Open usual pub hours. Also has a disco area.

Pink Beach @ Orpheus

Yorks Street. Lesbian, gay, straight club. Fri and Sat.

Women's Centre

19 North Street Arcade BT1 1PA. T:01232-243363 / 241676. Mon - Fri 10am - 4pm. Advice and information centre for lesbian and straight women.Provides mobile creche, outreach work and produces publications.

Cork

AIDS Helpline

T:(21)-276676. Mon - Fri 10am - 5pm. Telephone advice and information line for people affected by HIV.

Amazonia

Coast Road Fountainstown Co Cork. (21)-831115. Lesbian, gay, straight bed and breakfast about 12 miles west of Cork.

Art Hive

The Art Gallery McCurtain Street. Lesbian, gay, straight cafe.

Caidre

16 St. Peters Street. T:(21)-275837. Support group for people who are HIV+, asymptomatic or who have an AIDS diagnosis.

Gay Information Cork

P O Box 1 Cork. T;(21)-271087. Wed 7pm - 9pm and Sat 3pm - 5pm. Telephone service offering advice, counselling and information to lesbians and gay men. Also has a legal and medical referral service.

Icebreakers

Contact via Gay Information Cork. Lesbian and gay social group which enables people to meet without the pressures of the commercial scene. Meets 8pm last Tuesday of the month.

Lesbian and Gay Resource Group

c/o The Other Place 7/ 8 Augustine Street. T(21)-317660. Resource archive for lesbians and gay men.

Lesbian Line

P O Box 1 Cork. T:(21)-271087. Thurs 8pm - 10pm. Telephone service offering advice, counselling and information for lesbians. Also has a legal and medical referral service.

Loafers

Douglas Street Cork. Open usual pub hours. Lesbian, gay, straight pub.

Mont Bretia

Adrigole Skibberdeen Co Cork. T:(28)-33663. Lesbian, gay, straight bed and breakfast.

Other Place

Augustine Street. T:(21)-317660. Lesbian, gay, straight cafe, library and club. Disco Sat. Women's disco first Friday of each month.

Quay Co-op

24 Sullivan's Quay. T:(21)-317660. Lesbian, gay and straight cafe.

Derry

Bookworm

16 Bishop Street. T:01504-261616. Lesbian, gay, straight bookshop.

Lesbian and Gay Line

3rd Floor 37c Clarendon Street. T:01504-263120. Telephone service offering advice, support and information to lesbians, gay men and bisexuals.

Drogheda

Outcomers

Contact Dublin Switchboard for details. Lesbian, gay. Social group which meets second and fourth Friday of the month at The Resource Centre for the Unemployed 7 North Quay.

Galway

AIDS Help West

T:(091)-66266. Telphone advice and information for people affected by HIV/ AIDS.

Drop-In Centre

Contact Gay Help Line for details. Opens Sat afternoons.

Ensemble Youth Group

Contact Gay Help Line for details.

Lesbian and gay youth group. Meets monthly.

Gay Help Line

PO Box 45 Galway. T:(091)-66134. Telephone service offering advice, counselling and information. Tues, Thurs 8pm - 10pm.

Lesbian Line

P O Box 45 Galway. T:(091)-66134. Telephone service offering advice, counselling and information to lesbians.

Pluto

Details from Gay Help Line. Student lesbian, gay and bisexual group. Meets Thurs 8pm during term time.

Sheel-na-gig

The Galway Bookshop Cornstore Mall Middle Street. T:(091)-66849. Lesbian, gay, straight bookshop.

Waterfront

Ravens Terrace. Open usual pub hours. Lesbian, gay, straight pub.

Kerry

Lesbian and Gay Group

T:(01)-671-0939 or Dublin Switchboard for information. Lesbian, gay social group meets second Tuesday and fourth Friday in Tralee.

Kilkenny

The Motte Restaurant

Inistioge Co Kilkenny. Lesbian, gay, straight restaurant and bed and breakfast.

Limerick

AIDS Alliance

P O Box 103 Cecil Street Limerick. HIV/AIDS support group.

AIDS Helpline

T:(061)-316661. Telephone advice and information line for people affected by HIV/AIDS.

Forum

Details from Limerick Gay Switchboard. Lesbian, gay, bisexual social group which meets every second Wed at 8.30pm.

Gay Switchboard

T:(061)-310101. Mon Tues 7.30pm - 9.30pm. Telephone service offering advice counselling and information.

Lesbian and Gay Film Group

Contact Limerick Switchboard for details. Lesbian, gay social group.

Lesbian and Gay Youth Group

Contact Limerick Switchboard for details. Young lesbian and gay social group. Meets every two weeks.

Lesbian Line Limerick

T:(061)-310101. Thurs 7.30pm - 9.30pm. Telephone serivce offering advice, support and information for lesbians..

Women's Meeting

Contact Limerick Lesbian Line for details. Lesbian social group which meets on Thursday evenings.

Sligo

GALA (Gay and Lesbian Association)

Contact via Dublin Switchboard. Lesbian and gay social group which meets every month.

Silver Swan Hotel

Hyde Bridge. Open usual pub hours. Lesbian, gay, straight bar at weekends.

Waterford

Gay Line

T:(051)-79907. Wed 7.30pm - 9.30pm. Telephone service offering advice, counselling and information to lesbians and gay men.

Haricots

O'Connell Street Waterford. Lesbian, gay, straight vegetarian and wholefood restaurant.

Lesbian Line

T:(051)-79907. Mon 7.30pm - 9.30pm. Telephone service offering advice, counselling and information to lesbians.

Parents Information

Contact via the Gay Line or Lesbian Line. Support group for parents of lesbians and gays.

Wexford

GLOW (Gays and Lesbians Out In Wexford)

Contact Waterford Lesbian or Gay Lines or Dublin Switchboard for details. Lesbian and gay social group which meets every third Sun 5pm - 7pm in Wexford.

Sexual Politics

* ORDER FORM
To order titles direct from Cassell see the form at the back of the directory : here we list some 20 innovative and acclaimed new books in our Lesbian and Gay Studies, Sexual Politics and AIDS Awareness series.

* PUB QUIZ
Throughout 1995 Cassell and *The Pink Paper* shall be running a nationwide tournament of pub quizzes. If you run a pub and would be interested in taking part, contact Cassell's Sexual Politics Quiz, Villiers House, 41/47 Strand, London WC2N 5JE.

* MAKE CASH! HOLD A BOOK PARTY
If you are interested in hosting a book party for you and your friends contact Cassell's Sexual Politics Book Party, Villiers House, 41/47 Strand, London WC2N 5JE.

* MAILING LIST
For free information about our forthcoming titles, catalogues and news of special offers and book events in your area, fill in the form below and return to Cassell, Villiers House, 41/47 Strand, London WC2N 5JE.

Please include my details on the Sexual Politics Mailing List for receipt of details of forthcoming titles, news of special offers and of Cassell book events:

Name ....
Address ....
....
....
....

Send to Cassell Sexual Politics Mailing List, Villiers House, 41/47 Strand, London WC2N 5JE.

Index

Sexual Politics

Drag : A History of Female Impersonation in the Performing Arts by Roger Baker
'Baker has a deliciously wry style (and provides) a detailed historical perspective that is both coherent and wide-ranging.' Attitude

Male Impersonators : Men Performing Masculinity by Mark Simpson (Foreword by Alan Sinfield)
'A brilliantly positioned array of elephant traps and banana skins designed to trick conventional maleness into showing its true hand.' The Observer

Perfectible Body : The Western Ideal of Physical Development by Kenneth R. Dutton

Sadomasochism : Painful Perversion or Pleasurable Play? by Bill Thompson

Soft Core : Moral Crusades Against Pornography in Britain and America by Bill Thompson
'a good deal of scornful fun at the expense of Christian and feminist fundamentalists...a lot of valuable detail about 1980s campaigns and legislation.' Gay Times

Speaking of Sex : The Limits of Language by Antony Grey
'... beautifully written in his usual easy and felicitous style. The plea for sex respect should convince anyone...' Francis Bennion

Lesbian and Gay Studies

Broadcasting It : An Encyclopaedia of Homosexuality on Film, Radio and TV in the UK 1923-1993 by Keith Howes (Foreword by Ned Sherrin)
'Its range, rigour and thoroughness are breathtaking. More impressive still, it's a great read - fun, insightful and surprising.' Richard Dyer

Coming Out of the Blue : British Police Officers Talk about their Lives in 'The Job' as Lesbians, Gays and Bisexuals by Marc E. Burke (Foreword by Alison Halford)
'(This) pioneering study is in turn moving, anger-making and inspiring.' Jeffrey Weeks

Confessions of a Jewish Wagnerite : Being Gay and Jewish in America by Lawrence D.Mass (Foreword by Dr Gottfried Wagner)
'A daring, touching, sexy, funny, searingly honest confession. The title chapter is a must for every "opera queen", gay or straight.' William M. Hoffman

Hidden Holocaust ? : Gay and Lesbian Persecution in Germany 1939-45 by Gunter Grau

Impertinent Decorum : Gay Theatrical Manoeuvres by Ian Lucas
'This study of queer public manifestations provides an intellectual context for everything from Polari to Pride marches.' Attitude

Queer Noises : Male and Female Homosexuality in Twentieth-Century Music by John Gill
'always provocative and entertaining' Daily Telegraph

Safety in Numbers : Safer Sex and Gay Men by Edward King (Foreword by Cindy Patton)
'An astonishing achievement, at once highly intelligent, shrewd and accessible. This is a masterpiece of engaged criticism, written from the very heart of the worsening AIDS crisis.' Simon Watney

Scandal in the Ink : Male and Female Homosexuality in Twentieth-Century French Literature by Christopher Robinson

The Wilde Century : Effeminacy, Oscar Wilde and the Queer Moment by Alan Sinfield
'essential reading for anyone wanting to rethink gender and sexuality' Lynne Segal

Women on Women

Challenging Conceptions : Planning a Family by Self-Insemination by Lisa Saffron
'This pioneering book will be invaluable for lesbians contemplating motherhood.' Angela Mason

Daring to Dissent : Lesbian Culture from Margin to Mainstream edited by Liz Gibbs
'Radical, readable and feisty, this new collection of essays from very different dykes gives us all the courage to insist on our difference and the energy to dissent.' Patricia Duncker

Healing the Whole : The Diary of an Incest Survivor by Yvette M Pennacchia
'a poignant and moving story.' Clare Short

Lesbiot : Israeli Lesbians Talk About Sexuality, Feminism, Judaism and Their Lives edited by Tracy Moore

My American History : Lesbian and Gay Life during the Reagan and Bush Years by Sarah Schulman
'...combines a lively sense of recent history and some wise political reflections with vigorous and direct dispatches from the activist front line.' Mary McIntosh

Portraits to the Wall : Historic Lesbian Lives Unveiled by Rose Collis
'Written with a wonderfully light touch (it) brims with contemporary comments that put the histories into a meaningful context...completely brilliant.' Rouge

Talking Black : Lesbians of African and Asian Descent Speak Out edited by Valerie Mason-John

AIDS Awareness Series

How Can You Write A Poem When You're Dying of AIDS? edited by John Harold (Foreword by Pam St Clement)
'The unquenchability of the human spirit shines through this unique collection of poems provoked by AIDS. Grief, struggle, pride and loss are their heady themes.' Capital Gay

Positive Lives : Responses to HIV edited by Stephen Mayes and Lyndall Stein (Foreword by Edmund White)
'Every image challenges stock responses and assumptions...These photos are a humbling experience. They break your heart but they also give hope.' Time Out

Reports from the Holocaust : The Making of an AIDS Activist by Larry Kramer
'inarguably one of the most influential works of advocacy journalism' Randy Shilts

Safer Sexy : The Guide to Gay Sex Safely by Peter Tatchell (Photographs by Robert Taylor)
'Erotic, comprehensive and common-sensical.' Sir Ian McKellen

Reference

Cassell's Pink Directory : Lesbian and Gay Organisations, Businesses and Services in the UK and Eire compiled by Liz Gibbs and Tim Purcell

Cassell's Queer Companion : A Dictionary of Lesbian and Gay Life and Culture by William Stewart with Emily Hamer

Postcard Books

Get The Rubber Habit Photographs by Denis Doran with the Sisters of Perpetual Indulgence (Foreword by St Derek of Dungeness)

Pride and Protest : 32 postcards celebrating 25 years of lesbian and gay visibility and activism !

Sexual Politics

* ORDER FORM
To order titles direct from Cassell see the form at the back of the directory : here we list some 20 innovative and acclaimed new books in our Lesbian and Gay Studies, Sexual Politics and AIDS Awareness series.

* PUB QUIZ
Throughout 1995 Cassell and *The Pink Paper* shall be running a nationwide tournament of pub quizzes. If you run a pub and would be interested in taking part, contact Cassell's Sexual Politics Quiz, Villiers House, 41/47 Strand, London WC2N 5JE.

* MAKE CASH! HOLD A BOOK PARTY
If you are interested in hosting a book party for you and your friends contact Cassell's Sexual Politics Book Party, Villiers House, 41/47 Strand, London WC2N 5JE.

* MAILING LIST
For free information about our forthcoming titles, catalogues and news of special offers and book events in your area, fill in the form below and return to Cassell, Villiers House, 41/47 Strand, London WC2N 5JE.

Please include my details on the Sexual Politics Mailing List for receipt of details of forthcoming titles, news of special offers and of Cassell book events:

Name ....
Address ....
....
....
....

Send to Cassell Sexual Politics Mailing List, Villiers House, 41/47 Strand, London WC2N 5JE.

Order Form

All titles available from good bookstores or from Cassell Sexual Politics Department, Cassell plc, Villiers House, 41/47 Strand, London WC2N 5JE.

Tick the boxes below to indicate your choice(s) and send a remittance to cover the full cost of book(s) ordered plus postage and packing. P & P in the UK is £2.50 on all orders up to and including £25.00, £5 on all orders between £25.00 and £75.00. Orders over £75.00 in the UK are postage free. Outside the UK, please enquire at the above address.

Cheques should be made payable to Cassell plc. Credit card orders are welcome from holders of Access, Mastercard, Visa, AMEX or Diners Club cards. Please give card numbers and expiry date. All books are paperback except **Positive Lives**.

Sexual Politics

☐	Drag £14.99 0 304 32855 3
☐	Male Impersonators £12.99 0 304 32808 1
☐	Perfectible Body £16.99 0 304 33230 5
☐	Sadomasochism £13.99 0 304 34305 6
☐	Soft Core £12.99 0 304 32793 X
☐	Speaking of Sex £10.99 0 304 32698 4

Lesbian and Gay Studies

☐	Broadcasting It £19.99 0 304 32702 6
☐	Coming Out of the Blue £12.99 0 304 32714 X
☐	Confess.of a Jewish Wagnerite £12.99 0 304 3114 7
☐	Hidden Holocaust? £14.99 0 304 32956 8
☐	Impertinent Decorum £8.99 0 304 32797 2
☐	Queer Noises £12.99 0 304 34302 1
☐	Safety In Numbers £12.99 0 304 32701 8
☐	Scandal In the Ink £14.99 0 304 32705 0
☐	The Wilde Century £10.99 0 304 32905 3

Women on Women

- [ ] Challenging Conceptions £10.99 0 304 33076 0
- [ ] Daring to Dissent £12.99 0 304 32796 4
- [ ] Healing the Whole £11.99 0 304 33111 2
- [ ] Lesbiot £14.99 0 304 33158 9
- [ ] My American History £12.99 0 304 33167 8
- [ ] Portraits to the Wall £11.99 0 304 32851 0
- [ ] Talking Black £12.99 0 304 32965 7

AIDS Awareness Series

- [ ] How Can You Write...? £7.99 0 304 32904 5
- [ ] Positive Lives £19.99 0 304 32846 4
- [ ] Reports from the Holocaust £11.99 0 304 33171 6
- [ ] Safer Sexy £14.99 1 86047 000 9

Reference

- [ ] Cassell's Pink Directory £12.99 0 304 33085 X
- [ ] Cassell's Queer Companion £14.99 0 304 34301 3

Postcard Books

- [ ] Get the Rubber Habit £7.99 0 952 32290 0
- [ ] Pride and Protest £7.99 0 304 32966 5

- [ ] Please send me a 1995/6 Sexual Politics catalogue.